Dr Andrew Kilsby is an independent historian and published author who has had careers in military and diplomatic service both in Australia and Asia, in public relations & corporate communications, in property management and history and heritage. His history interests span military, business and biographical history. Dr Kilsby has convened and presented at history conferences, arranged exhibitions and written articles, histories, and biographies. Dr Kilsby holds a PhD in history from UNSW.

Also by Andrew Kilsby

The Big Garage: 65 Years of Motoring History 1923-1988

The Case of Eichengruen-Edwards and Continental Tyres

The Forgotten Cruiser: HMAS Melbourne I, 1913-1928

The Riflemen: A History of the NRAA 1888-1988

Co-author

A Reputable Set of Men: The Sandringham Club 1913-2013

Sigma Pharmaceuticals 1912-2012

First Published in 2023 by Echo Books

Echo Books is an imprint of Superscript Publishing Pty Ltd, ABN 76 644 812 395

Registered Office: PO Box 997, Woodend, Victoria, 3442.

www.echobooks.com.au

Author: Andrew J Kilsby

Title: Family Business, The Simmie Family of Simmie & Co
and Harpsdale: Andrew J Kilsby

Copyright © Andrew J Kilsby 2022

The moral right of Andrew Kilsby to be identified as the author of this work has been asserted.

ISBN: 978-0-646-86161-6 (softcover)

A catalogue record for this book is available from the National Library of Australia

Book and cover design by Peter Gamble, Canberra.
Set in Garamond Premier Pro Display, 12/17 and Minerva Modern.

www.echobooks.com.au

All rights reserved. No part of this publication may be reproduced, stored in a retrieval system, or transmitted, in any form or by any means, electronic or mechanical, without the prior written permission of the author and copyright holder.

FAMILY BUSINESS

The Simmie Family of Simmie & Co and Harpsdale

Andrew J Kilsby

Contents

Author's Note	vii
Introduction by Richard Simmie	ix
Chapter One – The Simmie Family to 1926	1
Chapter Two – Simmie & Co—1924–1941	21
Chapter Three – Simmie & Co 1942–1978	67
Chapter Four – Harpsdale 1940—1968	117
Chapter Five – Harpsdale 1969-2000	147
Chapter Six – Harpsdale 2001- 2022	165
Annex A – Harpsdale & the Brodie Legacy to 1906	179
Annex B – Harpsdale 1907 -1940	189
Annex C – Troodos, Arthur Dyson-Holland & Harpsdale	199
Endnotes	213
Select Bibliography	251
Index	257

Author's Note

It is always one of the most pleasurable tasks of the historian to reconstruct a challenging and complex historical tapestry over 100 years in the making. Here, I was faced with creating a complete narrative of not just a family history with all of its rich past and personalities, but also of two very different family businesses.

The starting focus of this story is the Simmie family of three brothers—John Ernest ('Jock') Simmie, George Herbert Simmie and William James ('Bill') Simmie, all veterans of World War One. First there was a building company of Master Builders—Simmie & Co. This was primarily managed by Jock Simmie in Canberra and co-jointly with Jock and his brother Bill in Melbourne. Over the period 1924 to 1978, the company was responsible for constructing a remarkable range of works, including some of the most iconic public buildings in Canberra. While architects, understandably, are noted for their designs, it was rewarding to flesh out the story of the equally important master builders behind them.

The other family business was at Harpsdale, purchased by Jock Simmie in 1940, which became a highly respected Dorset Horn Stud. Settled by the pioneer Brodie family in the 19th Century, this historic farmland and homestead is located at Yuroke, not far from Sunshine where the three brothers grew up before 1914. Then, with Jock's death in 1968, his son—also John Ernest Simmie—continued farming the land for more than 30 years, until his retirement in 2001. A grandson, Richard, continued to farm on what remained of the original Harpsdale property while restoring the homestead and grounds. Today Harpsdale is in the process of being sold. Another grandson, Peter, lives nearby with his family on old Harpsdale land at Belmont while a third grandson, Philip lives with his family in Queensland. So, the story began with three brothers and ends with three brothers, two generations later.

It would have been a near impossible task to bring these interwoven streams together into a coherent narrative without the help of Richard Simmie, with his keen interest in all matters of the Simmie family, the family's business enterprises and of Harpsdale itself. He has preserved a wide range of business records, especially of Harpsdale as a farming business (even some historic farm implements), and family memorabilia, ephemera, images and records which is being catalogued as the R J Simmie Collection. I would also like to thank a colleague, Dr Susan Walter, for her research into the colonial and early 20th Century land history of Harpsdale and to my Canberra researcher, Sarah Kilsby, for her work in the National Archives.

Finally, my heartfelt thanks to Richard Simmie for giving me the opportunity to work on this project with him and to bring back to life so many aspects of this Simmie family, Simmie & Co and Harpsdale.

Introduction by Richard Simmie

I would like to pay my respects to the traditional owners of this land, the Wurundjeri Woi Wurrung people, and to their elders past, present and emerging.

Harpsdale tells more than one story, not only that of the Brodies and the Simmies but also the Brock, Joyce and Gamble families (my forebears) who all played various roles in the early history of Victoria and Canberra, within government, the squattocracy, the Victorian Football League and Dookie College.

I have always considered myself a custodian of Harpsdale, a property that has fascinated me from my earliest childhood. As I explored the garden, I would create road names for all the paths I cycled around. I sneaked in through the west bay window when my grandpa (Jock Simmie) was in Canberra and wandered through the house, intrigued, and fascinated by its size and grandeur. Through the eyes of a 6-year-old, it appeared massive. It evoked love, fun, happiness, and mystery.

Christmas was always a very special time, Jock, surrounded by his grandchildren, Peter, Philip, Richard and Kate, would hand each of us

Harpsdale, 1940s—R J Simmie Collection

an envelope containing one of our Christmas presents, a £10 note, a princely sum in those days.

I was only 13 when Jock died and because my father had no involvement with the building company, Simmie and Co., and wasn't close to the next generation who took it on, I had little knowledge of what Simmie & Co did. Andrew Kilsby has uncovered more than I thought possible.

In 1975, aged 21, I was given my first heritage photo, by my aunt Helen (my mother's older sister). It was of 'Granny Hurst', formerly Brock, née Clarke, who was my maternal great-great grandmother. The photograph, printed on curved or domed porcelain, was taken at a fancy dress ball at Cliveden House, in 1889. This was the city residence of Sir William and Lady Clarke. Sir William, 1st Baronet of Rupertswood, was Granny Hurst's first cousin.

I eagerly accepted the photo and hung it in my room at college because it fascinated me, being a little piece of history and considering the story that went with it. I soon discovered a whole treasure trove of old photos, both at Harpsdale, in the den cupboard and at my aunt Helen's, 16 Roberts Streets, Essendon, which became Granny Brock's home after her original residence, 'Oak Hill' was sold in 1935. Granny Brock was the daughter-in-law of Granny Hurst, of whom more later in this story.

When I purchased my first home in 1981, I lined its long hallway with about 30 framed photos and have added to them ever since. In each home I have owned, the photos form an integral part of the décor.

My husband and I, in 2003, re-established a long-lost tradition of Harpsdale, its parties, well known during the 1940's and early 50's, when my grandmother Ivy was still alive. My parents, being hoarders by nature, meant there was a lot of history stored throughout the house, some on its walls, but mostly in cupboards, all waiting to tell their stories.

It wasn't until my father's death, in 2012, that I was able to bring Harpsdale to full life again, as we know it today. I was able to hang my photo collection on its walls, as if it was their homecoming, their rightful place, for all to see, in the home that had become so much a part of me.

Over more recent years, I started to appreciate that life is always evolving, there is always the potential for change. 2020 and 2021 were eventful years, which made me realise that nothing lasts for ever. I needed to record the history of Harpsdale, from its beginnings. The Brodie family arrived in the area in 1836. Simmie ownership spans three generations, but five generations have witnessed it, across a changing environment and world, over some 180 odd years.

Chapter One
The Simmie Family to 1926

This history must start with an acknowledgement of family historian Michael Hamblin's coverage of the early history of the Simmie family in Victoria (and NSW) in his *A Family History of Cornelia Creek & the Simmies*.[1] There is no doubt that his documentation of the setting as well as the lives of those early Simmie pioneers settling between Bendigo and Echuca and along both sides of the River Murray have greatly contributed to our knowledge today of the forbears of the branch of the extended Simmie family covered in this history.

The Australian story of the Simmie family branch in focus, starts with the arrival in the new colony of Victoria via Liverpool from their birthplace in Perthshire, Scotland of siblings and family members over 1852-1862. The forebear of the Simmies of this history, William Simmie, had been a farm labourer and ploughman in his native Perthshire. **William Simmie** (1825-1901), and his wife, **Flora** née **Penny** (1825-1897) emigrated along with their three children, as unassisted migrants, i.e., they paid for their own passage. They arrived in Port Phillip in March 1862. William's brother John (1823-1867) and his family also came in the same vessel, the *Marco Polo*, a three-mast clipper.

Another brother George (1828-1906), had migrated ten years before, arriving on the *Hibernia* at the start of the gold rush in 1852.[2] A sister, Annie (1830-1896), arrived two years later.

William and Flora had two more children after arriving in Victoria. Their five children were:
- Annie (1852-1891), who married Arthur Balding (1847-1923) – they had 15 children.
- Janet (1853-1941), who married Thomas Matthew Trewick (1846-1922) – no children from the marriage although Trewick had several children from a previous marriage.
- John (1857-1915), who married Jamesina Alice Harper (1861-1923) – they had four children.
- George (1862-1937) who married Elizabeth Ann Childs (1865-1938) – they had four children.[3]

and
- **James Simmie** (1865-1897), who married **Janet Aberline** (1866-1954) in Deniliquin, New South Wales (NSW) in 1889 – they had three sons.

The three sons were:
- William James ('Bill') Simmie (1890-1986)
- **John Ernest ('Jock') Simmie (1892-1968)**
- George Herbert Simmie (1895-1944)

On arrival in Victoria, William and Flora Simmie and brother John and his family lived in Carlton for a while before the brothers joined up with their younger brother George—who had established himself as a contractor in the ten years since his arrival in 1852 as stonemasons and blacksmiths. George by this time was also 'a partner in the firm contracted to build most of the Bendigo to Echuca railway line. They worked through to the finish of the line at Echuca [in 1864] and built many of the stone culverts that are frequent along the railway'.[4] About 1868 William selected land near Elmore north-east of Bendigo on the Campaspe River and named his farm 'Ruthven'. At the time it was about 76 acres (about 31 hectares); he farmed there at least until 1897.

His youngest son, **James Simmie**, married in 1889 at the Wesleyan Parsonage (Methodist) in Deniliquin, NSW. He was 24 and his wife **Janet** was 22. Their marriage certificate shows that he was a clerk, and she was a domestic servant, both residing in Deniliquin.[5] He had been born in Goornong, just south of Elmore in Victoria (presumably at his father William's homestead on 'Ruthven') and she at equally obscure Keilambete in Victoria, so both were some ways from their roots. Keilambete was a small dairy farming community near Terang in the Western Districts of Victoria. Janet Aberline's father, a dairyman, had by then died and her mother Janet (neè McFarlane)'s circumstances were unknown. However, Janet was the second of ten children; perhaps that was a clue as to why Janet Aberline herself was in Deniliquin as a domestic servant. If the family had fallen on hard times after the death of her father, she would almost certainly have been forced to look for a 'position' elsewhere.

In the case of James, it is known that a few years later, in 1891, he was appointed railway station master at Moama, in NSW across the river Murray from Echuca.[6] The Deniliquin and Moama Railway Company built a private railway in 1879 to connect with Moama, across the Murray River from the busy Victorian river port of Echuca. That town was connected in turn to Melbourne through the railway line which reached Echuca in 1864 via Bendigo. The new broad gauge railway track to Deniliquin was opened on 4 July 1876. A director of the Victorian private investment company which financed the railroad was William Simmie's younger brother, George, by now a wealthy landholder (including of the exceptionally large property of Cornelia Creek Run), politician and businessman investor.[7] As was later reported, James was 'in the employ of the Deniliquin and Moama Railway since boyhood.'[8] Hence his position as clerk at his marriage in 1889 in Deniliquin, and his subsequent employment as railway station master in Moama in 1891.

James and Janet Simmie moved into a house on Echuca Street, Moama with their infant son, William James Simmie ('Bill') born in 1896; two brothers followed William—John Ernest Simmie ('Jock') in 1892 and George Herbert Simmie in 1895. James Simmie established himself in the local community, noted as an auditor for the Moama Municipal Council in March 1896.[9] His eldest brother, Scottish-born John Simmie (1857-1915), had also settled in the area south of Echuca at Elmore and had become a Councillor in the Huntly

Janet Simmie and her three sons—George in her arms, Jock front left and Bill front right c1895
(RJ Simmie Collection)

Shire Council. He was also an early member and later Lodge Master for the Freemason's Millewa Lodge 47 in Echuca.[10] James Simmie, now the railway station master in Moama, a family man, and with a responsible position as well as auditor for the Moama Municipal Council, would have been an early candidate to join the Freemasons, no doubt at his uncle's invitation.

James Simmie appeared to be an up-and-coming young man, but tragedy struck on 4 March 1897 when he died unexpectedly at the age of 31 from 'consumption' (tuberculosis) from which he had been suffering for about 12 months.[11]

*James Simmie's Freemason's briefcase
(RJ Simmie Collection)*

His death 'followed a severe attack of influenza'. James Simmie was buried in Elmore and his funeral cortège consisted of '35 vehicles and a number of horsemen'.[12] At the time of their father's death, the boys were aged six, four and two. James' wife, now a widow with uncertain means and three young boys to parent, faced a difficult future, although James' will left the house and land and £514 in life insurance and savings (his life insurance with the Australian Mutual Provident Society was £500).[13] Janet Simmie placed a memorial notice in the *Riverine Herald*, with the poignant verse:

*Abide with me; fast falls the even-tide
The darkness deepens; Lord, with me abide
When other helpers fail, and comforts flee
Help of the helpless, oh, abide with me.*

*Swift to its close ebbs out life's little day
Earth's joys grow dim, its glories pass away
Change and decay in all around I see
O, Thou who changest not, abide with me*[14]

Only four days before James' untimely death, his father William, now in his 70s, sold out at 'Ruthven' and stepped back from farming, although continued to live at the homestead until at least 1900.[15] This sale could have been precipitated in part by the decline of his wife Flora's health as much as his own age as a farmer. **Flora Simmie** died several months after her son, on 21 July 1897, aged 72. *The Elmore Standard*, in its obituary, said; 'The death of Mrs Simmie happening so shortly after that of her youngest son, James, casts a gloom upon the event which will not be lightly dispelled'.[16] **William Simmie** lived to 77, cared for by his surviving daughter Janet Trewick (1853-1941). He died in 1901 from pneumonia and was also buried at Elmore.[17] His Estate was valued at £6,200 (472 acres) with liabilities of £688, net value of £5,512. His sons

John, William & George Simmie, c.1898 (RJ Simmie Collection)

George and John were the main beneficiaries of the land while his daughter Janet had a life interest in 72 acres and received £600. Grandchildren William (Bill) and John (Jock) Simmie received £50 each as did a grand-daughter, Janet Balding and his niece, Mary Simmie.[18] No-one knows why the youngest grandson George did not also receive £50; perhaps the will was made up before George was born and never amended.

Janet Simmie moved to Echuca with the three boys and no doubt received help from the extended Simmie family, including through the Lodge, but there is no doubt life would have been difficult for her. The boys attended Echuca State Primary School 208. In 1903, on the Victorian Electoral Rolls, she was noted as living in Pakenham Street in Echuca, and is listed as a 'confectioner', so by then was certainly back in employment to make ends meet. Janet remarried in 1904 to **John Ford Montgomery**, aged 42 (1862-1951), a carpenter of Sutton Street, Echuca East. He was a widower too; his first wife Lillie (née Edgell) had died in 1901. They had seven children, aged between 7 and 21.[19] Perhaps unusually they were married in Melbourne rather than locally at Echuca or Elmore, under the Free Christian Church. This church was located in Queen Street, Melbourne. In an advertisement in 1901 it was stated:

> Marriages celebrated by ordained clergymen, with due solemnity, in strictest privacy, at Holt's Matrimonial Agency, 448 Queen Street, Melbourne, opposite the old cemetery, or elsewhere, from 10 a.m. to 9 p.m. daily, Saturdays included. (No notice required).
>
> Fee ten shillings and sixpence; or marriage, with guaranteed gold wedding ring and necessary witnesses provided, £1 one shilling P.S.—No other charges whatsoever. All sizes, more costly wedding rings kept in stock if required.[20]

James Holt and his wife Annie were usually the 'witnesses provided' and were, in fact, the witnesses for John Montgomery and Janet Simmie in 1904. Janet Simmie, now Montgomery had one child **Eric Ford Aberline Montgomery**, born in October 1906 in Echuca.[21] Family lore states that when Janet married Montgomery, George Simmie (who died in 1906 with an estate valued at £178,000) disinherited her. The Simmie boys were then 14, 12 and 9, but came to regard John Montgomery as their father.

*Janet and John Montgomery wedding photo 1904
(RJ Simmie Collection)*

John (Jock) and William (Bill) became carpenters by trade. Jock Simmie later said that he had learned his trade with old building firm in Echuca, W W (William Watson) Moore & Sons. It is very likely that his brothers also did apprenticeships there as well.[22] The company built a range of buildings in Echuca and district and this exposure to the building trade in their teenage years would have lasting effect on all three. George, the youngest, appeared to have stayed with schooling as later his trade was given a 'clerk'.

By 1910, the family had moved to the new town of Sunshine, named in 1907 in honour of industrialist Hugh Victor McKay who had developed a factory there in 1904 which became known as the Sunshine Harvester Works. The new factory attracted many new families in 1909-1910. It was to become the largest (agricultural) manufacturing plant in Australia, employing at its peak more than 3,000 people.[23]

The evident attraction of employment opportunities in either the factory or in work in the district associated with it was almost certainly the catalyst for the move. The knowledge of this may well have come through Janet Montgomery's late husband's uncle, John Simmie, who had taken up a Sunshine Harvester Company agency at Elmore in 1906. By 1910 however the McKay Harvester Works was well known across the state. John Montgomery's youngest son from his first marriage, Albert Reid ('Bert') Montgomery, became an apprentice wood machinist at McKay's in 1910.

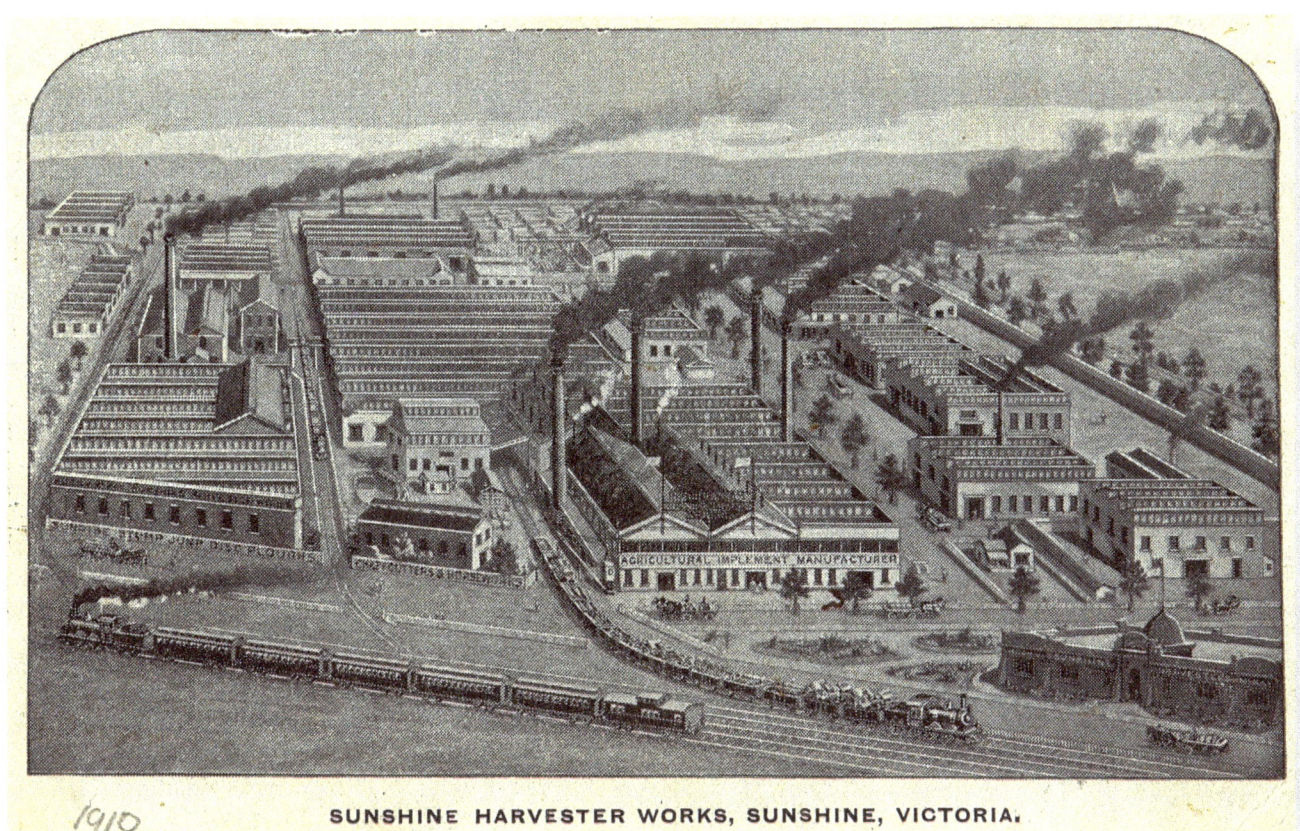

Sunshine Harvester Works, 1910
(Collections Museum Victoria)

When a major strike by unionised workers at McKay's in early 1911 got underway, 'football was one of the activities that kept going'. The local Sunshine football team included both Jock Simmie and Bill Simmie—the team went on to win the premiership that year.[24] Later, in 1913, the football club (now the Sunshine-Braybrook Football Club), went on to win the premiership again. In that team were both Bill and Jock Simmie, as well as Bert Montgomery—and John Montgomery as a team manager.[25] Jock Simmie was also involved in the local cricket team as was John Montgomery, and, no doubt, Jock's brothers as well.

Jock Simmie, Sunshine-Braybrook Football Club, c 1911 (RJ Simmie Collection)

At Sunshine, the Montgomerys and family took up residence in a rented concrete house in Ridley Street, provided by McKay's as part of the McKay 'factory town' estate developed by the industrialist to house the workers. 'Each allotment was big enough for a small orchard and also allowed room for keeping fowls'.[26] Janet and John Montgomery lived there until 1924, and after a few years at Kensington in Melbourne, returned to 1 Kororoit Street in Sunshine in 1928 where they lived until their deaths in 1954 and 1951 respectively. During the period in Melbourne, John Montgomery's son Albert lived in the house with his sister Violet Christina Montgomery, also a machinist at the McKay factory.[27]

According to Mike Hamblin in his family history, all three brothers worked for Harvester and George may have been a junior clerk at the company, as later shown on his Army enlistment papers.[28] However, it is also known that Bill Simmie, in June 1916 had his estate (such as it was) sequestered as an insolvent carpenter, 'through want of employment and pressure of creditors'— liabilities £193-3-2; assets just 5/-.[29] So Bill Simmie

Jock Simmie, (seated L) and John Montgomery (standing, top L),
Sunshine District Cricket Club, c 1911
(RJ Simmie Collection)

at least was by then working for himself. Years later a Simmie Street was named in West Sunshine after the family.

When war was declared by Britain against Germany in August 1914, Australia automatically followed. Patriotic fever swept the country and Sunshine was no exception. The Sunshine Harvester Works sprang into action to produce 200 wagons, 23 ambulances and 150 water carts in the first four weeks of the war. In that first flush of war fever,

35 employees from the Harvester offices in Australia and Argentina enlisted, including in Sunshine, Albert ('Bert') Reid Montgomery. George Herbert Simmie, Bert's stepbrother, also immediately enlisted in Sunshine; both were 19.[30] George's older brother Jock Simmie was not far behind, enlisting in the Australian Imperial Force (AIF) in January 1915. The oldest brother, William (Bill) Simmie, enlisted later—in 1917.

The service records of the three brothers in the First World War show more than a shared experience of Gallipoli and the Western Front, and more than the effects on their health both physical and mental later in life—it created a strong bond between them. Some years after the war it could be observed that George appeared to be somewhat distant from Jock and Bill Simmie, who had gone into business together. Nonetheless, George was witness at Jock's later marriage for example and wrote to him during the war as 'your loving brother'. But they all came back from war as mature men, were self-made in life and their own men as well.

George gave his trade on enlistment as 'clerk'. He was sent to the 4th Field Artillery Battery (FAB), in the 2nd FA Brigade of the 1st Australian Division.[31] The unit arrived in Egypt in late 1914.

J E Simmie upon enlistment 1915
(RJ Simmie Collection)

The brigade was then deployed to Lemnos at Gallipoli, with the 4th FAB having one of its field guns landed at Anzac Cove and firing by 6 PM on 25 April 1915; others followed.[32] George's service record does not notate Gallipoli or ANZAC—in fact there is a complete gap in his records between landing in Egypt and landing in France. But there is one telling entry—'Joined MEF 8/4/15'. The MEF or Mediterranean Expeditionary Force became the synonym for Gallipoli, and 2nd FA Brigade including 4th FAB embarked for Gallipoli on 8 April 1915.

When the Gallipoli campaign ended in failure, George then served in France as a driver-gunner.[33] On 2 August 1917 he was wounded in action with a gunshot wound to both thighs during the Third Battle of Ypres in Belgium.[34] Months of recuperation at the 1st Birmingham War Hospital followed. On leave afterwards he then contracted a dose of venereal disease—both gonorrhea and syphilis—in May 1918, leading to a further month in hospital. Such VD occurrence were common to soldiers at the time. George Simmie was entitled then to home leave as an original 1914 enlistee and the end of the war was at hand—he was discharged in March 1919 in Melbourne and returned to Sunshine. As late as January 1919 he noted to his doctor that there was still a fragment in his left thigh.[35] His wounds both self-inflicted, and inflicted on him, contributed to his premature death in 1944.[36]

Jock followed in 1915. He enlisted into the 21st Infantry Battalion, aged 22 and giving his trade as carpenter, on 21 January.[37] The 21st Battalion of the 6th Brigade was part of the newly raised 2nd Division. In late August 1915 it was deployed to Gallipoli, just missing the major August offensive there which had ended in failure. The transport ship bringing the unit to Gallipoli, HMT *Southland*, was torpedoed off the island of Lemnos—it sank, but slowly, allowing almost all aboard, including Jock Simmie, to get ashore safely.[38] The battalion landed at Gallipoli in early September 1915. Fortunately for Jock, it was a relatively quiet time, although Turkish artillery and snipers as well as poor sanitary conditions still led to many casualties. The campaign had ground to a stalemate and with winter on the way it was decided to withdraw from Gallipoli. In a remarkable deception campaign, the Allied forces successfully evacuated over 130,000 men by 20 December 1915. The men of the 21st Battalion were among the last infantry to leave, Jock among them. He was promoted to sergeant soon after.

Like his brother George, Jock was redeployed to France with his battalion after some training and recuperation in Egypt, arriving in March 1916. In July 1916, the 6th Brigade was committed to the

Battle of Pozières. The 21st Battalion was assigned to porterage duties in the leadup to the attack, engaged on building defence works and 'fatigues'—the demanding manual working parties needed to prepare for battle—as well as training in grenade and bayonet fighting, checking equipment and so on. On 29 July, the battalion moved into the front line trenches and relieved sister battalions in the front line. The war diary of the 21st Battalion noted that 'enemy's artillery very active' but does not record the casualties that day or the next.[39]

However, Jock Simmie, was a casualty—with a shrapnel wound to his right thigh on 30 July. He was evacuated to England and spent almost nine months in hospitals recovering—his war was over. He was returned to Australia and discharged in June 1917. It is not known whether the brothers had an opportunity to meet up in the brief time that they were both in France; coincidentally 4th FAB was in support of the infantry at Pozières that week of Jock's wounding.[40] Jock would walk with a limp for the rest of his life.

Jock's return may have given William (Bill) James Simmie his turn to enlist in the knowledge that one brother was arriving home to look after their mother in Sunshine. Another reason was that

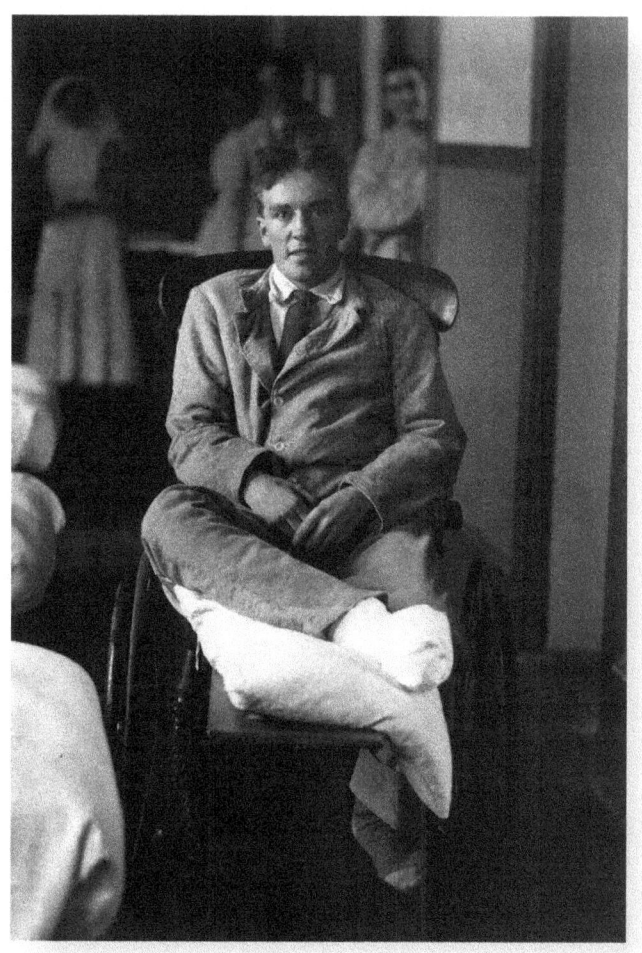

J E Simmie
Recovering from wounds 1916
(RJ Simmie Collection)

in June 1916 as we have seen, his estate had been sequestered the year before—Bill was broke. Aged 26, giving his trade as carpenter, Bill enlisted on

J E Simmie 1917
(RJ Simmie Collection)

7 May 1917. He was sent to France via training in England, joining his unit as reinforcements to the 24th Infantry Battalion in late November 1917. The 24th Battalion was, like Jock Simmie's 21st Battalion, part of 6th Brigade of the 2nd Division AIF. Like the 21st it had been at Gallipoli and was the battalion relieved by 21st Battalion at Pozières the day Jock was wounded.

By March 1918, the 24th Battalion was in the line near Messines. The German spring offensive got underway on 21 March. The unit war diary tells the story—'From 1 a.m. to 5 a.m. ...heavily bombarded by the enemy with gas shells, it being estimated that 5000 shells ...were fired into an area of 10 acres. Serious casualties...were caused to A & D companies which were billeted in dugouts...- two men were killed and 36-45 [were affected] by gas'. By the end of the day, the diary went on to say, '7 officers and 212 men were evacuated, most with eye trouble.'[41] One of the serious cases which were evacuated, returning to England for treatment, was Bill Simmie. He rejoined his unit in France nearly four months later, in mid July 1918.

Bill was to be wounded twice more—gassed again in July 1918 and hospitalised for two months and then suffering a gunshot wound to his right arm in heavy fighting at Montbrehain during the Battle of St. Quentin Canal in October 1918, just before the end of the hostilities.[42] He was returned to Australia, in January 1919 and was discharged to also return to Sunshine in June 1919. The three brothers together again after several years, all wounded veterans and no doubt nursing the long term psychological effects of their war experiences. Now they faced the challenge of adjusting back to civilian life and deciding where they would go from there. It would take them several years to put the building blocks in place for the next stage of their lives. All three started their lives again as carpenters. In Jock's case however, as he had returned in 1917 while his brothers were both serving in France, he was able to secure employment from 25th August, 1918 with the Office of the Auditor-General in Melbourne, initially working from Victoria Barracks, Melbourne.[43]

According to a later biographical vignette, Jock Simmie moved to this work while 'still on crutches', recovering from his war wound.[44] Electoral rolls place him in Sunshine until at least 1921, and it is known that Jock served as president of the Sunshine Branch of the newly established Returned Soldiers & Sailors Imperial League of Australia (RS&SILA) in 1919.[45] So, it is likely that he was able to secure new work in 1918 which later led him to Melbourne through the Repatriation Department, created in September 1917 to provide support for returned and especially disabled soldiers—as a wounded veteran of Gallipoli and the Western Front he would certainly have received help. Nonetheless, how Jock came to work there and why he went remains unknown, but we have some anecdotal insights:

The story goes that his supervising officer, Colonel Lang [Ling], asked him about his career plans. Jock replied that when fit enough he'd become a builder. The Colonel is quoted as saying 'Well my advice to you is to study accountancy while you are here with us, because no matter what you do later, it will stand you in good stead'.[46]

By 1922 he was described in electoral rolls as a 'public servant' with an address in Mitchell Street, Caulfield.[47] That year he moved to qualify for formal accounting and company secretary credentials. In May 1922 he was recorded as one of hundreds who passed the Commonwealth Institute of Accountants final exams.[48] In December 1922 Jock also passed the examination for the Degree of Associate (Parts I & II) set by the Australian Institute of Secretaries for joint stock companies and other public bodies.[49] Jock had married **Ivy Eliza Ann Joyce** (1890-1952) on 2 April 1921 in Melbourne; his brother George Simmie was a witness. Their daughter **Joyce Shirley Simmie** (1921-1981) was born 6 months later.[50] A son, also named **John Ernest Simmie** (1925-2012), was born on 20 September 1925.

On return from war service, both Bill and George remained at Ridley Street, Sunshine with their mother Janet, and John Montgomery. By 1924 Janet and John Montgomery (now listed as a coach builder in the electoral rolls) had moved from Sunshine to Kensington—and so had Bill and George, albeit in their own abodes. Bill had married in 1919 to **Constance Lillingston** (1894-1988). Their children were **Roy** William (1920-2004) and **John Ernest** ('Jack' aka 'Black Jack'—1923-1994).

It wasn't an easy transition; George Simmie struggled. In October 1921 he applied, not for the first time, for Government assistance under the Repatriation Department's Industrial Scheme. George, a clerk on enlistment, was employed as a carpenter—he'd been given assistance under the scheme for working tools to get started and sustenance of over £200. His first application was for training which he commenced at Swinburne Technical School as a wood worker in May 1919. He hadn't done so well. 'Placed in employment under the Scheme as a carpenter ... on 22/10/19, 40% efficient. Transferred from that employment on the recommendation of the Soldiers' Industrial Committee and commenced in the employ of Mr W Simmie, 17/11/20.'[51] By October 1921 he was deemed to be 90% efficient but a further period of six weeks' training was approved.

By this time, it appeared that Bill Simmie had settled down relatively easily, with family and a working trade sufficient for him to take George under his wing in 1920. By 1924 the brothers had stabilised sufficiently to establish a building company—Simmie & Co. It was registered by George, as William had a legal impediment holding him up and Jock still employed with the Office of the Auditor-General. It was not long before all three brothers were engaged in the enterprise. In 1927, George Simmie also married, to **Eileen Mann** (1898-1963). A daughter **Shirley** (1929-2005), died a spinster.

18 Family Business – The Simmie Family of Simmie & Co and Harpsdale

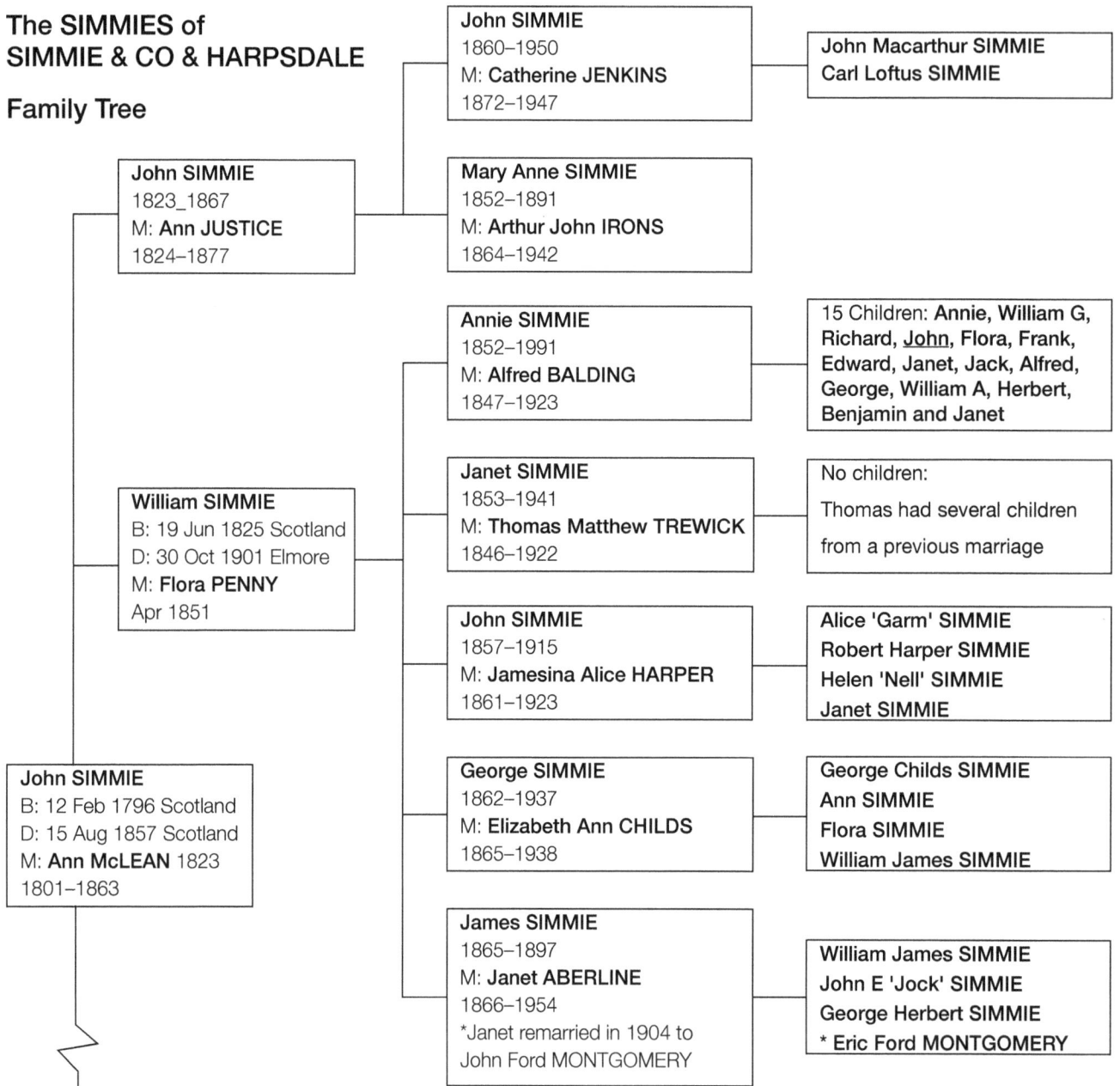

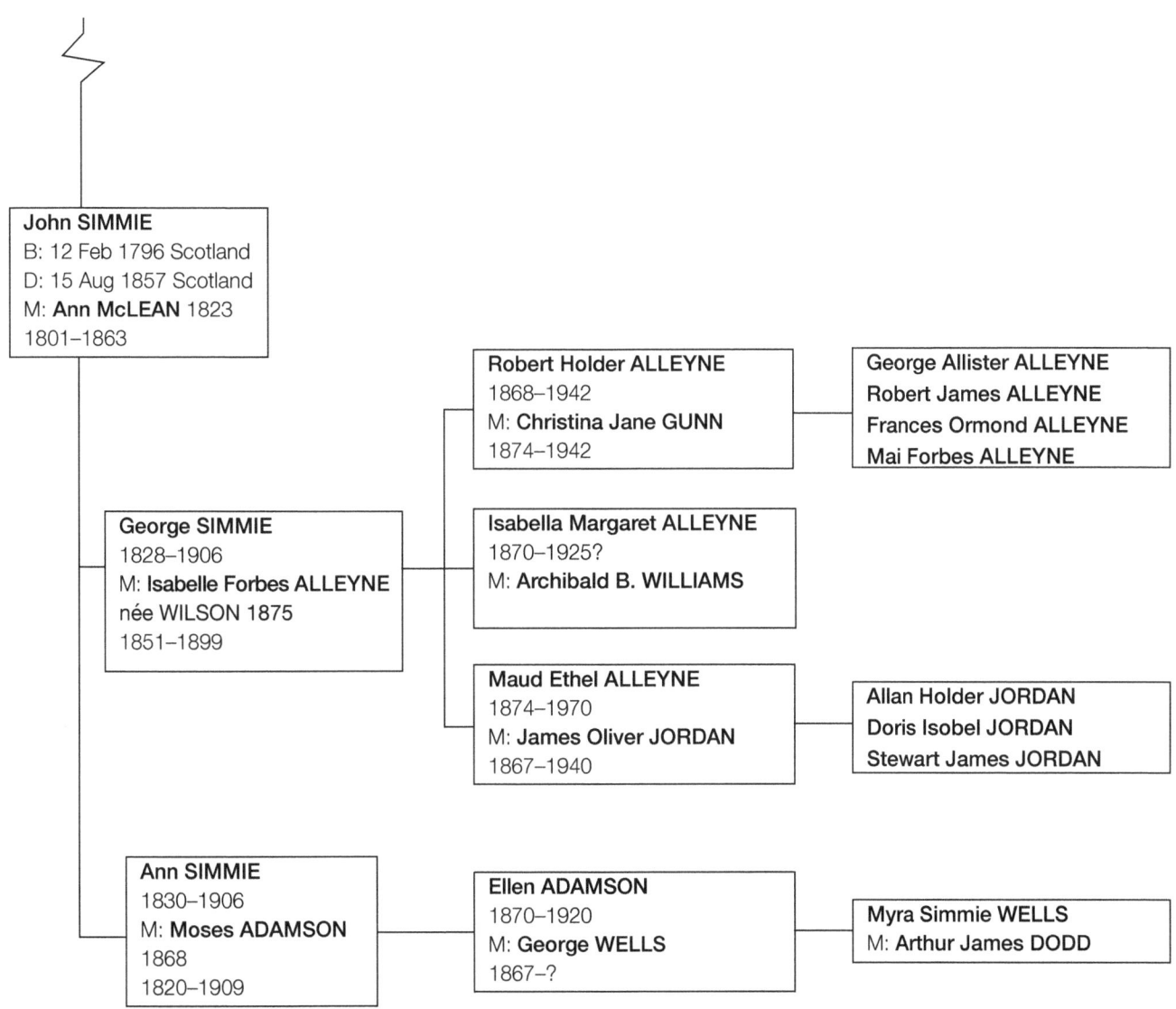

Simmie Family Tree
(From A Family History of Cornelia Creek Run & the Simmies)

William James 'Bill', John Ernest 'Jock' and George Herbert SIMMIE Family Tree

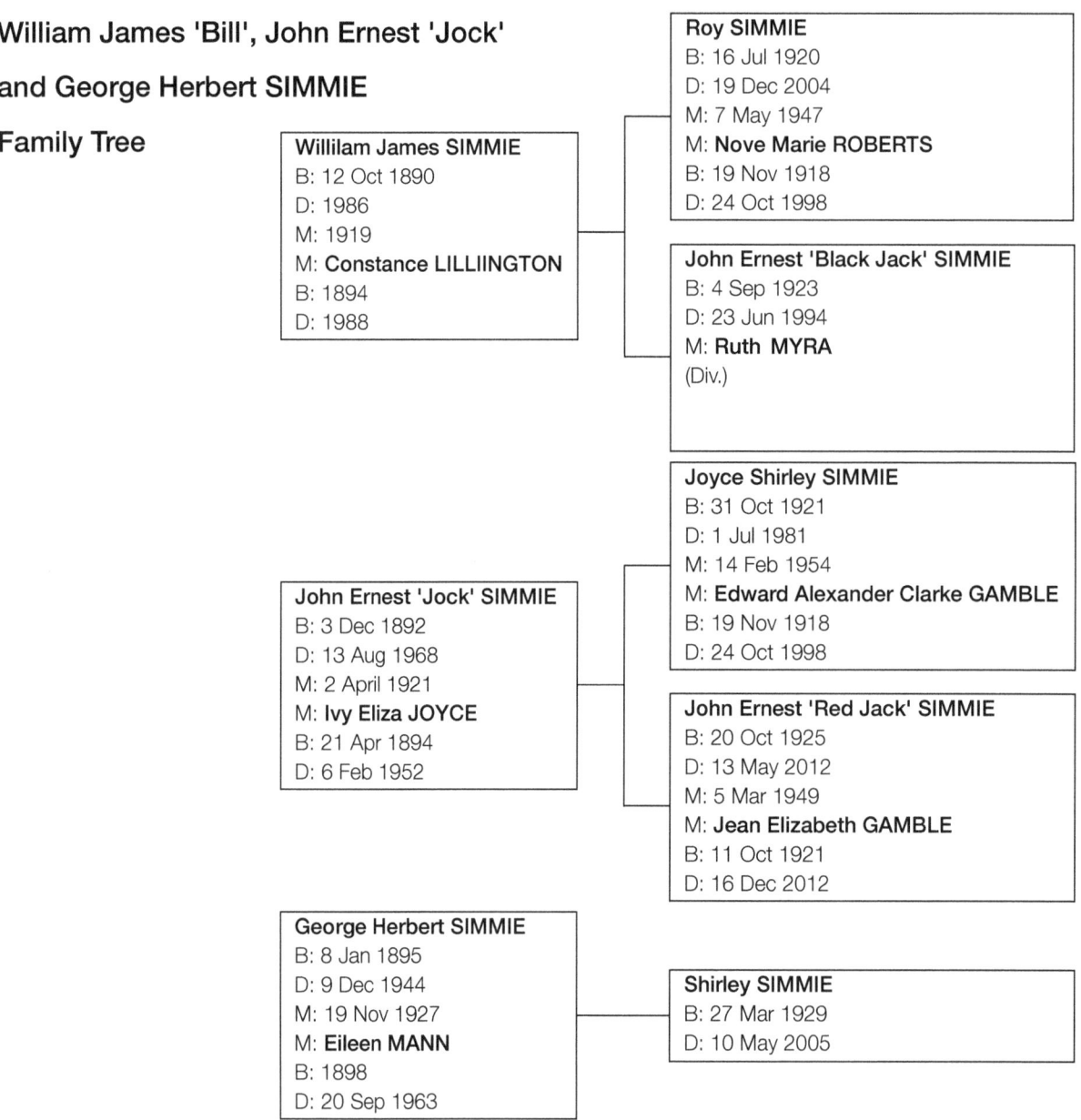

George Herbert, John Ernest (Jock) and William James (Bill) Simmie family trees. (RJ Simmie Collection)

Chapter Two
Simmie & Co—1924–1941

On 25 July 1924, George Simmie formed Simmie & Co Pty. Ltd. with David Balderinnie Hedderwick of Kew, 'for the purpose of builders and general building contractors.'[52] Hedderwick, described in the registration papers of the company as an architect, but in the 1924 Victorian Electoral Roll as a contractor, was related to the principal of the legal firm of Hedderwick, Fookes & Alston, which prepared the registration papers. Even before the registration of the company, an advertisement in the *Age* under 'Simmie' at the registered offices of the law firm in Flinders Street, Melbourne, called for 'Scaffolding and Builders plant'.[53]

The first recorded Simmie & Co project in Melbourne was when the Federated Builders' Association of Australia's magazine *Building* recorded in 1924 a two storey garage being built in Carlton for Yellow Cabs of Australia Ltd. at a cost of £30,000.[54] Other early projects included the Alexander Smith office building in Queen's Street, completed in 1928, a new dairy produce section for the Victoria Markets at a cost of £26,981 for the Melbourne City Council in 1928, and the first telephone exchange in Oakleigh for the Works and Railways Department for £4,784 that same year.[55]

Sketch, the Alexander Smith offices (*Building*, 1928)

Once Bill Simmie's old insolvency from 1916 was finally cleared in mid-1924, he too became a partner:

> The INSOLVENCY ACT—in the Court of Insolvency, Central District, at Melbourne—In the Matter of WILLIAM JAMES SIMMIE, of 22 Ridley Street, Sunshine, Carpenter, an Insolvent—A First and Final DIVIDEND to be Declared in the matter of the abovenamed insolvent, whose estate was sequestered on 13 June 1916. Creditors who have not proved their debts by the 5th day of August 1924, at 5 p.m., will be excluded. Dated this 15th day of July 1924. A. McK. Hislop, F.I.CA., official assignee, 20 Queen Street, Melbourne.[56]

Despite this, it did not take Bill long to establish himself in the Melbourne building industry. By 1928 he was already noted as a delegate to the national convention of the Federated Master Builders Association of Australia.

On 22 October 1926, Jock Simmie resigned from the public service to join his brothers in the new building company, Simmie & Co, established

FEDERATED MASTER BUILDERS' ASSOCIATION OF AUSTRALIA
22nd. Convention, Melbourne, 1928

William 'Bill' Simmie, a delegate from Melbourne, 2nd row, 4th from right.
(Building, 1928)

by George in 1924.⁵⁷ Jock Simmie formally joined the firm in December 1927, but he had already been active developing Canberra business since 1926.⁵⁸ The registered office of the company moved from their lawyers' offices in the city to the corner of Rankin's Road and Smith Street in Kensington in November 1929; the company remained there until its liquidation in 1987.

Another director was L F Pyke, builder, who was listed from 1929-1931. The Jewish, later Sir, Louis Frederick Pyke became a close associate and friend of Jock Simmie as will be described, but also with George.⁵⁹ George Simmie remained as a director in the company until 1931, when he left to become a director in the Colonial Spark Plug Co.⁶⁰ It is not known whether George left the company he established because he was unhappy in the arrangement with his brothers or just decided that this was not the business for him after all, especially, as we have seen, he was not a 'natural' carpenter/builder like his brothers. However, despite the apparent distance between the brothers as they got older and the family circles got wider, the bonds between the brothers would not have been easily disturbed, although a business falling out in particular between George and his brothers cannot be entirely discounted.

The Colonial Spark Plugs Company in South Melbourne was registered in October 1921 with £20,000 in capital.[61] One L F Pyke was recorded as the director in 1931.[62]

George was noted in December 1931 as a co-applicant in Canberra for Letters Patent for an invention by Arthur Edward Geere (engineer) and himself (contractor) for 'Improvements in Spark Plugs'.[63] The patent was granted in May 1933. Arthur Geere was the chief engineer and factory manager at 64 Sturt Street, South Melbourne. It seems that spark plugs were attractive items—over 10,000 were stolen in a robbery at a loss to the company of £1,000.[64] George himself died prematurely in Brighton on 19 December 1944, with occupation given as metal worker. His cause of death, liver failure, suggested heavy drinking as a possible cause with war trauma as a contributing factor to his early demise along with treatments for his self-inflicted wounds in World War One.

Meanwhile, Bill Simmie managed Simmie & Co in Melbourne which worked on a wide range of projects; Jock supported in the early years and more directly after he returned to Melbourne from Canberra in 1931:

> William was the other Partner in Simmie & Co. He was, from stories told, the one to best manage the workers on the building site (he had a sharp tongue and colourful language) and Jock was the brains behind the business and did all the quoting. Jock studying etc with Accountancy would have been of valuable assistance.[65]

In 1926 a Canberra branch of Simmie & Co was formed when Jock Simmie and his wife Ivy left for Canberra in time for the opening of Parliament by the Duke and Duchess of York in 1927—and became part of the story of the building of the nation's capital.[66]

Simmie & Co Canberra 1926-1931

In 1926 Jock and his wife Ivy moved to Canberra where Jock set up Simmie & Co there. It was auspicious timing with a building and

Ivy Simmie in the Canberra environment
(RJ Simmie Collection)

construction boom for the new Federal capital about to get underway. What prompted Jock to take that step is not known . He may well have been encouraged to do so by Masonic, veteran and building industry contacts that he would have developed by then, as well as a shrewd assessment of the opportunity coming in what was known then as the Federal Capital Territory to build a national capital from the ground up. It took quite a bit of entrepreneurial spirit, some capital and connections to take that plunge. No doubt the move also gave Bill and Jock both room to move and be their own men whilst providing mutual support and business leads. It certainly didn't take long for the first contracts to be won in Canberra.

At this time, Canberra was set in sheep-farming country, with little shelter from '...sharp-edged winds. Unsealed roads and unpaved footpaths turned to slush in wet weather, and yielded clouds of red dust when they were dry. What houses existed 'were far too small for the families...and they lacked screens on windows and doors to keep at bay the millions of blowflies which swarmed in from the surrounding sheep-country'.[67] Hundreds of building industry workers were accommodated in tents, and many were separated from their families for whom there was no accommodation, let alone schools, shops and other amenities.

It was in this 'frontier' environment that Simmie & Co in Canberra, on 4 November 1926, announced that it was in business.[68] One of the first areas for construction was the small Civic Centre which provided for a small commercial focus for the city. By the time Simmie started work with some projects, the *Canberra Times* said: 'The face of Civic Centre No. 1. Subdivision has changed noticeably since July last when there was no sign of buildings'.[69] Simmie and Co were already hard at work with two storey buildings in Civic Centre for offices and shops and the first banking building in Canberra, for the Commercial Banking Company of Sydney (CBCS) and then the Commonwealth Bank as well.

The CBCS was to be managed by James David Aubrey, father-in-law of up-and-coming Sydney architect (and Freemason) Malcolm Johnson Moir (1903-1971), who later worked with Jock Simmie in Canberra on several iconic projects, as shall be seen.[70] The supervising architect on the CBCS project was former Melbourne-based architect Kenneth Henry Bell Oliphant, another Freemason and World War One veteran, of whom more later.[71] Jock Simmie later told an anecdote, without naming the bank concerned, 'about the bank manager who lost the key to the strongroom door of his new bank an hour before it was to be ceremonially handed to him by the Bank's Chairman of Directors.'[72]

There is little doubt that Jock Simmie used his credentials as a Gallipoli and wounded Western Front veteran to build connections and develop business in Canberra when national pride in developing the new capital was supported and managed by so many war veterans, from builders to senior officials in the burgeoning public service. Additionally, Jock Simmie was a Freemason, like his father before him. In Canberra (and in Melbourne) his veteran status and Masonic connections dovetailed in the personal and business relationships needed to successfully develop Simmie & Co business from a standing start. Many veterans had joined Lodges after the war. A possible example of this was an early contract in 1927 to build shops and offices on four leases along Northbourne Avenue in Canberra's Civic Centre for the Lariston Investment Company. This company was owned by none other than Senator for Victoria, Harold Edward Elliott or Major-General 'Pompey' Elliott CB, CMG, DSO, DCM, VD and member of the United Grand Lodge of Victoria's Naval & Military Lodge No 49.[73]

Another important early contract was to build an assembly hall, later known as Albert Hall, near the Hotel Canberra and Parliament House in mid-1927.[74] When it was listed on the Register of Significant Twentieth Century Architecture for the ACT (RSTCA—ACT) in 1984, as a 'late and rare example of the 1920's Classical Revival', it described the importance of the building as:

> ... historically and socially important as the first venue for concerts, dances and other occasions for the early residents of Canberra. The building served the Canberra community

as its main theatre, exhibition hall, conference and convention centre, ballroom, and concert hall until the construction of the Canberra Theatre Centre in 1965.[75]

As Canberra's only performing arts venue for its first 40 years, and able to hold an audience of up to 700 persons, Albert Hall influenced the growth of flourishing musical, operatic and dramatic societies, such as the Society for Arts and Literature, Canberra Relief Society and Canberra Repertory Society. It was also the venue for tours by the Royal Ballet and the Australian Ballet, and even housed exhibitions of paintings and sculpture before a national gallery emerged. The Albert Hall was opened by Prime Minister Stanley Bruce in March 1928, and he declared that it 'would radiate the liberalising

Albert Hall under construction 1927
(National Archives of Australia)

movements of national significance which played so important a part in the development of the community.'[76]

In a speech to the new Master Builders Association of the Federal Capital Territory in 1927—of which Jock Simmie was already a member—Sir John Harrison, a member of the Federal Capital Commission (FCC) said:

> 'If I were a younger man, who was able to commence life anew, this is the place where I would put up my shingle. There is a lack of enterprise in regard to Canberra on the part of the Sydney builders. There are big opportunities here waiting to be seized.'

Debutante Ball at the Albert Hall, 1956
(National Archives of Australia)

Sir John added that some big building work would be available during the current year for builders. Tenders would be received during the next two or three weeks for the foundations of the main administrative buildings. Other work would follow...[77]

Jock Simmie and Simmie & Co was to be advantaged by the slow take up of opportunities in Canberra by Sydney construction firms. Yet Sydney firms were certainly prominent in the tenders for the foundations of the Commonwealth Administration Offices for example. A Sydney firm won the tender, and no less than six others among 13 tenders were from Sydney—Simmie & Co was 9th. However, as Harrison had described, there was no shortage of opportunities. As one of the first locally domiciled contractors, Simmie & Co went on to create a prominent place in the Federal Capital Territory, thus cementing his position as one of the 'builders of Canberra'. In August 1928 Jock Simmie was elected Treasurer of the Master Builders Association and he would play a prominent role in the Association for many years thereafter.[78]

In May 1928 Jock Simmie became a member of the Canberra sub-branch of the Returned Sailors and Soldiers Imperial League of Australia (RS&SILA—

later the Returned Services League (RSL). Ivy Simmie also joined the Ladies Auxiliary as soon as it was formed, in March 1930. Jock and Ivy also saw opportunities to join the small coterie of influential persons in Canberra by joining the Canberra Golf Club in 1927—they were noted as playing in a mixed fours game led by the Prime Minister following the opening of the first nine holes of the club's new course in November that year.[79] Ivy was also a keen tennis player and joined in the Eastlake Tennis Club's opening tournament in March 1928.

In the meantime, as it tried to establish itself, Simmie & Co took on what, by the standards of some of the very large projects to come, were relatively small jobs—a seven room villa in Braddon and a six-bedroom cottage in Red Hill for example, came in August 1928. But both were architect designed, by Kenneth Oliphant with whom Jock Simmie had been involved on his early bank construction in 1926.[80] Construction of ordinary houses in Canberra for both workers and professional people alike was at a premium as the capital rapidly took shape and the population increased, given impetus by the opening of the first Parliament in May 1927.[81] It was probably no coincidence that the home in Braddon was for one Dr Arthur James Cahill, who happened to have joined the Canberra sub-branch of the RS&SILA on the same night as Jock Simmie. A fellow Victorian, Cahill had served in England and France as a medical doctor during the First World War.[82]

August 1928 saw a new, but modest, public building project.[83] Simmie & Co won the contract to build an 'insectory' for the new Council for Scientific and Industrial Research (later the CSIRO)—two modest hot-houses at a cost of £2,700.[84] These were quickly dignified as Entomology Laboratories. Two more houses in the suburbs of Reid and Forrest completed the year. 1929 saw a leap forward in the company's fortunes, winning more work at the CSIR for £17,900 and described as 'the largest undertaken in Canberra in the last 12 months'. It was to be for the first section of buildings for a National Museum of Zoology (by 1929 called the Australian Institute of Anatomy).[85]

This was followed almost immediately, in April 1929, by a large £65,951 contract to construct the final stages of the Institute of Anatomy. 'Construction of the Institute began in April 1929, and it had sufficiently advanced by January 1930 for the building to be occupied soon afterwards, though work on it was not

The Entomology Laboratories with the start of the Institute of Anatomy on right
(National Library of Australia)

Construction workers in front of the Institute of Anatomy 1929
(National Film and Sound Archive)

completed until late that year or early 1931'.[86] The buildings of the Institute were specifically intended 'to house Professor Colin Mackenzie's gift collection of specimens of Australian fauna'. The Institute would be erected next to the site for the future University of Canberra in Acton.[87] The *Canberra Times* wrote the company up:

> The builders, Simmie and Co, have contributed a large portion of the buildings in Canberra since commencing operations here in 1926. The Albert Hall, Commonwealth Bank, Commercial Bank of Australia, the Commercial Banking Co. of Sydney, the Bank of Australasia, Lariston Buildings, Snow's Corner, a large shopping block for Canberra Shops Ltd., and various other buildings have been erected by them. They have In hand at present the Entomological Laboratories, the Institute of Anatomy, as well as various residences in various suburbs.[88]

The final cost of the building, as noted in October 1931 was £72,392-3-0, per the meticulous accounting of the Federal Capital Commission; the building was finally completed in August 1931.[89]

Years later, in 1984, the building was placed on the RSTCA—ACT. The architect who was largely responsible for the design and supervision of the

The Australian Institute of Anatomy c 1935
(National Library of Australia)

Institute of Anatomy was FCC architect Malcolm J Moir, a fellow Freemason with a strong Scottish heritage like Jock Simmie. They would form both a strong professional relationship and personal friendship in the years ahead.[90]

Jock Simmie also got involved with other business opportunities, perhaps in part due to the downturn in construction work as Canberra's economy slowed with reduced Government expenditure and the effects of the Great Depression were quickly felt in Canberra after early 1930. For example, in May 1929 he and two others registered the company of Esmond's Garages Ltd with a nominal capital of £30,000 in 20,000 ordinary shares and 10,000 preferential shares of £1 each. With head office in Queanbeyan NSW, Esmond's was established to 'carry on as manufacturers, engineers and as agents for motor cars, cycles and aircraft'.

The company was named after fellow director and founder John Esmond, 'one of the best-known identities of Canberra and Queanbeyan during the construction days of the national capital'. [91] Esmond's continued as a very successful motor dealer, holding the General Motors (and Holden) franchise for the ACT. Following the departure of John Esmond from the business in 1940, Jock Simmie appeared to control the company. In 1929 Jock also moved forward with his Masonic interests. On 6 March 1929 Jock was admitted to Capitol Lodge 612 of the Uniting Grand Lodge of NSW. The Lodge operated in Queanbeyan. [92] Like Simmie & Co in Melbourne, the Canberra company also built some churches and associated

St Andrew's Presbyterian church under construction 1929
(National Archives of Australia)

constructions.

Unlike in Melbourne, the denominational churches in Canberra were often the first to be built there—such was the case with the St. Andrew's Presbyterian church on Capitol Hill (less nave and parish hall), the contract of which was announced in May 1929. The church underway, in August that year Simmie and Co also won a tender for the Methodist School Hall on a central site catering for both Presbyterian and Methodist denominations. It was designed to seat 100, and include a kindergarten hall, classrooms and kitchen.[93] By the end of 1929, Simmie & Co had won more work with the CSIR as approved by the

St Andrew's Presbyterian Church, completed 1932 (National Archives of Australia)

Federal Capital Commission. Having completed the Entomology Laboratories, this time it was for Botanical Laboratories at a cost of £16,333. It was scheduled for completion in under six months.[94]

Into 1930 however, the impact of the Great Depression was already evident; 'cutbacks in government spending during this period quickly brought an end to Canberra's growth spurt.'[95] In May 1930, the FCC (along with its Architect Department), was abolished and replaced by the Canberra Advisory Council.[96] Through 1930 and 1931 Simmie & Co managed to survive with a range of small projects—the larger public projects dried up. Indeed, the Government, to alleviate unemployment, in June 1930 even allowed the erection of semi-detached homes in the suburb of Manuka to be built by day labourers, leading to an immediate protest by the Canberra Master Builders—including Jock Simmie—who expected the jobs to be put to tender. The protest was to no avail. Small jobs came Simmie & Co's way but it was share all work between all the builders.

There was a house construction in Forrest, but little else but residential that year—the opening of the Methodist School Hall in May 1930 was small consolation for the downturn in work. Carry over work from earlier, such as at St Andrew's church, kept work crews together until it opened in August 1932. Jock Simmie kept his key people together as best he could, even forming a company cricket team to play local clubs.[97] In early 1929 architect Moir had formed a Canberra Men's Hockey Association—it became the Federal Capital Hockey Association (FCHA) and Moir was its first secretary.[98] Jock Simmie joined the FCHA committee as a Vice-President; another on the committee was fellow Freemason Thomas Mitchell Shakespeare who was later patron of the FCHA. He was a good contact for Jock Simmie for another reason—his son Arthur Shakespeare was also a member of the new Canberra Advisory Council.[99] Ivy Simmie kept herself busy with activities in the Horticultural Society, entering the best garden competition but without success—Mrs Annie Shakespeare was also a member. Golf continued; Jock donated a trophy for a competition in April 1931.

Jock also ramped up his Masonic activities by also becoming a Royal Arch Mason on 6 February 1931 at a meeting in Canberra of the Australian Chapter No 87.[100] Another new business opportunity for Jock Simmie arose at the end of 1931. A new Companies Ordinance was passed in

Canberra and the second company to be registered under its provisions was the Civic Theatre Limited. Jock Simmie joined a group of three other investors as a director in the new company, which issued a prospectus for a new and modern sound film theatre to be constructed in Canberra City which would seat 1100 patrons—with capital of £20,000 in £1 shares.[101]

At the same time as the announcement of this new venture, the Simmies put their six-bedroom villa in 5 Baudin Street, Forrest, where they had lived since 1928, with tennis court and 'garden well-laid out', up for sale.[102]

Family Life 1926-1940

The Simmies had decided to relocate to Melbourne and Jock would start spending less time in Canberra. The main reason was the death in Melbourne of Ivy Simmie's mother, Emily Joyce, as much as the downturn in business in Canberra. Jock was close to his in-laws and no doubt Ivy was concerned for her father Jack. Jock and Ivy went to live with Jack Joyce at Martin Street, Elwood from 1931 until August 1935; Jack Joyce never remarried. Jock and Ivy Simmie then moved to the house Jock built at 42 Halifax (on the corner of Hall) Street,

Flyer for the Weatherly Estate sale in 1934
(RJ Simmie Collection)

Brighton following his purchase of the block in November 1934. Jock's parents, Janet and John Montgomery had already returned to Sunshine in retirement.

The house was on a double block and had a tennis court. Ivy Simmie's father Jack Joyce went

House at Halifax Street, Brighton
(RJ Simmie Collection)

with them. Ivy wanted for nothing, including a full-time live-in home help. Jock continued to travel to Canberra to oversee and manage the Canberra arm of Simmie & Co.[103]

It is easy to forget in the detailed history of Jock Simmie's business life with Simmie & Co, his other business interests and the later Dorset Horn Stud at Harpsdale that he was also a father and husband with a growing family. When Jock and Ivy moved to Canberra in 1926, they took with them their two children Joyce Shirley Simmie aged five, and John Ernest Simmie aged just one. John was called 'Red Jack' to differentiate him from his cousin, also John Ernest, who was 'Black Jack'. When Jock and Ivy and the children returned to Melbourne in 1931 Ivy was able to rely on house help to manage the household and the children. Jock

Before the Dance, Lorne 1930s
(RJ Simmie Collection)

Simmie was away as much as at home managing his growing business in Canberra and also working closely with his brother Bill in Melbourne. He would travel to Canberra by train and later, years after World War Two, started to fly commercially.

Once Jock and Ivy with son John and daughter Joyce had returned to Melbourne from Canberra in 1931, they often went to Lorne on the Great Ocean Road which had opened in 1924, with other family members and other holidaymakers and guests to that area. Large groups would gather at Erskine House (guesthouse since 1877); Lorne was a fashionable place to go and be seen.[104] Jock had purchased some land in the lower Dandenong Ranges near Emerald and also was a keen member with Ivy of the Emerald Country Club and its golfing fraternity and was noted as Club Captain on New Year's Day in 1940.[105] Once Jock purchased the historic Harpsdale property in 1940, his land in Emerald was superfluous and the Club too far away to travel just for golf. Visits to Lorne however, given the travel arrangements to get there and back alone, would have made them especially anticipated by all the family.

Simmie & Co Canberra 1931-1941

With the Depression in full swing through 1932 before a gradual recovery began in 1933, the Canberra building scene was flat. Jock, however, was

John, Ivy and Joyce Simmie, 1936
(RJ Simmie Collection)

always on the lookout for new opportunities and in 1932 he was noted as one of four applicants before the Prospecting Board for the extension by 400 acres of a gold prospecting lease near Queanbeyan.[106] Presumably until then they had had no luck; it's not known if there was any subsequently.

In 1933 work started to pick up. Simmie & Co won the contract to build 'extensive additions' to the Government Printing Office for £7,355. This was followed soon after by a Department of the Interior contract for the concrete work for the new Black Mountain Reservoir; another £7,197 earned.[107] The Reservoir was commissioned by the end of January 1934, but other work was in hand, both large and small. On 9 February 1934 Simmie & Co won arguably its biggest ever contract and its most prestigious, namely the Museum section of the new Australian War Memorial (AWM).[108] It could be seen that the contract was also aimed at employment, with a clause in the contract stipulating local workers only were to be employed. Work got underway immediately.[109] Jock Simmie reported to the *Canberra Times* that he already had 15 local men employed. As a reminder of the times his contract was set in, the newspaper reported:

The (first) National Library, off King's Way, Canberra 1935 (National Library of Australia, Mildenhall Collection)

All the plant is on site, and today [22nd February] a start will be made by tractor to plough one portion of the basement. This earth will be removed by a huge scoop, tractor drawn. In addition to this scoop, *six horse-drawn scoops will also be put to use*. [author's italics][110]

Then in April 1934, another prestigious project was awarded to Simmie & Co—the first section of the new National Library, on King's Avenue.

The contract was worth £10,639; Simmie & Co won the contract against 11 other contenders.[111] The building was completed in June 1935.

When the building was demolished in 1968 with the opening of the current National Library in Parkes, a remarkable discovery was made. Simmie & Co workers had placed inside one of the columns they had completed at the building entrance, along with a 1935 newspaper, the following 'document':

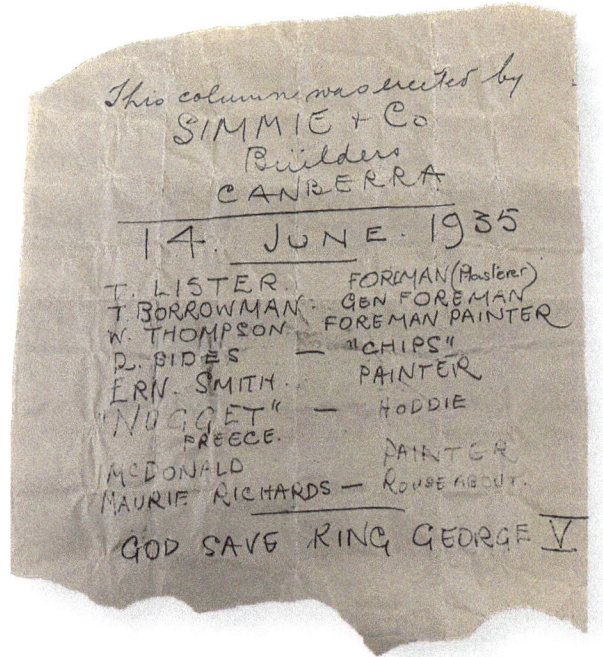

Workers note left in column of National Library 1935 (National Library of Australia)

'This column was erected by SIMMIE & Co Builders CANBERRA

14 June 1935

T. LISTER.	FOREMAN (Plasterer)
T. BORROWMAN.	GEN FOREMAN
W. THOMPSON	FOREMAN PAINTER
R. SIDES —	"CHIPS" [Carpenter]
ERN. SMITH.	PAINTER
"NUGGET" PREECE. —	HODDIE
J McDONALD	PAINTER
MAURIE RICHARDS —	ROUSEABOUT

GOD SAVE KING GEORGE V

Thomas ('Tom') Borrowman (1887-1957), who had emigrated from Scotland in 1912, worked for Simmie & Co in Canberra from 1928. He had been the site supervisor for several projects including the CSIR (later CSIRO), Black Mountain Reservoir, the Civic Theatre and the National Library. His obituary noted that he then 'took over the supervision of Simmie & Co's joinery shop and examples of his exceptional craftsmanship are to be seen in the National Library, the Australian War Memorial, American Embassy and more recently the Netherlands Embassy'. During the Second World War he was a member of the Volunteer Defence Corps as well as the Queanbeyan Rifle

Club, and he was a long-time supporter of the Queanbeyan Football Club, in which he served as President during the war years.[112] His Scottish antecedents would have been well regarded by Jock Simmie.

With the opening in September 1934 of St Andrew's Presbyterian Church—'the magnificent building which occupies a commanding site...and impresses one with its height, strength and dignity' (in 2017 the church was listed on the RSTCA-ACT as a prime example of 'inter-war Gothic' style)[113]— Jock Simmie and Simmie & Co would have been a well-known name in Canberra and among Parliamentarians, civil servants, and workers alike. There is no doubt that in under 10 years and from a start-up position, Simmie & Co had come far and fast. Jock Simmie's credentials, connections and networking had paid off handsomely and Simmie & Co had developed a first-class reputation. Yet Jock Simmie did not let it get in the way of accepting lesser works as well—like the three brick residences being built in Forrest and Griffith. The fact that he had to ask for an extension of the contract because of the huge demands of the AWM and National Library contracts did not prevent him from finishing.

It was another 30 years before Jock Simmie stepped back from work in Canberra. In the book, *On Solid Foundations—the Building and Construction of the Nation's Capital 1920-1950*, Jock was described thus:

> A typical Australian of many fine parts— with a delightful sense of humour—able to mix in any company—a keen businessman of undoubted ability—who in his success was always mindful of the needs of others, ready to assist. Jock Simmie's word was his bond in all things.

> Jock also observed the custom of having a drink on-site with the boys, handing out the Christmas pay packets, a few personal remarks, and a hearty handshake with each one. This ritual was always well received, although on one occasion he recounted that he overheard one wag observe that like all accountants, Jock's largesse was not likely to start an unruly inflationary surge![114]

With the AWM work underpinning the company's prosperity well into 1935, Jock Simmie continued to seek and win numerous contracts in the years leading up to World War Two. In 1935 as a sign of better times, Simmie's cricket team was revived, but could not withstand the Printers Quarters XI in a friendly match. Esmond's Garages Ltd was reconstituted in 1935 as Esmond's Motors Ltd. with a branch in both Queanbeyan and in Canberra. The new company saw Jock Simmie continue as a major shareholder and director, registering capital of £30,000 divided into 20,000 £1 shares and 10,000 cumulative preference shares, also £1 each.[115]

In another sign of returning confidence, the new Civic Theatre, the second theatre in Canberra, started construction in July 1935 as another Simmie & Co project. The theatre, first mooted in 1931, would open in early 1936 and would seat 850 patrons.[116] As has been noted, Jock Simmie was an investor himself and, as a director of the company, was public in his support for the project. One of the other investors was Lieutenant-Colonel Harold Edward Jones the former patron of the Hockey Association. M J Moir, whom Jock Simmie had worked with on the Institute of Anatomy project, was the driver of this project too. Moir just happened to be the manager of the existing Capitol Theatre in Manuka and the architect for the new one in Civic.[117] Canberra, with its small population of less than 12,000, was a small place indeed.

Breaking the first sod for the Civic Theatre 1935. Jock Simmie 4th from L; Malcolm Moir 3rd from R and William H B Dickson with shovel (National Library of Australia)

Almost counter-intuitively, even after Ivy had relocated to Melbourne Jock remained a member of the Canberra Horticultural Society and contributed 'a handsome bowl' as a perpetual trophy for the 'most successful member exhibitor of vegetables at the principal exhibitions.'[118] This appears to be another example of Jock's ability to mix with all types of people but also see the networking opportunity in a simple bowl; as we have seen, some very influential people were members of that society.

He made sure Simmie & Co was seen to be part of the community as well. For example, Simmie & Co fielded two teams for the tug-of-war

Civic Theatre, 1938
(National Library of Australia)

—'strenuous training was being carried out'—at the Canberra Highland Gathering in September 1937.[119] On another level altogether, Jock continued to develop his Masonic-cum-veteran connections. In Canberra, he was a founding member of the Remembrance Mark Lodge 133.[120]

The first of several Department of Interior contracts at the Royal Military College (RMC) Duntroon began in 1936. First, the new Science Block and classrooms for £13,197, then, a few months later, on the sixth large administration block for a further £5236. These buildings were cited on the RSTCA-ACT in 1984.[121] As we will see, the Melbourne 'division' of Simmie & Co

J E Simmie Masonic medal, Remembrance Mark Lodge 133 (RJ Simmie Collection)

was also benefitting from Jock Simmie's defence connections in Canberra. In late 1936, a private residence was also built at 3 Wilmott Avenue in Forrest from late 1936 for solicitor and Freemason William Hay Baker Dickson, which was later placed on the RSTCA-ACT, described as a style of 'interwar functionalist'.[122] It was the latest project with architect, Malcolm Moir. In mid-1937 Simmie & Co started on the first section of a new public school at Ainslie, the 'fine, modern building' was expected to take 12 months to complete at a cost of £29,785.[123] That year Jock Simmie became a Fellow of the Association of Cost Accountants of Australia.

He also invested in two new companies in Canberra. In July 1937 came Capital Motors Limited, in the suburb of Manuka, with a capital of £15,000, which later advertising described as a sub-dealer of Esmond's Motors (Canberra). Jock was listed as the first signatory, and another was Gwilym Thomas Evans, a prominent Canberra accountant, who was also a director of Esmond's Motors. The Manuka service station completed in 1938 and leased by Capital Motors, was designed by M J Moir. It was a consortium led by Moir and which included G T Evans, which had won the lease of the site, for 99 years.[124] In a cover-all, the objects of Capital Motors were described as:

> .....the business of manufacturers, engineers, agents, dealers, or hirers, repairers, storers [storemen], and warehousemen of automobiles, motor cars, motor lorries, aeroplanes and other commercial vehicles and all machinery, accessories, and other appliances capable of being used therewith.[125]

In September came FCT (Federal Capital Territory) Investments Limited, with share capital of £15,000; and the same signatories as Capital Motors. This company described its objectives as '... to purchase and otherwise acquire real or personal property of any description and to acquire, hold and deal in freehold, house and land property'.[126]

One of the project managers in employ in Canberra at that time was Louis Frederick Pyke, who as previously described was a director in George Simmie's Colonial Spark Plugs venture in Victoria in 1931. According to Pyke's biography, Pyke had joined Simmie & Co (in its early years) after completing a carpenter apprenticeship. Later he described himself as a 'lousy student' and a poor carpenter, but '...he loved building'. He became a project manager with Simmie & Co and worked on large construction jobs including buildings in Civic Centre and the AWM. He was made a junior partner of Simmie & Co in 1939.[127] After World War Two, Pyke and Jock Simmie developed business together in Melbourne, as will be described. Meanwhile the work got underway at the AWM and was due to be completed in 1940. Who was to know that by then Australia would once again be at war?

This ground-breaking, monumental project was not without its problems, not least due to the disagreements about design features between the two architects namely John Crust and Emil Sodersteen—from different firms—who had jointly won the architectural competition for the best design. That was not the only issue facing the builders of the AWM. Michael McKernan's history of the AWM, *Here Is Their Spirit*, takes up the story:

> The builder, Simmie and Company of Melbourne, had estimated that the completion of stage one would take 60 weeks and had commenced work in February 1934. By May 1935 the firm's directors, both of them ex-servicemen, were asked to explain the obvious lack of progress and they listed a number of factors: much more rock in the excavations than had been allowed for; the wettest year on record in Canberra; a complete shut-down for 2 months while plans were altered; and uncertainty of supplies when materials could only be ordered after alterations had been agreed to. The builders refused to give an approximate completion date until they had been told that there was agreement on all the details of the design.[128]

In another significant contract, in October 1937 it was announced that Simmie & Co had been awarded a £151,616 contract for the final and completion stage of the Australian War

Australian War Memorial forecourt under construction c1937
(RJ Simmie Collection)

Memorial, a two-year project. The exhibition galleries had been completed in 1936. Simmie & Co now had the prestigious and perhaps most publicly important parts of the undertaking—the Hall of Memory and Dome, the courtyard and the cloisters, the Roll of Honour in bronze or marble (it would be bronze) and the facing of the whole structure in white Hawkesbury sandstone.[129]

It was the costliest building project on the 1937-38 construction plan for Canberra and needed more than 100,000 cubic feet of sandstone—the same type that Simmie & Co had used on the Institute

Australian War Memorial forecourt under construction c1937
(RJ Simmie Collection)

of Anatomy project in 1929. The Australian War Memorial contract was a triumph for Simmie & Co and especially for Jock Simmie, whose standing could not have been higher. In 1984 the AWM was listed on the RSTCA—ACT.[130] The iconic building project was nearing completion in early 1941 and it was hoped to open it on Anzac Day that year. [131]

McKernan relates that through most of 1938 architect disagreements continued until finally Sodersteen resigned in December that year, leaving Crust to complete the design features. Jock Simmie must have been considerably relieved. However, issues continued:

The Australian War Memorial nearing completion, 1941
(Australian War Memorial)

In April 1940 [Crust] asked Simmie and Company for an expected completion date but the builders could give no realistic forecast 'owing to the inability to obtain supplies and difficulties in transport owing to the Coal Strike'. In August the builders complained to the Department of the Interior that the Hawkesbury Sandstone Company was causing delays by not providing sufficient quantities of stone.[132]

The Prime Minister, R G Menzies, apparently did not like the finished building. When it was opened by the Governor-General in November 1941, Jock Simmie—the principal of Simmie & Co which had completed one of the most expensive and largest national buildings to date—was not placed on the dais although the two estranged architects were sat next to each other.[133] Was the slight intended because Jock had been forthright as to the reasons for the delays? It didn't seem to matter however, as Simmie & Co continued to be a major force in the building of Canberra for almost 30 more years.

Smaller projects continued to come to Simmie & Co. For example, in July 1938 the firm began construction of the two-storey Returned Soldiers Club in Civic Centre, a £7,500 project. It was opened in February 1939 by the Governor-General.[134] A 'refuse destructor' (or 'modern garbage incinerator')—housed in a brick three storey building was constructed in Westridge in May 1939 followed by additions and alterations to the Hotel Kingston.[135]

The advent of World War Two in September 1939 meant defence contracts began to come in—both in Canberra and Melbourne. A hiccup occurred in late 1940 when the company was informed that it had not registered in the ACT as a 'foreign company' under the Territory's Companies Law. Simmie & Co's consulting accountant, G T Evans, was quick to rectify the oversight, for the penalty was £5 per day for every day unregistered—and Simmie & Co had already been operating in the Australian Capital Territory (ACT) for almost 15 years![136]

In Canberra, Simmie & Co was well placed with Jock Simmie's evident veteran, masonic, master builder and community connections. Additionally, in April 1940, Jock Simmie became a foundation member of the newly inaugurated Canberra branch of the Commonwealth Institute of Accountants.[137] In November 1939 construction of two 'general service hangars' got underway at the Royal Australian Air Force (RAAF) base at Canberra aerodrome, for £41,997. This was followed by another hangar immediately afterwards, for £22,508 in the first half of 1940.[138]

Simmie & Co also built smaller prestige projects as well. For example, in 1941 it constructed two, two-storey residential properties in the 'Interwar Mediterranean' architectural style at 58 and 60 Arthur Circle in Forrest. No 58 (later heritage listed) was built for Charles and Elizabeth Chandler. No 60 was built for Harold and Edith Raggatt.[139] Another residence was built at 4 Normanby Crescent in Deakin. The architects for all three were long standing associate, M J Moir and his second wife and architect Heather Sutherland.[140]

The suburb of Forrest, named in 1928, contained the 'Blandfordia 4 Housing Precinct'

Canberra Aerodrome hangars c1940
(RJ Simmie Collection)

(which includes Arthur Circle and 5 Baudin Street, where Jock Simmie lived to 1931); and now includes several heritage-listed properties. The precinct itself was registered for heritage listing in 2007, and although that did not occur, it is worth describing why that was proposed and how that application in 2007 helps to explain why Jock Simmie both lived there himself, built numerous residences there, and made so many connections essential to his ever-expanding business:

> The original housing designs were all by professional architects, including many of Canberra's most notable architects, along with architects of renown from elsewhere in Australia.... The precinct is also remarkable for its....strong associations with Australia's

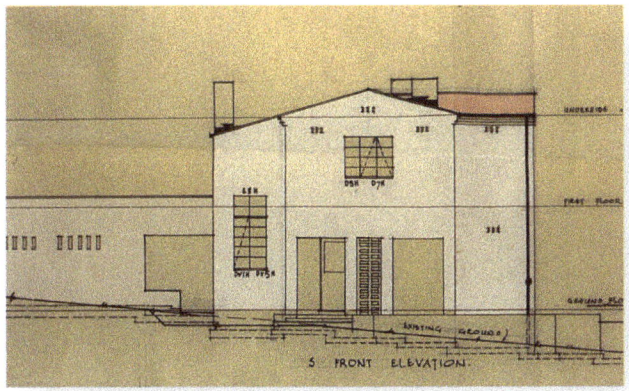

Elevation, 58 Arthur Circle, Forrest, 1941
(Courtesy Peter Freeman)

political, administrative, economic, intellectual, and cultural history since the first residents moved in in 1926. …Adjacent to the present 'embassy belt', this neighbourhood housed the first British High Commissioner and numerous other foreign diplomats…. The Blandfordia 4 Housing Precinct was also home to prominent architects and builders, to political journalists, and to a number of Cabinet ministers. There are close associations with three prime ministers…[141]

Simmie & Co Melbourne 1924-1941

An inventory of Simmie & Co projects in Melbourne and Canberra between 1924 and 1939 saw the company competing successfully in a wide range

Advertising residential sites in Blandfordia 1928
(National Library of Australia)

of building projects from small to large. The company survived not only the highly competitive building scene in Melbourne, but also the Depression and World War Two periods. The company was appointed

The St Kilda Sea Baths c1932
(State Library of Victoria)

to some very large projects while completing more 'bread and butter' constructions to maintain cash flow between the large jobs, for example, additions and alterations to a used car dealership in South Yarra in 1933.[142] Among the first of the large projects was the rebuild of the St Kilda Sea Baths (1930)—a project worth £50,830. As this work was in the Great Depression, it was 'intended to use all the labor [sic] possible to assist in relieving unemployment'.

Bill Simmie told the *Age* that:

> The office organisation would be expedited so that men could be put to work on the site quickly. He expected that within a fortnight about 60 men, chiefly labourers, with a sprinkling of artisans, would be needed. As the work progressed the number of persons employed would increase to about 150 before

St. Monica's Church, Moonee Ponds
(State Library of Victoria)

the end of the year. …local labour would be given the utmost possible preference. All the cement, steel and timber…would be Australian.[143]

Less than a week later, Bill Simmie was on the back foot, as 'a large number of unemployed turned up at the baths…..in the hope that men would be taken on. Later in the morning they were informed that no jobs were available'. Bill explained that more would be taken on once the work had been laid out but that 'all labour would be engaged through the local municipal unemployment bureau' and that 'employment would be restricted to residents of St. Kilda.'[144]

Monastery at Croydon for the Missionaries of the Sacred Heart 1939
(*Building*, 1939)

At its opening in October 1931, St Kilda City councillor and former mayor, World War One hero Albert Jacka VC, extended congratulations to Simmie & Co Bill Simmie responded.[145] When World War One began, Catholic, 'sporting identity and businessman', John Wren, announced that he would give a gold watch to Australia's first Victoria Cross winner—which was won by Jacka at Gallipoli in 1915. Jacka later became a business associate of Wren (who was also known to the Simmie brothers through Jock Simmie's father-in-law). Wren in turn was a strong supporter of Archbishop Daniel Mannix of the Catholic Diocese in Melbourne. These connections would lead to much business in the years ahead for Simmie & Co.

One of the first of many Simmie & Co projects for the Diocese was the beautiful St Monica's Church in Moonee Ponds, which replaced the old church built in 1884, which was demolished to make way for the new. Archbishop Mannix laid the foundation stone in early 1934. Completed at a cost of £30,000, the nave, lady chapel, entrances and baptistry opened in December 1934; it could seat up to 1200 people.[146]

*Monastery cloisters at Croydon for the Missionaries of the Sacred Heart 1939 (*Building*, 1939)*

This was followed by the equally impressive Monastery for the Society of Missionaries of the Sacred Heart in Croydon (1938)—now a heritage listed building—on a 46-acre site:

> The building has been planned in the form of a 'U' enclosing a centre courtyard about 150 feet across, the whole of this courtyard being surrounded by a cloistered arcade. The Chapel, ...at the open end of the 'U', forms the dominant feature.....and is linked to the cloistered arcades on both sides by open cloisters. The material employed.....is cream brickwork, the quality of which is of a very high character, the architect complimenting the builders, Simmie & Co, on its very high standard. The main building...provides accommodation for 65 students, in addition to priests and lay-brothers. There are more than 100 rooms, comprising classrooms, library, common rooms, dining hall, and 80 bedrooms.[147]

Other works came in the aftermath of the Depression. The Plaza Theatre in Northcote (1934) was followed by a new wing of the Bethesda Hospital in Richmond and the Albany Court offices and shops building in Collins Street, Melbourne (1936)—the Albany Court project was a contract worth £65,000. Designed by architect Marcus Barlow, the building had 14 floors, a basement and sub-basement.[148] Factories followed for R & WH Symington in West Melbourne, another for Lamson Paragon in Richmond for £25 000 project—and in Brunswick, West Brunswick and South Melbourne

Plaza Theatre, Northcote c1935
(State Library of Victoria)

Albany Court under construction, 1936
(State Library of Victoria)

Albany Court showing Simmie & Co sign 1936
(State Library of Victoria)

Open for business—Albany Court, Collins Street 1938
(State Library of Victoria)

Symington Factory, West Melbourne, c1938
(State Library of Victoria)

Eyelets Factory, Windsor, 1939
(State Library of Victoria)

Open for business, Qualeta House, 1938
(Decoration & Glass)

Qualeta House, 1938
(State Library of Victoria)

New concrete stand at Royal Agricultural Show arena, 1939 (University of Melbourne Archives)

through to 1938, including the Eyelets factory in Windsor. Simmie & Co also built a new building in King Street in the City for the Victorian Butter Factories Cooperative, later registered as a significant 20th century building by the Architects Association.[149] Qualeta House, an eight-storey warehouse building was also built that year in Flinders Lane, featured in *Decoration & Glass* magazine.[150]

An amusing story at Jock Simmie's expense brought 1937 to an end. He was playing golf at Kingston Heath Golf Club in Cheltenham, Victoria, shortly before Christmas. The club was even then regarded as one of the best golf clubs in Australia and not far from his new home in Brighton. The *Argus* takes up the story:

> The tranquillity of the links was disturbed by the rampages of a mad cow. "Strawberry" had broken through a fence and was standing in front of the 14th green with evil thoughts in her mind when "Jock" Simmie hailed two committee-men ....who were standing on the 15th tee, facetiously demanding that they should officially remove the bovine stymie. He had scarcely spoken when the cow charged Simmie's partner, Keith Howe, and then turned its attention to Simmie. Simmie, who is very lame as a result of a war injury, had not run for more than 20 years, but those who were present said that his sprint would have earned him a place in the Empire Games team had the selectors been present. An unceremonious dive into a deep bunker saved him from further attentions from the cow.[151]

In 1938, Bill Simmie was elected to the Committee of the Master Builders' Association of Victoria.[152] Other works over 1938-1939 included an additional storey on the Nurses Quarters, along with the second section of the Women's Block and the connecting link to join the Women's Block with the main institution, at the Victorian Benevolent

Home & Hospital for Aged & Infirm in Royal Park (its name changed to Mount Royal in 1939). The architect was Joseph Plottel, who had collaborated with Simmie & Co on other projects in Canberra—where he designed Jock Simmie's house in Forrest—and in Melbourne.

Another interesting job for Simmie & Co in 1939 was the construction of a new concrete stand for the Royal Agricultural Show Society. [153] The concrete was poured by the Reinforced Concrete and Monier Pipe Construction Co. Ltd., a company founded by Sir John Monash before World War One. The company pioneered reinforced concrete construction in Victoria and no doubt there was much exchange of building expertise and knowledge between it and Simmie & Co.

Further work was carried out at the offices and warehouse (bulk and general stores) for Alfred Lawrence & Co, in Kensington, along with a factory and showroom at 501 Swanston Street in the City followed in 1940, built for Wake's Mail Order Co. and Swanston Used Cars. [154] Next came extensions to the St Andrew's Presbyterian Hospital in East Melbourne (1940). In Sunshine, returning to the area where Bill and Jock Simmie had spent formative years, the company built a new Catholic church—

Our Lady of the Immaculate Conception Church, Sunshine under construction 1940
(Courtesy Our Lady of the Immaculate Conception Sunshine History Group)

Our Lady of the Immaculate Conception (1940).[155] Even small jobs were not passed up, such as a villa construction in Camberwell in 1941.

The Catholic Church in Sunshine was built to replace the old wooden church which had burned down in 1939. Patrick Joseph O'Connor, the architect for the new church, asked for tenders in February 1940. [156] The church was opened on the new commemorative day—Australia Day—on 26 January 1941.

> ... a magnificent new church has been erected that is a source of pride to the Rev. F. Ryder,

parish priest, and parishioners. Built of brick and of attractive design, the new church in its graceful proportions and appointments is a fine addition to Our Lady's block of parochial buildings and is worthy to rank amongst the best Catholic churches in the archdiocese. The architect, Mr P. J. O'Connor, and builder, Mr Simmie, are to be warmly congratulated on their splendid work. ... the church has ... well been described as a gem of ecclesiastical architecture. In its design the architect has departed from many of the old conventional lines, and the church possesses many notable features, the Sanctuary and central Altar being especially noticeable. The solemn blessing and opening ceremony was performed on Sunday afternoon, January 26, by Archbishop Mannix...[157]

Alfred Lloyd was Simmie & Co's construction foreman (and a later director of the company), on wages of £6/4/- per week and his brother Edward was one of the workmen. In a letter written to a Church member in 2001, Alf Lloyd said:

> According to my note book of that time the church was started on 1-4-40 & finished 26.1.42 & the construction was stopped for some months when we all were sent to Darley to build the Army Camp.[158]

New wing for St Andrew's Presbyterian Hospital, 1942. (Building, 1942)

The Darley military camp was located near Bacchus Marsh and urgent construction got underway in July 1940 by a consortium of three contractors led by Lou Thompson of Thompson & Chalmers, including T R and L Cockram, and Simmie & Co, for £133,751. Up to 400 men were involved in the work and another 300 in waterworks and road construction. The logistics around catering and housing those workers alone was a major task within a major construction effort. It was no wonder that Simmie & Co, to meet the deadline for the camp's construction by 31 August and meet its contract obligations, had to pull workmen off the Church site in Sunshine.[159]

Over 1940-1942, Simmie & Co in Melbourne also constructed a new wing for the St Andrew's Presbyterian Hospital in East Melbourne.

Simmie & Co had another source of income too, from a stream of Commonwealth military related projects in Victoria which could well have been helped along by Jock Simmie using his veteran and Canberra connections in the Department of the Interior, still located in Melbourne at this time. From 1935, Simmie & Co started to make successful tenders for work at the Explosives Factory Maribyrnong (EFM) and later Ordnance Factory. This followed the Commonwealth Government's announcement in late 1933 of a major rearmament programme, accelerated in 1935.

The contracts started with works including guns and carriages shops (1935). In 1938 and 1939, a box store and shell painting building, metrology and metallurgy wings, a headquarters building for the inspection department, a sheet metal shop, and even latrines. Between 1940-45 an instruments building, an administrative building, and numerous structures 'near Melbourne', including one of steel and asbestos cement, followed—all for the Department of the Interior.[160] These projects brought into the company revenue of almost £250,000 over the years before and during World War Two.

The post-war period brought a whole range of new risks and opportunities for Simmie & Co, but in some respects the next 20 years would surpass the first 20. Jock and Bill Simmie were perhaps at the peak of their endeavours in this period and the company was mature and well-known and respected. Inevitably however, the age of the brothers, and for Jock Simmie, the demands of running the business in Canberra and its associated travel, working closely with Bill Simmie in Melbourne, his own farming pursuits and growing wider family and personal interests all meant that succession planning began to loom larger in the company management.

Chapter Three
Simmie & Co 1942—1978

Simmie & Co Melbourne 1942-1978

After World War Two, building and labour shortages were endemic in both Canberra and Melbourne, but Simmie & Co sustained its viability. It took work across Melbourne wherever it could be found including building works on established sites, building residences and school extensions, small telephone exchanges and amenities blocks. Construction sites and works included at Maize Products Pty Ltd in Footscray (1942), the Hopetoun Kindergarten and Nursery—a project worth almost £20,000 (1944)—and the Sunshine Technical School (1946).

In 1947 alone it was working simultaneously on projects for a new kindergarten in Fisherman's Bend, new buildings for the Deaf & Dumb Institute in Burwood, new buildings for the Gordon Institute in Highett, a new factory for the Electricity Meter Manufacturing Company behind British Xylonite in Moorabbin, the Kindergarten Teachers Training College in Kew, Craig's Buildings in Elizabeth Street (for the Commonwealth Bank), the Ada Mary A'Beckett Free Kindergarten in Fishermen's Bend, and the Melbourne City Council's electric supply sub-station in Gallagher Place in the City.[161]

Hopetoun Kindergarten and Nursery, Flemington, c1945
(State Library of Victoria)

Ecclesiastical works included St Joseph's Parish Church in Brunswick and construction of the Kildonan Children's Home in Burwood for the Presbyterian & Scots Church Children's Aid Society (1948), St Theresa's Church and School (1951), then more extensions at St Joseph's in Brunswick (1951). It built extensions to the St Vincent de Paul School in North Essendon (1952) and worked on St Joseph's Convent in Kew and St Francis Church in the City (1953), as well as constructed Our Lady of Good Counsel Parish Church in Deepdene (1954). That project alone brought in a very large part of the total cost of building and furnishings at £65,000 to the company.[162] That year it also worked on extensions to the Holy Spirit Church in East Thornbury.

In late 1946, the *Age* reported:

> Full-scale production of prefabricated homes for Victoria will begin early next year, plans having been made to coordinate the activities of 15 firms which will, be engaged solely on that work. .....Houses built under this plan would save 40% in time and 30% in cost, and less time would be lost through bad weather. Priority in materials supply would be given to a number of firms best equipped for the rapid production of houses, but details would be settled by the special state committee on prefabricated homes set up by Mr Cain, Premier.[163]

This was a business opportunity which the Simmie brothers moved on quickly. Jock Simmie and Louis Pyke (later Sir Louis Pyke), former director of Colonial Spark Plugs with George Simmie, building partner with Jock Simmie in Canberra, and who had been made a junior partner of Simmie & Co since 1939, joined together to form Pyke-Simmie Pty Ltd in 1947. According to Pyke's biography, 'The firm initially built mass-produced, imported prefabricated houses for Victorian Electricity Commission workers, but later extended to general industrial contracting.' In 1956 Pyke left to start up on his own account.[164] At the time Pyke left 'there was talk about at the time that Simmie & Co was at a crossroad of the possibility of expanding to the next level of size'. Jock Simmie's grandson Richard takes up the story:

> I remember meeting Sir Louis Pyke and his wife, in the late 1970s at Harpsdale. I think Pyke was knighted at the time, which means at least 1978. He kept in contact with my father [John Ernest Simmie 1925-2012]. Pyke was 15 years Jock's junior. I remember he had just purchased a Mercedes Benz 300 SEL, a car which I thought

The interior of St Joseph's Parish Church, West Brunswick 1952
(RJ Simmie Collection)

Our Lady of Good Counsel Parish Church, Deepdene
(State Library of Victoria)

Interior, Our Lady of Good Counsel Parish Church, Deepdene
(State Library of Victoria)

*The new Odeon Theatre,
1951*
(State Library of Victoria)

was it and a bit. He was reminiscing about Jock and Simmie & Co about expanding. The sum of £500,000 was talked about for the expansion.

My grandfather didn't, couldn't or wouldn't embark on that journey perhaps due to his age (Jock was then in his early to mid-60's) and maybe due to his concern about managerial issues within the company as he didn't have a great relationship with his nephews Roy and Jack, Bill's sons. He thought they lacked managerial skills, and it would be a big risk at that age.[165]

The 1950s saw Simmie & Co in Melbourne move from strength to strength, no doubt bolstered by the extra energy in the company with more of Jock Simmie's presence and standing in the industry. In 1947 Jock became a Fellow of the Chartered Institute of Secretaries and in 1953, an Associate of the Commonwealth Institute of Accountants. In 1950 the company continued with projects small and large—from two residences in Toorak to renovations to the Liberty Theatre in Bourke Street (1950) before it was burned out by fire—and then appointed to build its successor the Odeon (1951), the first new picture theatre in Bourke Street since World War One. Other projects in 1950 included

The celebration party hosted by Greater Union after its debut screening at its new Odeon Theatre, at the Argus Hotel on 1 November 1951. Shown L-R are GU managing director Norman Bede Rydge, Bill Simmie, Jock Simmie, and theatre manager Frank Alan Budd
(Film Weekly 1951)

for Melbourne Distillery in Port Melbourne, Australian Glass Manufacturers in Spotswood, and a new electric supply control room for the Melbourne City Council.

Work commenced on transforming the old grand ballroom of the Exhibition Building—the dance venue known as Palais Royale—to a new grand hall in which the Queen would dine in 1952. Small projects included a new residence in Malvern along with a bakery in St Kilda (1951), along with another Brighton residence (1952); and a bakery in

Simmie & Co employees in the Simmie & Co yard, corner Rankin's & Smith Street, Kensington c1947 L-R—George Boucher (joiner), Burt Hurley (plumber), Ron Aberline (mechanic), Jack Carlin (wood machinist), Raymond Veal (carpenter apprentice), Roy Simmie (son of Bill Simmie), Frank Conway (carpenter), Fred Johnston (labourer). Front— Ron Yates (carpenter apprentice, Unknown (plumber apprentice) (RJ Simmie Collection)

Fairfield, a small block of flats in North Melbourne, a new residence in South Yarra and a small shop-office in Ashburton (1953). A new Youth Centre was also built in West Footscray in 1953 along with work for Bruce Small Pty Ltd, owner of Malvern Star bicycles in South Melbourne.[166]

In 1952 Simmie & Co then won a stunning major project—the contract to build the new 1939-1945 forecourt at the Shrine of Remembrance to commemorate the sacrifice of those Victorians who fell in World War Two. The idea of a new commemoration addition to the Shrine of Remembrance was controversial when first mooted in 1948. The cost, at first estimated to be £60,000 in 1948, then £90,000 by 1951 and then soon revised to £160,000 once the first construction tenders were received that year. The Shrine Trustees appealed to the public to subscribe to funding the new forecourt.

Critics suggested the money be better spent on schools or hospitals or even country memorials; calls from ex-veterans decried malign 'communist' attacks on the plans—the first shadows of the Cold War to come. An Empire-wide concept competition in 1947—only open to veterans—was won by Ernest Edward Milston (formerly Ernst Israel Mühlstein) a Jewish immigrant from Czechoslovakia. He arrived in Australia in 1940 and served in the Directorate of Fortifications and Works in Land Headquarters and then the Army Engineers 1942-1946. Milston transferred from South Australia to Victoria in 1945 and was naturalised in 1946, just in time to enter the competition.[167] An architect of pre-war renown, Milston went on to win the second design competition.

The Shrine and forecourt, c1955
(State Library of Victoria)

For such a prestigious public project, there was remarkably little publicity around the construction tenders, to be submitted by February 1951, or the outcomes. Only a small regional newspaper, the *Wodonga & Towong Sentinel*, in a very long article about the Shrine project, mentioned in passing that the contract to build the 1939-1945 forecourt had been won by Simmie & Co.[168] Both Bill and Jock Simmie were veterans, and the track record of Simmie & Co in Melbourne and most important, Jock Simmie's status in Canberra where Simmie & Co had built the Australian War Memorial would have been considered for the tender. It may also have helped that Jock Simmie was a foundation member of the establishment of the Masonic Peace & Commemoration Lodge 519 in 1936, centred around the Shrine. Perhaps Simmie & Co did not want publicity given the initial controversy around

The 1939-45 Forecourt of the Shrine, c1955
(State Library of Victoria)

the project, or around the undoubtedly high revenue achieved from the project. Whatever the reason, it was uncharacteristic of Simmie & Co.

Simmie & Co constructed a seven-storey building in Lonsdale Street for the Federated Pharmaceutical Service Guild in 1953 along with a new residence in Malvern. A major project worth £63,272 came in 1954 with the construction of seven, two-storey blocks for Housing Commission flats in Reservoir East.[169]

Other projects that year included an amenities block at the City Abattoirs, ecclesiastical works in Deepdene and East Thornbury, a new commercial building in Northcote, a new office building for the Metropolitan Melbourne Tramways Board in Preston, another residence in South Yarra, building works at the Braybrook Hotel, and at Rowntree in Brunswick. Indeed, Simmie & Co was progressing

J E Simmie Masonic medallion, Lodge 519, 1936 (RJ Simmie Collection)

Jock Simmie caricature, as president of the MBA Victoria (Bulletin, 1956)

so well that year that it built a new head office for itself in Rankins Road, Kensington. Jock Simmie's grand-daughter, Kate Gamble, recalls that in the Centennial Hotel (now a private residence) next door to Simmie & Co, Jock Simmie had built on a special little bar area where he could go and drink with the locals and his employees after work.[170]

The Simmie brothers were very well known in the building industry and both Bill and Jock Simmie were involved with the Master Builders Association of Victoria over the years, as time permitted. Jock was elected senior vice-president in 1955 and then president of the Association over 1956-1958, but between 1927-1930, in 1936-1939 and again in 1952-1953 he had been elected as a committee member, demonstrating over 30 years of involvement. His committee tenure in 1953 also included membership of the MBAV's Finance Committee, reflecting the recognition of Jock Simmie's business acumen. Bill Simmie was also elected to Committee in 1940-41.

In 1954 Jock Simmie was also appointed to a sub-committee of the MBAV's Industrial Committee to

Housing Commission housing, Reservoir East, 1954
(State Library of Victoria)

define industrial policy for the Association, and in 1956, while president, he also served as a MBAV representative on the Department of Works and Housing Regulations Committee. In April 1968 he was awarded Life Membership of the Association.[171] There is no doubt that the involvement of both Bill and especially Jock Simmie in the MBAV both deepened their professional knowledge and networks within the industry as well as in Government. It also shows just how much Jock Simmie was involved in Victoria and helps to explain the periods of slow business in Canberra at that time for Simmie & Co.

Simmie and Co. continued on in Melbourne through the rest of the 1950s. The roll call of companies as clients as well as locations across Melbourne lengthened. Works in 1955 included for the British Australian Lead Manufacturers paint factory in Port Melbourne, more Housing Commission flats and shops in North Melbourne, warehousing in Brooklyn, for Neon Electric in South Melbourne, the Grandview Hotel in West Brunswick, and a store and showroom in Braybrook. In 1956 works included for

Interior, the Stadium, nearing completion
(University of Melbourne Archives)

Exterior, the Stadium 1956
(University of Melbourne Archives)

the Commonwealth Bank in the City, a 'stadium' in West Melbourne, and a new store for the Melbourne City Council in the City; in 1957 for H Rowe & Co manufacturers in Notting Hill, and a new shop in Glenroy.

The original West Melbourne Stadium had been constructed in 1913 and was taken over by John Wren, the then chairman of Stadiums Pty Ltd, in 1915. The stadium quickly became a major venue for entertainment, principally boxing (it was known as the 'House of Stoush') until it burned down in 1955.[172] A tender to rebuild was made by Architects Cowper, Murphy & Associates in October 1955. They were the leading theatre architects of their day and closely related with Wren.[173]

Although there is no evident link between the architects and Jock Simmie/Simmie & Co, builders of theatres in Canberra and of the Liberty and then Odeon in Melbourne in the early 1950s, there is a strong probability that Jock's father-in-law, Jack Joyce, introduced Wren to him.

There was a football connection through Collingwood, as well as theatres, and Wren attended Jack Joyce's funeral in 1945 where Jock may well have renewed his acquaintance with Wren. Simmie & Co managed to finish the rebuild in time for the 1956 Olympics, where it was the venue for boxing, basketball, and gymnastics events. The stadium was rebuilt to hold more people (10,000) and was air-conditioned, at an estimated cost of £150,000.

Interior, the Stadium, ready for Olympic boxing 1956
(State Library of Victoria)

No details of the winning tender were ever made, and only a small advertisement for 'laborers.— Stadium job, Dudley St., W. Melb.' by Simmie & Co hinted that they had won the tender.[174]

In 1959 projects included flats as part of the Hotham Gardens project:

> ...an ambitious and much publicised slum reclamation program, on the site bounded by O'Shannassy, Curzon and Arden Streets, North Melbourne, jointly initiated by the Housing Commission of Victoria and the Master Builders' Association, which included inputs from some of Melbourne's most prominent architects of the day.[175]

Other works in 1959 included for Brooklyn Quarries in Brooklyn and the Reserve Bank in the City.

In 1960 works were underway for the Victoria Hotel in the City, McKenzie & Holland in Spotswood, and for a large plaster mill and gypsum storage building and warehouse extensions for Australian Plaster Industries Pty Ltd in Fisherman's Bend. Further works that year included a new State Electricity Commission depot in Newport, a Commonwealth Bank branch in Blackburn, an office and factory building for British

Hotham Gardens Project of public housing, c1963
(University of Melbourne Archives)

Christian Brothers Juniorate in Bundoora under construction, 1958
(Edmund Rice College Archives)

Oxford University Press building, Melbourne 1960
(State Library of Victoria)

Automatic Telephones in North Melbourne, for Oxford University Press in South Melbourne, Essendon Anglican Grammar School in Keilor and for a new motel in Flemington (the site is still used as a motel today).[176]

Ecclesiastical projects continued, for St Claire's Catholic School in Box Hill (1956), extensions to the Tempel Beth Israel synagogue in St Kilda (1957), for the Christian Brothers Juniorate in Bundoora (1958), St Joseph's Church again in West Brunswick (1958), St Anthony's Convent in Alphington (1960) and at the Presbyterian Donald Cameron Home for Elderly Women in Kew (1960).

Simmie & Co Canberra 1942-1969

In January 1942, Simmie & Co was awarded yet another prestigious project in Canberra, namely the construction of the new American Legation (later Embassy) ambassadorial residence and chancery building along with a second residence for the first secretary. It was yet another co-operation with architects Moir & Sutherland, under supervision of a US State Department architect.[177] Peter Freeman, in his book *Thoroughly Modern*, which detailed the life and times of the architects, related that 'amongst the builders of the Simmie construction team

US Embassy under construction
(Courtesy Peter Freeman)

were [building supervisor] Conrad Tobler and Jack McNamara, and a number of more experienced builders'. McNamara had joined Simmie in 1935. He told Freeman that:

> Jock Simmie was a good man and a good judge of men. He was good natured, he had to be, and he had been injured in World War One, and wore an iron brace on his leg. He was a top-grade accountant as well as being a top builder....His tenders were usually successful, and he was an astute businessman.[178]

American Embassy c1943
(RJ Simmie Collection)

The embassy was occupied in December 1943. The chancery, residence and precinct was listed in 1984 on the RSTCA—ACT. Apart from the Virginia-colonial style the now Embassy is regarded as:

> ...historically and socially important in Canberra, as one of the first diplomatic mission to acquire one of the special sites set aside for foreign missions in Yarralumla. (The accepting of the building tender and signing of the building contract occurred on the day Japan attacked Pearl Harbor and excavation commenced immediately).[179]

Other building works non-military in nature also continued during the war years. These included alterations and additions to existing quarters for nurses and domestic staff at Canberra Community Hospital (CCH -1942); construction of additional accommodation for Ministers and members of the Senate at Parliament House for £10,531 (1943); and alterations and additions to Canberra Telephone Exchange No1 for £17,363 (1943). In April 1943, the Apple and Pear Board decided to establish a permanent depot in Canberra and leased a section of Capital Motors in Manuka for the purpose. Jock Simmie was one of the directors of Capital Motors.[180]

The depot would have made up for the loss of trade during the war years when the motor vehicle trade was severely curtailed. In 1944 continuous work was underway—erection and completion of seven brick houses in Griffith for the Department of the Interior (presumably for wartime staff—this later grew to 10 houses for £12,996); a new TB (tuberculosis) isolation ward at the CCH for £16,000; and wooden office buildings for the Prices Branch of the Department of the Interior.[181]

Then in 1945, a change of emphasis—helping to meet the demand for housing with the expansion of war time Canberra and Commonwealth Government functions. An order came to build 27 brick houses in the new suburbs of Griffith and Narrabundah, a handy £49,291 contract following the downturn in defence contracts as the war came to an end. In early 1946, another housing contract for with 41 houses in Griffith and a further 11 in Narrabundah. 364 demountable homes known as the Narrabundah 'prefabs' were built in Narrabundah between 1947-1952.

Simmie & Co built the last 180 of these—they proved to be 'very successful in attracting families to Canberra, many of whom were families of building industry tradesmen', a win-win for Simmie & Co.[182] A comment was made in the *Canberra Times* that 'in regard to the private houses and those being erected by Simmie & Co, difficulty is being experienced in obtaining materials. Almost every kind of material used in the buildings is in short supply'. [183]

Additions to Lieutenant-Colonel H E Jones' Moir-designed residence at 45 Melbourne Avenue in Forrest were made in 1945, and an 'ice storage chamber' was installed for the Commonwealth Cordial Co Ltd (another Moir design) in Braddon as well. Simmie & Co also continued to pick up other Government works such as extensions to the Commonwealth Offices (West Block) in early 1946.[184] Other civil works included additional classrooms for Telopea Park School at a cost of £27,719.[185] Extensions were made to the Moir residence at 43 Melbourne Avenue, Forrest in 1948.

In 1949, a new private residence was to be built for Professor Marcus Oliphant, then based in England, who had accepted the new post of Director of the Research School of Physical Sciences at the newly established Australian National University (ANU).[186] It was the first residence to be built on the former sheep station 'Weetangera', now the Belconnen area. The architect for the ANU, Brian Bannatyne Lewis, the then Professor of Architecture at the University of Melbourne and master planner for the new university, had been suggested as the architect for the Oliphant residence, but he clashed with Oliphant when they met in Easter 1948. So, when it came to designing a house for him, Brian Lewis suggested that it might be better if the scientist selected another architect. Oliphant agreed, saying '...I might then get a competent one'.

Following his fracas with Lewis, Oliphant commissioned the Moir & Sutherland practice to design the new residence. However, Oliphant and his wife Rosa continued to have disagreements with the new architects over design and cost. Meanwhile, the winner of the 1949 building tender for the Oliphant residential project was announced, and this was Simmie and Co, with a bid of £15,426. However, after the long saga, the Oliphants never lived there, disliking it and regarding it as beyond their budget. They moved instead to a more modest home near the ANU campus at Acton, provided by the university. The ANU was obliged to build the original house, being under contract, anyway—so Simmie & Co completed the house. The house remains at 199 Dryandra Street, O'Connor.

Civil works picked up again in 1951 but for several years it was quiet for Simmie & Co in Canberra, mostly due to a general downturn in projects due to

199 Dryandra Street, O'Connor 1997
(Courtesy Peter Freeman)

an acute post-war shortage of building materials. It may also have reflected Jock Simmie's new interests in farming in Victoria as well as the Shrine project and masonic pursuits around that project, such as the new Peace & Commemoration Lodge of which he was a foundation member. On 15 April 1947 he was also admitted to Broadmeadows Lodge 564.[187]

It was not until 1951 that Simmie & Co were again in the news starting with projects in Narrabundah once more—a new but modest Play Centre and then 'weatherboard cottages' for which the company was advertising for carpenters, offering two years of work at six days a week. This looked to be a large project. In February 1952, the company was still looking for tradesmen including carpenters and painters for the weatherboard cottage project. These were almost certainly the simple houses constructed to house the ever-growing number of workers building the post-war boom town that was Canberra. Until then many lived in tents and other temporary camps. Wages rose steadily—carpenters were awarded an extra 15/- a week in April 1953 by the ACT Conciliation Commission—Simmie & Co was one of several building companies named as respondents in the case.[188] The death of Jock Simmie's wife Ivy on 6 February 1952 will also have accounted for a relatively quiet period for Simmie & Co in Canberra; Jock was hard hit.

Then in 1953, more defence work. In a return to RMC Duntroon, Simmie & Co won a contract from the Department of Army to build for cadets undergoing a new science course, a brick and concrete engineering and testing laboratory, for £34,462.[189] This was followed that year by the construction of a new infant school at Griffith (£116,946), to relieve overcrowding at the Telopea Park School that Simmie & Co had worked on in 1946. Canberra was growing fast. Less than two years later, Simmie & Co were contracted to build the new Griffith Primary School (£157,591) slated for completion in February 1956.[190] Still a member of the Master Builders' Association of the ACT (MBA-ACT), Jock Simmie was one of two delegates representing that association at the annual convention of the Master Builders' Federation of Australia, held in December 1954.[191] Simmie & Co was described as 'one of the oldest-established building organisations in the ACT'.

The work in Canberra was now steady and lucrative—and 1954 saw Simmie & Co maintain their momentum as one of the pre-eminent building companies in Canberra with projects both prestigious and standard. Early 1954 saw a return to Civic Centre when Simmie & Co began excavation for a new commercial building for Chic Salons Pty Ltd. It might not have sounded as prestigious as Simmie & Co's next project that year, but it was 'one of the largest commercial premises erected in Canberra and should be the forerunner of other commercial development on the Brisbane Buildings site'.[192] In May the Governor-General Field Marshal Sir William Slim opened the extensions of the Canberra Club in the City, another Simmie & Co project at which the architect, Kenneth Oliphant, paid tribute to the builders.[193] It was worth £30,000 to Simmie & Co.

Then in late 1954 it won the contract to build the new Dutch (now Netherlands) Chancery building in the embassy precinct for completion in March 1956 'if existing building difficulties can be overcome'— namely 'the lack of sufficient labour and supply of local materials'. At this time, the government was embarking on the next stage of Canberra development, which was to bring a further 2,000 public servants to the capital as their departments transferred from State capitals. According to the secretary of the MBA-ACT in December 1954, 'in

Jock Simmie, c1958
(RJ Simmie Collection)

the past eighteen months the labour force of the ACT has been reduced to approximately 1,500, and it is anticipated that approximately 3,300 tradesmen, etc., would be required....[194]

As well, as housing continued to be in high demand in Canberra, the Dutch were not the first to be asked to build their own accommodation in their Embassy grounds. It was the second embassy collaboration by Simmie & Co with the architect Malcolm Moir, who had supervised design at the US Embassy, also built by Simmie & Co in 1942.[195] In faint praise, one writer described the Dutch chancery as a 'pleasant, unobtrusive building whose only unusual feature is its curving half-moon shape'.[196]

On Anzac Day 1955, the foundation stone was laid for the construction of the St James Anglican National Memorial Library—a contract worth £62,00 to Simmie & Co. The work would take about 15 months to complete, the first of a group of buildings to be developed in Barton to be known as the Collegiate Church of St Mark's. The Library was opened on 24 February 1957 in front of 2,000 people, and was dedicated to 'the nurses, chaplains, doctors, missionaries and all non-combatants who died in Australia's wars.'[197]

Master Builders like Jock Simmie and his company were engaged in a wide spectrum of building projects involving many trades of which many were heavily unionised. Inevitably this led to conflict and disputes from time to time. 'Industrial troubles' rose in frequency into and through the 1960s. But working for the ACT and Commonwealth Government also had its pitfalls. In 1956 for example Simmie & Co was working on two schools—at Turner and Griffith. It laid off 52 tradesmen engaged on the sites in April because the Department of Works failed to make its progress payments to the company, without which workers could not be paid on time. This led to protests led by the Builders Workers Industrial Union (BWIU) under Pat Clancy—but outside of Parliament House and not against Simmie & Co.[198] In the case of the Turner Primary School, Simmie & Co took over the contract after the main construction company had failed 'to play the game by the trade union movement' and which had fallen well behind on the work schedule.[199]

Simmie & Co would not always be so fortunate regarding the BWIU. Sometimes it would be caught between competing unions—the BWIU was antagonistic towards the Builders Labourers Federation (BLF) and both were antagonistic

St James Anglican National Memorial Library 1957
(National Archives of Australia)

to employers, such as Simmie & Co. The BLF were as quick as the BWIU to 'declare black' jobs where the company in its eyes had 'breached the award' for that group of workers.[200] In general however, Jock Simmie maintained respect and good relations with union men, not least because of his own impeccable credentials as a former carpenter and war veteran in tune with the common man. Accidents on work sites also occurred from time to time, and rarely but tragically sometimes even fatal accidents. However, it was unusual to see Simmie & Co in the law courts either in Canberra or Melbourne, a testament to its good overall safety record.

Late in 1956, Simmie & Co won a new project, namely, to build the Federal Republic of Germany (FRG or West Germany) Embassy chancery and ambassador's residence in Yarralumla, near the site of the American and Dutch Embassies, both built by the company. Plans for the building came from the FRG Planning Body and a Melbourne firm of architects were commissioned—Gerd & Renate Block—under a supervising architect from the FRG.[201] Later, at the handing over ceremony of the Embassy in March 1958, Jock Simmie was naturally invited. Later he told a story in a 'good natured way' about the occasion:

Jock Simmie speaks at the 'richfest' ceremony at the unfinished FRG embassy in March 1957. Seated behind is Richard G Casey, Australian Minister for External Affairs
(RJ Simmie Collection)

He whispered to a fellow guest that when he was lying in the mud on the Western front, examining the mess a piece of German shell had made of his leg, he'd never imagined one day he'd be enjoying a drink in Australia's national capital with a smartly uniformed German military attaché.[202]

Simmie & Co also built the High Commission of the Federation of Malaya (now Malaysia), which was opened by Prime Minister, Tunku Abdul Rahman, in September 1959. The embassy was designed by Neville Ward of the Moir, Ward + Slater, the former Moir & Sutherland.[203] Subsequently, Simmie & Co won the contract to build the Philippines Embassy with construction underway in November 1962 and handed over on 2 December 1963 in another collaboration with architects Moir and Slater (and Illustre of the Philippines). It was the first purpose-built embassy for the Philippines in any overseas country and cost around £200,000.[204]

The late 1950s and early 1960s saw a mature Simmie & Co at work in Canberra, winning contract after contract. In 1959 it moved offices to Fyshwick near the airport in a new industrial office zone although it seemed that if Jock Simmie was not in town the quest for new work could slow down too. Projects over these years included the five-storey MLC office building in London Circuit, Civic Centre for the Mutual Life and Citizens Assurance Company Ltd (1957) in yet another collaboration with architects Moir, Ward + Slater; a factory and offices for the Bega Co-operative Society Ltd for £39,000 (1960); the Rugby Union Club along Northbourne Avenue to be used by 30 rugby clubs in the ACT and built in two phases over 21 months for £90,000 (1960-61); four blocks of flats to help meet a rapidly growing population (1961); and a contract to build the R G Menzies Library at the Australian National University (ANU) the same year.[205] Jock Simmie actually loaned the Rugby Union Club $14,000 unsecured; the terms being arranged with the President of the Club at the time on a mutual understanding that the principle would not be required to be paid until 30 June 1971 with 7% interest per annum. There was nothing in writing. It was eventually paid by the due date.[206]

Jock Simmie's interest in Esmond's Motors saw some evolutions following the acquisition of the firm by Commonwealth Motors in 1957. Commonwealth Motors was established in Canberra in 1953 by Wright Brothers London Ltd (itself established in 1895) and with the acquisition of Esmond's Motors, became the General Motors (and later Holden) dealers in the ACT, as well as for Pontiac, Chevrolet and Bedford. In 1961 they opened Lyneham Motors to support the growth in that dealership.[207] At the time of the acquisition, one of Esmond's directors—Edward George Stubington—moved to the new firm as its manager.

Somewhat presciently, and perhaps arising from the death of the founder of Esmond's

The MLC Building, 1957
(National Archives of Australia)

Motors the year before, Jock Simmie (5241 paid up shares), reached an agreement with Stubington (185 shares) in 1955 that if Esmond's were liquidated or sold to a third party or the shares transferred, he would share the difference in the price of the shares equally with Stubington, 'as his and my rightful share of the appreciated value and goodwill of Esmond's Motors'. By this time Jock

Simmie was well established in his farm in Victoria bought in 1940, but he was still travelling every third week to Canberra as he done religiously ever since 1931. The accounts for Esmond's in June 1956 showed a net profit of £17,496.[208] As Jock Simmie looked to be the majority shareholder in Esmond's at the time of the acquisition the following year by Commonwealth Motors, his investment in Edmond's paid off. By that time Stubington, who by then had been a director with Esmond's for 29 years, also profited from Jock Simmie's generosity.

Another residence at 38 Holmes Crescent in Campbell came Simmie & Co's way from Moir & Slater in late 1962. Built for public servant Daniel Nutter and his wife Edith, 'a sparse and elegant building, epitomising the suave 'Post-War International' style'.[209] It was not realised at the time, but the residence was the last work completed with Malcolm Moir—it had been a long and fruitful association for over 30 years. That must have been a happy job compared to the rest of 1962, which saw the return of industrial strife from unionists—and Simmie & Co this time was in the middle of it. The firm was one of several builders at work across Canberra that year. In Simmie & Co's case, it was constructing Garema Place (also called the Garema Building) in Civic. On its completion in August 1962, it would hold 24 businesses, both offices and retail businesses. Simmie & Co had been given permission to carry out work on a weekend for pipelaying only.

Today it seems almost quaint that the Master Builders Association should give such permission in a public advertisement in the *Canberra Times*, but trade unionists at that time were quick to react.[210] By July 'industrial action' had begun, with trade unions, especially the BWIU, threatening 'black bans' on Simmie & Co and other builders as well for only using one trade on the weekends (such as plumbers or bricklayers) but not others (like carpenters). The builders wanted the flexibility to not have to pay weekend wages to all of their contractors, but the union view was that the builders had to employ *all* of the trades involved on the weekend if any one trade was used, or not work at all! The unions subsequently banned all Saturday work.[211]

The dispute escalated. Another Simmie & Co project—alterations and extensions to the Canberra Hotel—soon was caught up as well as BWIU carpenters walked off the job, because plumbers, wall tilers and painters had worked on Saturday but not them. The union demanded Simmie & Co pay all the workers the same wage on weekends whether they were employed or not: '...union policy was that if one man was called in on Saturday, all must be called in'. In August 1962, carpenters, and builders' labourers at Garema Place asked Simmie & Co to

Garema Place 1965 with the Simmie-built MLC Building behind
(National Archives of Australia)

pay them £3 a week more because they had not been given Saturday work. Finally, the BWIU and BLF unions told its members to return to work following an order by the Conciliation and Arbitration Commission. By January 1963 Simmie & Co had completed its projects and industrial peace reigned once more. The Garema Place project for Finance & Guarantee Co Ltd was worth £140,000 to Simmie & Co. [212]

A highly prestigious building project had come the way of Simmie & Co in 1961—the R G Menzies Library Building at the ANU, later to be heritage listed. The architect was John Francis Deighton Scarborough in association with Collard, Clark & Jackson. Scarborough was known to Simmie & Co—they had built additions to the Nurses Memorial Centre in St Kilda Road in Melbourne under Scarborough's design in 1956. [213] The library was opened on 13 March 1963 by Her Majesty, Queen Elizabeth II, accompanied by the Duke of Edinburgh. PM Robert Menzies also attended. Unusually for a builder, Jock Simmie was invited to attend and was introduced to the Queen:

> They said Jock didn't wash his hand for some time after shaking hands with Her Majesty. It was said in a jocular way but also with some awe. It was like the pinnacle of Jock's life to meet Royalty.[214]

In 1963 yet another project with Moir & Slater, Simmie & Co won the contract to build the new Rugby Union Club headquarters in Blackall Street, Barton (Simmie had built the original Club in Braddon in 1960). [215]

Simmie & Co—The end of an Era

By the early 1960s, Jock Simmie was stepping back from work as he was now over 70, but still travelling to Canberra to lead the business there. In one of the last projects in Canberra, work was awarded the offices of the *Canberra Times*.[216] It was fitting in a way that the *Canberra Times* was established in 1926 by Jock Simmie's long term acquaintance and fellow Freemason Thomas Mitchell Shakespeare.[217] Another project in 1964 was the award of a contract from Canberra Grammar School to construct a new 'Chapel of Christ the King' at a cost of about £25,000.

The chapel, which was designed to seat 350 people, was built in brick (Bowral browns) with a slate (from Wales) roof and was circular in construction. A photo taken at the time of the contract signing sees Jock Simmie looking on, closely observing the client the Right Reverend

Student reading in the landscaped surroundings of the R G Menzies Building of the University Library, 1964
(ACT Heritage Library)

Canberra Grammar School chapel contract signing 30 July 1964, Jock Simmie on left.
(RJ Simmie Collection)

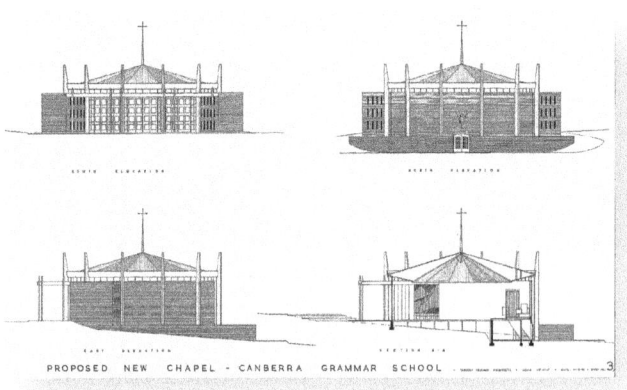

Architect drawings, proposed chapel at Canberra Grammar
(Courtesy Peter Freeman)

Kenneth John Clements (the Bishop of Canberra and Goulburn) as he signs, overlooked by the architect George Holland. [218]

Dedicated in August 1965 by Bishop Clements, the school news sheet, the *Red Hill Outlook,* said:

> The architects, Yuncken & Freeman, and the builders, Simmie & Co, must be congratulated for their painstaking efforts in producing a building worthy of its name as they had many difficult constructional problems to overcome.[219]

Simmie & Co continued with projects in Canberra right up until, and even after, Jock Simmie's death in 1968. These included the Liberal Party Headquarters (1965) and the $200,000 ACOA building in Barton (1966). Simmie and Co tendered for the construction of Ursula College at ANU (1967—opened by PM Malcolm Fraser in 1968); for brickwork and blockwork at the ANU's Psychology Building and for the Phillip Fire Station (1968)—with unknown results. One of the last contracts awarded to Simmie & Co was for the construction of the National Memorial Youth Hostel in O'Connor, for $36,637.[220] The hostel site was adjacent to the Oliphant house project at 199 Dryandra Avenue, O'Connor.

Yet another contract for $157,322 was awarded after Jock Simmie's death in 1969, for a bulk store for the Bureau of Mineral Resources in Fyshwick to be completed by January 1970 while it also competed for tenders to construct the Biochemistry block at ANU and the Weston Creek Primary School (1969).[221] The company continued on, finding itself in court over a dispute with Leighton Contractors in 1973 but wound up in Canberra not long afterwards, leaving Simmie & Co in Melbourne to continue on to 1978. Ironically what outlasted Simmie & Co in Canberra, apart from its iconic building projects, was the Simmie Bowl for the best vegetable section exhibitor at the Spring and Autumn Flower Shows. The last mention of this was 1987.

In Melbourne, Simmie & Co continued on through the sixties and seventies. However, changes to management and the age of Jock and Bill Simmie began to tell on the vigour and direction of the company. In 1960, the annual return of the company under the Companies Act 1958 showed Jock and Bill Simmie as directors and Roy Simmie, Bill's son, as Company Secretary.[222] In 1962 the shares in the capital of the company, increased to £100,00, were increased four-fold to 400,000 shares.[223] Then in 1964, Jock Simmie wrote a codicil to his will stating that if his nephews were to take on managerial roles in Simmie & Co, he wanted to be bought out of the Company. This happened in 1966, for a sum of $80,000.[224] So that year, 1966, Simmie & Co was left in the hands of Bill Simmie and his son Roy.[225] Even then, Jock Simmie continued to travel to Canberra to ensure projects kept underway, until poor health overcame him. Additional directors were also added to Simmie & Co—Alfred Lloyd and Clarence Albert Walker, both long-time managers within Simmie & Co. Even with failing health, and even after formally leaving the company, Jock Simmie continued to travel to Canberra to oversee the firm's work, almost to the very end

of his life.

The 1960 annual return of Simmie & Co also showed Jock Simmie as a director of Pyke-Simmie Pty Ltd, Tomlins-Simmie Pty Ltd and of Marshall Shoes. Pyke-Simmie continued until 27 April 1967 but had not been commercially active since the mid-1950s. In 1963 Jock Simmie helped with the winding up of Joyce & Howe Shoes after its acquisition by Marshall Shoes (and acquired in turn by Julius Marlow/International Shoes). John James Joyce (the 2nd) and Jock's brother-in-law, was retiring that year along with Keith Howe; both their fathers started the business.[226] Jock was very close to his in-law side of the family; his payment was a new Mercedes Benz 220S.[227]

Years later, Jock Simmie's grandson Richard reminisced about the aftermath of winding up Joyce & Howe:

> My uncle [Jack Joyce] bought himself a Rolls-Royce Silver Cloud 3. I used to be in awe of that car when Jack and Ruth would come out to visit Jock at Harpsdale. In the late 1970's, I dragged my mother along to see Uncle Jack and Aunty Ruth, mostly to have a look at the car. Uncle Jack said would you like to go for a drive, of course I said yes. He was concerned the battery might be flat as he hadn't used the car for some time. Fortunately, she kicked over and away we went around Kew Boulevard. He even allowed me to drive it, still a highlight to this day.[228]

Tomlin-Simmie Flour had been started up by Jock Simmie's uncle John Simmie (1860-1950) in 1912 at Bendigo and later John was joined by his brother George (1862-1937). By the 1920s the company had interests in Richmond in Melbourne. The company had passed to George's children, including William James, Flora 'Flo', Ann and George. With the death of William in 1958, the less experienced directors began to struggle, and the company was soon in financial trouble. In January 1959 Jock Simmie was asked by Flo Simmie to help her as a director of Tomlins-Simmie Flour to sort out the business and get it back on track.[229] Jock Simmie helped out and presumably became a director in doing so. The company was later bought out by Robert Hutchinson & Co of Glenroy in 1972.

Through this period Simmie & Co worked on a number of building projects. In 1962 these included the North Suburban Club in Moonee Ponds, Sunshine Technical School, a MCC electric supply sub-station in Parkville, and the Green Room Club in South Melbourne. In 1963 projects included a War Memorial Tower at the St Alban's Anglican Church Armadale while in 1964 contracts for work with Colvan [food] Products in Fitzroy, the Farrer Hall of Residence at Monash University in Clayton, works at the Mount Royal Hospital in Parkville, and for Crestknit in Hawthorn.

The Tower project at the Armadale St Alban's Anglican Church was an interesting example of Simmie & Co's connection with war memorial construction in both Canberra and Melbourne. It

The Green Room Club, South Melbourne 1962
(State Library of Victoria)

Farrer Hall, Monash University 1964
(Monash University Archives)

was a long time in gestation. The parish had raised the question of completion of the Church with a spired tower as early as 1957, with the Secretary at St Albans submitting a plan to the Diocese at St Pauls Cathedral 'as the memorial to those who fell in two world wars' in early 1958. The church estimated the cost at £7,500 with an additional £1,000 for the spire. Construction of the tower would also 'complete a beautiful building which has been unfinished since 1898'. A fund-raising effort—the Wells Pledge Canvass—was underway in March 1958, but building was not expected to commence until 1961.[230] The architect was English-born architect Wystan Widdows and his partner David L Caldwell.[231]

Diocese funds for the project remained tight—it had to borrow £2,000 from the National Bank in Prahran, but Widdows' plans were finally approved in April 1962. Tenders for the construction of a 'brick and concrete-framed tower' were called for by Widdows & Caldwell on 30 June 1962, less the spire, omitted 'on account of lack of funds.'[232] Simmie & Co's tender of £8,987 was the lowest of eight and after further adjustments to price, it was approved as the builder on 29 November 1962, with C A Walker [Clarence Albert Walker] as the Simmie & Co point of contact. It began demolition

*War Memorial Tower,
St. Albans, Armadale, 1963*
(Anglican Diocese Archives, Melbourne)

of the old porch and erection of construction screens before the end of 1962 but delays in final council approvals meant that work did not begin until 18 February. The footings were poured in early March 1963. The Foundation Stone, which came from St Alban's Cathedral in England, was laid at the end of that month.

The construction was estimated to be completed by 29 March 1963. However, by May 1963, work was behind schedule due to increasingly acrimonious relations between the Vestry at St Albans and the architects. The Vestry, frustrated by Widdows' poor communication and slowness to act on changes, began to deal directly with contractors and calling for prices without Widdows being informed. In a letter to the Vestry, Widdows expressed his annoyance, stating that 'it is obvious that the Vestry has no confidence in either my artistic or administrative ability as an architect', and wondered 'whether it would not be better all round for the Vestry to dispense with our services for the remainder of the contract...' [233] Although this low point was overcome, constant changes on both sides also meant relations did not improve either. Simmie & Co continued its work under these challenging circumstances and provided practical solutions to both Vestry and the architects as issues arose.

The 75 feet high tower was finally completed in September 1963 and was dedicated on 29 September by the Victorian Governor Sir Rohan Delacombe and Eleanor, Lady Delacombe and the Anglican Archbishop of Melbourne, Dr Frank Woods, ChStJ. [234] It had taken six years to conclude and even though the Dedication was regarded as the completion of the Church building, the apparent purpose of the tower as a war memorial seemed to be quickly lost, and no records appear to remain of how its War Memorial Chapel was arranged. A World War One Honour Roll was certainly in place at the time but only 10 years later, in 1973, the Church was sold to the Coptic Church, and the Honour Board 'lost'. It is not known if a World War Two Honour Board was ever made, despite the intention of the Vestry in 1957 to memorialise both wars. Now, the tower remains but the original purpose has all but forgotten. Without its spire, even then the Church building was not completed in all of its planned glory.

Meanwhile Simmie & Co continued on. Other projects through the balance of the 1960s included for Dickies Ltd in Yarraville (1965), the SEC in Coburg, for Crabtree & Sons in South Melbourne, Malley's in Moreland

(1966), the Flemington-Kensington RSL in Rankin's Road, across from the Simmie & Co head office, St Michael's School in St Kilda, for the Commonwealth Aircraft Factory in Port Melbourne, and the Malvern Library (1967).

Company employee records show that in June 1963, the company had a full-time wages list of 36 tradesmen, plus 10 apprentices paid at the award rate.[235] Edward Lloyd, the brother of Alf Lloyd and who also worked on the Catholic Church in Sunshine in 1941, was still listed as an employee in 1963. Others included John Ernest ('Black Jack') Simmie (Bill Simmie's youngest son), as a foreman—he would later become a director of the company in 1965 with Jock Simmie's departure. Black Jack's role in the company was to supervise the building sites (as did his father, Bill). One anecdote about Jack probably summed up his attitude to his work:

> There is a story told by a relative of Roy Simmie that Roy received a call from a building site asking to know the whereabouts of Jack as he hadn't been there that day. Roy investigated to find that Jack had left the country and was on holidays in Fiji. Jack hadn't told anyone, just got up and left the country. Jack wasn't keen on working.[236]

McCaughey Court, Ormond College, University of Melbourne
(State Library of Victoria)

Building works continued following the death of Jock Simmie in August 1968. Works at the Footscray Football Ground and the construction of the hexagonal 'Brutalist' design McCaughey Court for married students at Ormond College, University of Melbourne (for which the architects Romberg and Boyd won a national award) were underway that year, along with work for Clarks Shoes in Abbotsford and again for H B Dickie in Yarraville.[237] In 1969 works included at the Essendon Technical School, further construction of the Kindergarten Teachers Training College in Kew, the Pharmacy College in Parkville, again at St Michael's Church in East Burwood and the Footscray Swimming Pool.

The 1970s however, saw a definite slowing down of projects underway in Melbourne. These included, in 1970, work at the RAAF No 1 Store at Tottenham, the Elderly Citizens Club in North Melbourne, again for the Reserve Bank (Note Issue Department) in Fitzroy, for Cemetery Works and Grassmere Investments in the City, and works at Lowther Hall at the Anglican Grammar School in Essendon. Fewer projects got underway in following years. A significant two-storey civic centre was built for the Flinders Council in Rosebud—the project cost was $1,600,000 of which Simmie and Co earned nearly $900,000—and a gas and fuel depot in Brooklyn, in 1973; Engineering Building 6 at Monash University Clayton; works at Crabtree Vickers in South Melbourne, construction of 18 'maisonettes' (flats) in Box Hill in 1974, and work at the Sunbury High School in 1975.

One of the last major projects for the company

Flinders Shire Office and Civic Centre 1976
(Courtesy Rosebud Library)

was the Footscray Psychiatric Hospital built from 1974 and opened in 1977. The design by an architect within the Public Works Department, James Fong, was created in 1969 but it wasn't until 1973 that the Federal and State Governments announced funding for the building, behind the existing West Footscray Hospital. In February 1974 in *Building & Construction* magazine, it was reported that a tender for construction of the (initially named) Footscray Psychiatric Centre for $1,965,161 had been accepted from F T Jeffrey Pty Ltd. However, in May 1974 the *Victorian Government Gazette* reported that the contract had been given to Simmie & Co for $1,907,032 instead.[238] A former

Footscray Psychiatric Hospital
(Courtesy John Jovic)

project manager at Frank Jeffrey noted that the firm was selling out at the time to another firm, A J Galvin, and he confirmed that the contract for F T Jeffrey did not proceed. Simmie & Co, presumably the next on the tender list picked up the contract for their original quote instead.[239]

A 70-bed facility, the completed hospital was not without controversy. Described in the architectural book *Australia Modern* as a 'brooding hulk' and later became known as 'the bunker'.[240] Nonetheless, in 2020 it achieved heritage listing as a prime example of 'Brutalist' design, thanks in large part to photographer John Jovic. Heritage Council Victoria, in its determination of the heritage status of the building, found it 'to be a striking, prominent, highly intact and notable example of a Brutalist building which demonstrates key elements of the style'.[241]

The 1973 Annual Return of Simmie & Co showed capital of $200,000 in 400,000 shares of which 79,020 were fully paid up or otherwise than in cash—the bulk of the shares were held by Bill Simmie (36,920) and Roy and Jack Simmie (15,000 each), with 2000 shares each to Alfred Lloyd and Clarence Albert Walker.[242] As Bill Simmie lived on for more than a decade past this point, it is worth describing what happened to him and to Simmie & Co with its demise less than two years after his death, in December 1987. Richard Simmie, Jock Simmie's grandson, noted that:

> Jock was very good at advising people about how to secure their financial future. William Simmie had no interest in farming so with Jock's advice built an apartment block in 1941 as his strategy whilst Jock started acquiring land on the outskirts of Melbourne as his investment in the future.[243]

The apartment block was at 519 Mt Alexander Road in Moonee Ponds and consisted of six art deco apartments for rent and a larger two-storey maisonette that became home for him and his wife Connie [Constance] until his death in February 1986 at the age of 95. Connie died in 1988. Their newly married granddaughter Susan and husband Keith Ball lived in Unit 1 in 1975 for a time. The block was listed in 1983 on the Register of Significant Twentieth Century Architecture—Victoria and as an historically significant building in Moonee Ponds. The block was also notable for 'Extensive English style gardens in raised garden beds…..; much of which survives today'.[244]

By 1973 the firm was pushing on, but Jock Simmie was dead, and Bill Simmie was already over 80.

Furthermore, according to Keith Ball, Roy Simmie's son-in-law, it appears that Roy stopped building works by the late 1970's.[245] By 1975 the Simmie & Co annual return showed that Bill Simmie's shares had been reduced to 1,920, but Simmie Nominees P/L, showing the company address in Rankin's Road, Kensington, and a new entity now controlled 35,000 shares with the remaining shares as per the 1973 return.[246] Family lore has it that Roy had a 'run in' with Norm Gallagher, leader of the militant BLF, and after this Roy decided to cease the business. Roy's brother Jack (John Ernest) Simmie wasn't interested in the business, neither was his son, Bruce, or son-in-law, Keith Ball.[247]

Eventually, a report by the company auditors, Coopers & Lybrand, in December 1975 gives some credence to the family story about a 'run-in'. The accountants noted:

> The company is involved in certain contracts the results of which cannot be determined with reasonable certainty at this time. We have therefore not been able to satisfy ourselves that adequate provision has been made in the accounts against all possible losses in arriving at the value of $110,986 ....the accounts have been drawn up on the basis of the continuation of the company as a going concern which is primarily dependent upon the outcome of these disputed contracts.[248]

On 30 June 1976, Coopers & Lybrand noted 'the company is involved in legal proceedings in relation to certain contracts', but the value of the company was now $264,848.[249] Newspaper reports in the *Age* that year listed Simmie & Co as one of

Simmie & Co letterhead 1977
(RJ Simmie Collection)

The former Simmie & Co wall sign, head office, Kensington, 2022
(Courtesy David Mitchelhill-Green)

32 companies which had been awarded 'no tender contracts' by the Victorian Labor Government over 1970-1978—it had been given contracts worth $735, 409. [250] All to no avail, for in June 1978 Simmie & Co—'retiring from business'—advertised the sale of its woodworking, building and fabrication equipment along with office furniture and motor vehicles.[251] It was the end of an era. The company finally was liquidated in 1987. Bill Simmie's Probate, in 1986, showed just $59,000 cash and no real estate. When Roy Simmie died in 2004, he didn't leave a huge estate, just $700,000 in cash. [252]

*The former Simmie & Co head office
in Kensington, 2022*
(Courtesy David Mitchelhill-Green)

The former Simmie & Co head office in Kensington, 2022
(Courtesy David Mitchelhill-Green)

Dorsets at Harpsdale, homestead in background c1950
(RJ Simmie Collection)

Chapter Four
Harpsdale 1940—1968

By the late 1930s Jock Simmie had started acquiring land northwest of Melbourne as he looked to his future. He had purchased some land near Emerald (he was noted as the Captain of the Emerald Country Club in 1940), but in 1940 he purchased 'Harpsdale', an historic property near Craigieburn and Sunshine.[253] His mother and John Montgomery had moved back to Sunshine in 1928. In October 1941 Jock and Ivy moved to Harpsdale, selling their Brighton home in October 1941 for £3,725, supposedly for what it cost him to build. On moving to Harpsdale, Ivy found that she had to be much more self-sufficient, with no live-in help anymore. She rose to the challenge. Now Jock Simmie was to split his time between Harpsdale and Canberra, managing a farm in Victoria where he established Dorset Horn Stud No 768, and a very large and very demanding building business in Canberra and Melbourne.

In January 1941, Jock Simmie installed as manager at Harpsdale one Arthur Kirke Dyson-Holland, for wages of £5 per week.[254] Dyson-Holland also managed a Soldier Settlement farm adjacent to Harpsdale, called 'Troodos'.[255] He was an experienced farmer but down on his luck following a long drought. At that time his wife had also been in hospital for a month, and he had been unable to get to Melbourne to pay his instalment. By May he informed the Soldier Settlement Board that he had sold his sheep at a loss due to the low market prices.[256] By this time, Dyson-Holland had renegotiated his lease to reduce the instalments by extending the purchase period.

The new one, dated 1 March 1939, with a debt of £1,005-3-0 his 78 half-yearly instalments of only £26-7-7 over 39 ½ years, would have seen him making his final payment in September 1978.[257] The old one was only cancelled on 1 August 1941, due to Dyson-Holland misplacing it for some time.[258] Despite the reduced instalments, Dyson-Holland had not paid his September 1941 instalment by October.[259] The inspector noted that he thought Dyson-Holland would sell the allotment to his employer, Simmie, who had approached him on the subject, and the inspector thought this was a wise move.[260] Dyson-Holland paid his September 1941 instalment in February 1942, just before the March 1942 instalment was due.[261]

What the Inspector and the Board did not know was that because of their shared World War One connection, Jock Simmie had taken over Dyson-Holland's mortgage on Troodos (£3,600 in 3 instalments) and allowed Dyson-Holland and his wife Leila to continue to live there. In return, Jock made Arthur manager of the farm on the understanding that when Arthur retired, he would hand over the title of Troodos to him.[262] The inspector's assessment on the allotment of July 1942 seemed more upbeat, with a report that it was a 'good prospect'. Dyson-Holland was a 'good settler' who had 300 ewes at present lambing.[263] In September 1946 however, there was no stock, it being out on agistment, no plant and just 270 fowls on the land.[264] Dyson-Holland was still working as manager for Harpsdale. The stock were frequently 'on agistment' over the next few years, during which time he remained employed by Simmie.[265]

In August 1947 the inspector noted that Dyson-Holland took 'particular interest' in controlling vermin and noxious weeds. [266] Then, with little explanation as to the source of the funds [money from Jock Simmie], Dyson-Holland sent the Board a cheque for £778-5-3 on 30 March 1955, this being the balance owing on the property.[267] Once Dyson-Holland found his copy of the lease, which he had again mislaid, the Board of Land and Works approved the issue of a Crown Grant for the land in June.[268] The grant was issued on 16 June 1955, and Troodos once more became privately-owned land.[269]

The agreement with Jock Simmie about handing over the title on Arthur Dyson-Holland's retirement was a verbal agreement as Jock Simmie's word was his bond in all things. The day Arthur died—18 October 1963—and according to the story passed down in the Simmie family, he had been to town to retrieve the title to give to Jock, as he had retired. However, before handing over the title he had to bury his dog that had died that morning—while doing so, Dyson-Holland had a heart attack and died as well.

Leila Dyson-Holland then refused to hand over the title for several weeks but eventually did after much legal threatening and a Supreme Court case which ruled in Jock Simmie's favour.[270] According to the court records, the case was heard by Sir Henry Winneke in December 1964, following probate being granted on Dyson-Holland's estate the previous March. Winneke, an alumni of Scotch College and a member of the Victorian Masonic Grand Lodge, had been appointed Chief Justice of the Victorian Supreme Court that same year.[271] The court found that an agreement had been made between Jock Simmie and Arthur-Dyson-Holland in 1942, although 'The deceased didn't execute in his lifetime a registerable [sic] transfer of the said property to the Plaintiff.'

> Plaintiff [Jock Simmie] agreed to buy from the Deceased [Arthur Dyson-Holland] the whole of the Right, Title and Interest of the Deceased in Property called Troodos, 200 acres 14 perches. Crown Allotment 18A, Parish of Bulla Bulla, County of Bourke for £3,600.[272]

Jock Simmie's name finally went on the title to Troodos in June 1965.

The Harpsdale Dorset Horn Stud was founded on 5 November 1941 by Jock Simmie with the purchase of 22 ewes from George H Earp of 'Athlea', via Glenrowan, which were in lamb to Athlea ram 83/39.[273] Then 20 more 2T Stud Ewes were bought direct from Athlea, which were mated to Stud Ram, Newbold 351/39 on 5 February 1942. This ram was purchased from William J Dawkins, of 'Newbold', South Australia for 20 guineas (a guinea =21 shillings or £1-1) at the Newmarket sales yards in Melbourne on 7 November 1941. Then, on 19 May 1942, 18 more ewes from Athlea were purchased which were in lamb to various Athlea sires.[274] The lambing of

1942 showed 1,061 lambs from 1,038 X-bred ewes and 59 Dorset Horn (DH) flock ewes. By June 1942, an insurance note noted that Harpsdale was carrying 500 lambs, 900 ewes, 500 wethers and 40 rams.[275]

Jock Simmie bought small numbers of cattle, usually less than 15 in number on and off over the years, but they were never a real feature of the farm. During World War Two, there were poultry sheds constructed and there were two sheds full of white laying hens with breeding facilities to raise chickens. His daughter Joyce was supposed to look after them but did very little towards their maintenance. Jock received an extra petrol ration of 44 gallons per month because of the poultry and breeding program. There was also always at least one milking cow. Harpsdale records show that in January 1942, a purchase of an American-type No.31, 15 Gallon Diabolo separator, for £13-5-6.[276]

By June 1943, the Dorset Horn Stud was well established, with farm records showing Romney Cross ewes 1,050, DH ewes 64, DH rams 36, DH Harpsdale-bred rams 37, DH Stud ewes 112 and DH stud weaners 49. From that point stock numbers were ~ 900–1,400 X-bred ewes, 300–600 wethers, DH Stud ewes 95–100, Stud DH rams 1–4 and flock DH rams 70–90. By 1946, the selling of DH rams and ewes, bred at Harpsdale, was well established and the stock being sent all over Victoria and interstate—for example, to Ballarat and Sale, Harkaway, and Toongabbie on the south-east of Melbourne.[277] By December that year the farm expanded a little more with Allotment 6A in Parish of Mickleham, a purchase of unused road for £9-10-4, taking the rates notice for Konagaderra from 48 ½ to 54 ½ acres.[278]

The increasing tempo (lambing rates were generally 84–92 percent) and size of farm operations meant an equally increasing commitment to maintaining fencing. Over 1946/47 fencing at Harpsdale consisted of a mile of boundary fence of stonewall topped with post and 3 wires, 3.25 miles of internal fencing of stonewall topped with post and 3 wires, four miles of new fencing, 4.5 miles of other existing fences in good condition and 3.75 mile of post and wire boundary fences.

The Newmarket sales yards began business in 1859 and were situated between Racecourse Road and Epsom Road in Melbourne. Harpsdale began showing Dorset rams there, and winning prizes. In 1949 Harpsdale won first prize in the show pens at the Australian Society of Breeders of British Sheep December 1949 sales at Newmarket.[279]

First Prize certificate, Dorset Horns, Newmarket 1949 to J E Simmie (RJ Simmie Collection)

Jock never worked the farm. His passions were the stud sheep and his garden which occupied all his spare time when he was in residence. He also developed an extensive orchard—Richard Simmie remembers 'Jock always up a ladder pruning his precious apple, plum, pear and quince fruit trees.'[280] Arthur took on more of the work of managing the farm. The earliest records for wages are in 1943. Arthur Dyson-Holland—£317, Jock's son John Ernest Simmie—£156 and another employee William McAuliffe—£106. The amount for John, who was just turning 18 that year, probably reflects his age at the time. It wasn't until 1947 that John was paid a similar but still lesser wage than Dyson-Holland and it wasn't until the 1960s that John earned the same as Dyson-Holland.[281]

There was much work needed initially with renewal of much of the fencing, constant pasture improvements and fertilizing as much as he could depending on Government rationing. William McAuliffe was responsible for the lion share of the new fencing; if he wasn't fencing, he was working in the garden for Jock and Ivy.[282] Jock Simmie also did a lot of subcontracting to local farmers in the area in the early years—Reg. Hartley Poole, Hutton Troutbeck and sons, and Herbert Cliff—next door neighbours at Mickleham—and the Lloyd family, to name a few—for chaff production, ploughing and sowing paddocks, dam works, stripping crops etc.[283] The 1950s also saw the purchase of dozens of rabbit traps to try and control the rabbit population along with the use of carrots doused with 1080 poison. One year several thousand rabbits were killed in a few baitings but were never entirely eradicated.[284]

Dyson-Holland's children also featured during the 1940s helping with shearing, stooking hay and other activities needing labour.[285] There were

Arthur Dyson-Holland with prize-winning Dorset Horn rams at Newmarket Sales, Melbourne 1949
(RJ Simmie Collection)

certainly enough crops to justify a new chaff cutter in 1948, a new tractor, model 30K H V MacKay Massey Harris (to replace the old Fordson which came from the ACT and had all metal wheels) in 1949, and in 1952 a new Sunshine Harvester.[286] Richard Simmie recalls:

> In the 1980's the now old chaff cutter was towed into the upper shearing shed paddock and set alight by my father; he wasn't very good at removing rubbish. When he renewed fencing the old fencing was usually left lying on the ground.[287]

In January 1951, the agricultural magazine *Australian Farm and Home* wrote about the Harpsdale Dorsets. In particular, at the October 1950 Newbold Sales in South Australia, Jock Simmie paid the world breed record price of 510 guineas for the ram Newbold 162 of 1949. The annual Newbold sales were the largest stud sales in Australia, held at the Newbold Sheep Stud near Gawler in South Australia.

> This purchase represented another step in the progress of a stud which may well be challenging older Victoria studs for supremacy in the next year or two. In nine years, by consistent use of Newbold sires and capable handling of the

The 510 guineas Dorset Horn ram bought by Harpsdale at the Newbold Sales, South Australia 1950
(RJ Simmie Collection)

> flock by his manager, Mr. A. Dyson-Holland, Mr. Simmie has built up a very fine stud... Harpsdale has been developed into an almost pure Newbold blood flock. The breeding flock at Harpsdale now comprises about 300 ewes... The stud has always marked more than 100% of lambs.[288]

The magazine went on to say:

> The property of 1,350 acres.....has been highly improved since the stud was founded. Remarkable results in pasture development have been obtained by applying 4cwt to 5 cwt of lime every second year, followed by 1cwt of

superphosphate. About 60 acres of oaten hay is grown each year. Carrying capacity is now high, for, in addition to the Dorset Horn stud, Mr. Simmie maintains a flock of about 1200 Border Leicester-Merino cross ewes, which produce over 1,000 lambs annually when mated to Dorset rams. About 400 crossbred wethers are also carried.[289]

Wool remained an important income stream for Harpsdale. A peak in wool sales was reached in 1951 at the height of the Korean War but even by 1955 Harpsdale wool was achieving premium returns. For example, the top Merino wool price at the Melbourne wool sales in 1955—where 13,200 bales were put up for auction—was 95d (pence)/lb. Harpsdale had six bales of 'aaa comeback' wool in the sales that day and they sold at 73¾d, which put the sale for that grade of wool among the notable high points in the sales report.[290] Jack Burt and Co. of 'Kalkallo', not far from Harpsdale, became the shearing contractor for many decades. Sheep were often railed to Craigieburn and mustered up Craigieburn Road to the farm. This practice continued into the mid-1960s.

Looking towards security for himself and family and strongly attracted to country life as he had experienced in his youth and after World War One (including in Canberra which remained largely rural in aspect right into the 60s), Jock Simmie bought the Harpsdale property in 1940 (for £12/acre); settlement was Australia Day 1941. Even with the Japanese attack on Pearl Harbour in December 1941 the war would still have seemed far away from Harpsdale. On the day Jock and Ivy moved into the homestead, they experienced a thunderstorm and all the rooms leaked—but the house was renovated by Simmie & Co and completed in October 1941. Jock's name finally went on the title in 1944. A further 196 acres—'Belmont'—was purchased in 1941 from William Henry Poole for £3,773.[291]

By 1956, Harpsdale was already being described as one of the well-known studs in Victoria. In June 1955 Harpsdale DH rams were selling at 20–30 guineas each.[292] In November the following year, sales of 1955 drop ewes from Harpsdale reached up to 55 guineas each at the Newmarket sales in November 1956.[293] In 1957, Jock Simmie employed another person, Rowan McClusky, to help on the farm. He originally boarded with the Dyson-Hollands. Rowan met a nurse, Shirley, who worked at the Greenvale Sanatorium, got married and they moved into Harpsdale house and helped look after Jock. Rowan eventually moved onto greener pastures in the mid-1960s. Jock Simmie then employed various farm help who lived in the house at Troodos and the last, at 'Belmont'.[294] By the late 1950s, Harpsdale was selling DH ewes and rams to Stanley Theo Hawkins and family of 'Springfield', Finley, NSW, who owned the famous Poll Hereford Stud.[295]

Other developments at Harpsdale included, in 1957, a brief period of increased cattle production, mostly due to John Simmie's interest. That same year Jock Simmie sold several Harpsdale-bred DH stud rams for 100-150g each. A new shearing shed was also built on site of the old one, about 500 metres from the homestead, and in 1956 a silo was installed for £298. Harpsdale's average incomes over these years was:

1955/56 = £20,077
1956/57 = £21.193
1957/58 = £11,478
1958/59 = £14,237
1959/60 = £10,885.[296]

Jock liked to be seen at events and take his place among far more well-established farmers and graziers, such as the National Sheep Dog Trials. In an emulation of his trialed and true method used in Canberra to put himself forward in a modest way in the Canberra building scene by making modest donations to various organisations, he donated £20 as third prize for the champion dog at the 1957 national trials held in Canberra that year.[297] His donation would have been noted. More important to him were the Newbold stud sales in South Australia. Jock and Arthur went to the October Rams Sales in SA every year, with John Simmie taking on that role after 1963 after the death of Arthur Dyson-Holland. Early on they drove. John 'talked about going to Adelaide in the Humber Snipe (a 1949 purchase) and how it tackled the terrible roads with great aplomb'. Later on, they would fly.[298] In 1960, when a Dorset Ram sold at the Newbold sales for a world record price of 1150 guineas, Jock Simmie was there—and bought a Dorset Horn ram for 500 guineas (£525).[299]

Jock Simmie continued to subcontract local farmers, in particular Reg. Poole, of 'Lancedene' (which was immediately to the east of Harpsdale), for ploughing, sowing new pastures etc. As John got older, he started doing more of the work himself.[300] As a sign of some diversity in the farm production of Harpsdale, Jock Simmie was also interested in stud cattle. For example, in 1961 he was noted as buying the Angus stud bull 'Holmwood Grand Slam' for 260 guineas at the Newmarket annual stud beef cattle sales that year.[301]

Newbold Sales, South Australia 1960. Jock Simmie sits on right with pipe in mouth, as usual
(RJ Simmie Collection)

December 1964 Harpsdale saw a major purchase of land, when Jock Simmie bought Lot 5 in the Parish of Darraweit Guim in the Shire of Romsey, 477 acres across the Deep Creek from Ted and Joyce [Simmie] Gamble's farm, connected by a shallow ford that was passible most times of the year. This was to be Joyce's inheritance when he died. This land abutted the property owned by Joyce and her husband **Edward Alexander Clarke Gamble** (1919-2013). Edward started buying land there, later called 'Cooinda', in the 1950s, at least 780 acres which increased to over 1200 acres after Jock Simmie's death. Edward ran wethers and cattle. The sheep on this land would be driven overland from the railway siding at Clarkefield.[302]

By the early 1960s, John Simmie was generally running the farm 'although he used to complain about having to convince two old men about implementing changes' in the way the farm was managed and run. The farm books from 1963-1966 showed the transition underway, with John Simmie's handwriting increasingly evident as he took on more of the management and responsibility especially in the face of his father's declining health. Eventually John Simmie was able to gain power of attorney over Jock's affairs as Jock started to fail, mentally and physically.[303] The farm itself, however, was facing a long drought. Rainfall had been on the decline since 1965—in fact the first six months of 1967 were the driest January-June period for the 20th Century over large parts of Victoria, and it was the driest year in 140 years of records in Melbourne. Limited rain and extremely dry conditions continued into 1968.[304]

Family Life at Harpsdale 1941-1968

When Ivy moved to Harpsdale, Jock never quite got around to hiring the help she was promised.[305] However, as the social couple they were, this did not stop Jock and Ivy hosting several dances a year at Harpsdale by 1942 with all the locals invited.[306] With their son John and daughter Joyce now at home there would have been quite a 'gay crowd' (in the parlance of the time), from the local rural district and adjoining

Harpsdale, mid-1940s. Jock Simmie in the new rose garden beds
(RJ Simmie Collection)

farms enjoying the hospitality of the Simmies. There was the Easter Saturday tennis tournament followed by a supper dance with a 3-piece band in the sitting room (drum, sax, and piano). There would be dancing from 8.30 to 2 am. The other major party of the year one was New Year's Eve.[307]

John had returned home after leaving school at Intermediate (today's Year 10) from Scotch College in 1942. He had been described by his Principal the year before:

> His conduct has been very good throughout and he is reliable and trustworthy. I am sorry that he is leaving School on the account of his inability to attend earlier in the day. He has worked steadily and is now a member of

an Intermediate form. I can recommend him as a well-behaved, sound, steady boy.[308]

With World War Two underway and when the military took over Wesley College for 6 months, Scotch had to share its premises with Wesley, Scotch in the morning and Wesley in the afternoon.[309] John would have spent months travelling from the farm to Kensington and then onto Scotch by public transport—and he would have had to leave the farm at least an hour earlier to get there on time. His father Jock wasn't keen, and John wasn't interested, in boarding, so it was easier to leave school. John Simmie's son Richard later reflected on this:

> Even though Jock did his accountancy after the war, I am not sure how he valued a complete education at his son's age and as I have mentioned, his own war experience would have swayed in Johns favour of leaving school and becoming a farmer, After the war I would imagine the issue of going back to school was just as complex.[310]

John turned 18 on 21 September 1943. That he did not enlist, unlike his cousins Roy and John ('Jack') Simmie (Bill Simmie's sons), who served in the Air Force and Army respectively, was possibly in part at least to Jock Simmie's assumed aversion to war arising from his own experiences in World War One on the one hand and even more likely due to the fact that Jock felt he needed help on the property—which made John one of those forbidden to enlist because he was in a 'reserved occupation'—in agriculture this included 'Farm hands, singly employed'.[311] With steady pressure from Australian society at the time to enlist regardless, John managed to resist this, even if he was wanting to do so, by the greater pressure from his father not to do so.

John Simmie also had a busy social life as a teenager and young man. There was tennis at the Greenvale Tennis Club (est. 1914) where he would meet the Websters from nearby property 'Dunhelen', especially James (later a Victorian Senator for the Country Party and in 1949, best man at John's wedding); the Millar girls—Mavis and Joan and **Jean Gamble** (1921-2012), John Simmie's future wife.[312] Mavis and Jean had been friends since age 6. There were also local dances at Greenvale, at Craigieburn Hall, and in Moonee Ponds, and a lot of horse riding. Horses would have been the main mode of transport until John Simmie got his license.[313]

Even before John got his car licence, Jock Simmie purchased an ACME motorcycle for him when his son had taken up working for him and

Dyson-Holland at Harpsdale.[314] As related by John's son Richard, his father often spoke about it later in life. When he had a pillion passenger, they would not be able to get up the Broadmeadows hill, heading back to Harpsdale, on Mickleham Road, without getting off and pushing it up. Richard Simmie recalls that the passenger would have been James ('Jim') Webster; Jim and John Simmie were only three months apart in age.

They were 'as thick as thieves', always getting up to mischief especially in Jock Simmie's straight eight-cylinder 1940 Oldsmobile, where John would make his older and future brother-in-law, Bill Gamble, the driver. Bill was a teetotaller and 'maybe he was the driver before John even got his licence' in 1943.[315] Richard Simmie recalls that the car was always in the repair shop after John and his mates used it on a weekend—once with a cracked chassis after having too many people in the car going over bumps too fast and with the weight of the gas producer on the back. The way the story was told to Richard, Jock would mutter and grumble, get the car repaired and John would be able to have the car whenever he wanted—"I think my father was somewhat indulged".[316]

George Herbert Simmie, the youngest of the three Simmie brothers, died prematurely on 19 December 1944, in Brighton. His occupation was noted as 'metal merchant'. His cause of death, liver failure, suggested heavy drinking as a possible cause with war trauma as a contributing factor to his early demise along with the arsenic-based treatments for his self-inflicted wounds in World War One. George's wife Eileen outlived him by nearly 20 years. They had a daughter, Shirley who died a spinster in 2005. According to Jock's grandson Richard, George was never mentioned as he grew up and the three brothers rarely socialised:

> My father's [John Ernest Simmie's] 21st birthday is key in telling who was not there [including] his uncle Wm. and family (Connie, Roy and Jack), Janet Montgomery (paternal grandmother) nor his uncle George's wife, Eileen and daughter, Shirley. The only time I knew of Shirley's existence was when my father told me she had died in 2005. My father occasionally spoke about Jock's war story but never mentioned George's.[317]

George of course had left Simmie and Co in 1931 to pursue his own business interests. Whatever the reason for George's absence the essential blood relations and shared experiences of the brothers' early years and especially of World War One would still have kept them close, even if they saw less of each other over time. Nonetheless, less is known of George than either of his older siblings. He died more than two years before his nephew John Ernest Simmie's 21st birthday in 1946.

John Simmie married Jean Gamble, on 5 March 1949 and they moved into the house at Belmont. Jean Simmie was the youngest of four children born to Desmond and May Gamble. She was born at 'Brocklands', Greenvale, the dairy farm acquired by Desmond Gamble in 1921. The farm was 300 acres and the family hand milked 40 cows. Electricity came in the 1920s and machine milking was made possible. Jean went to the local Greenvale state school but finished at year 10. While she had an opportunity to attend Penleigh Girls School it would have meant that she had to live with her grandmother, Granny Brock, at 16 Roberts Street Essendon.[318] Jean didn't like her grandmother so left school instead.

Jean was a very determined and often stubborn person which was to show itself throughout her life. She was a shy person by nature, but it never stopped her from doing things, for example marrying John Simmie against the family's wishes. She took on the running of the household (her sister Helen had married in 1939)—cooking for the family and any employees, managing the vegetable garden, washing clothes, and taking animals to the Metropolitan Meat Market in North Melbourne. She still found the time to play tennis at the Greenvale Tennis Club where she met her future husband.[319]

Her relatively tough upbringing growing up, her hard work and knowledge of the rural setting placed her in a good position when she moved to Belmont, and later, after Jock Simmie's death, at Harpsdale. Richard Simmie later recalled:

> Our mother was a good seamstress, making a lot of our clothes when we were young, preserving fruit using the Fowlers Vacola kit, gardening etc. She was also a loyal friend and good sibling especially to her sister, Helen. Helen never had a car licence and Jean would take Helen, each Tuesday, to the Victoria market.

> Jean and Helen spoke most days and for considerable time. Helen would always ring at morning tea or lunch time as she knew Jean would be in the house preparing things. This would annoy our father immensely as he would come for his tea or lunch to find nothing was on the table ready because Jean

John Simmie (L), Jean Simmie (R) and Ivy Simmie in background, sheep drenching
(RJ Simmie Collection)

was on the phone to her sister—he would exclaim "For glory sake woman, where is my lunch/morning tea, I haven't got all day". How Jean would have loved a cordless phone. It would have saved her a lot of grief over the years.[320]

Throughout 1949, Jock and John did the renovations to the house, consisting of demolishing the old rear section which had dirt floors and building a new section consisting of a bedroom, sunroom, kitchen, bathroom, and laundry. The old part of the house (stone) was replastered, and all five rooms renovated. In late 1949, the power was put on. John and Jean's early life at Belmont was tough until the renovations were completed. Most never were, according to Richard Simmie, as his father John 'was a perfectionist and never had enough time to complete most things'. However, for all of his procrastination and best intentions John was nonetheless an accomplished carpenter.

John also did carpentry work for others including his sister-in-law, Helen Souter (née Gamble, Jean's older sister). For example, he put in sliding doors that opened up the dining room into the sitting room in her home at 16 Roberts Street, Essendon, a house she had inherited from her maternal grandmother, 'Granny' Bessie Brock (née Warner). He would later add to the sunroom, doubling its size. John was also working long hours often seven days a week on occasion, helping

Arthur Dyson-Holland and his father Jock Simmie as a general farm hand at Harpsdale. Jean, like all country wives, were expected to add their labour on occasion as well as raise their families and support their husbands at home and during busy periods such as shearing when meals had to be prepared for all. In this Jean had a great role model in her mother-in-law, Ivy Simmie, at least until Ivy's premature death in 1952.

Bessie Brock, Jean's maternal grandmother, was always known as **Granny Brock**. Born in 1867, she died at the age of 82. She was remembered by her family as an utter snob. The Brocks were well known in the Bundoora and Preston districts. Granny Brock's mother-in-law Elizabeth Hurst, formerly Brock, née Clarke, was a first cousin to Sir William Clarke, 1st Baronet of Rupertswood. She died in 1922. The Hursts attended balls at Cliveden House, the city residence of Sir William and Lady Clarke and were probably also guests at the Clarke's Rupertswood mansion in Sunbury.

Granny Brock's father-in-law, Alexander Brock, was part of the early Victorian 'Squattocracy' in the Romsey region then later had extensive property interests in Shepparton, Yark, Avoca, Janefield, Bundoora and Preston. Alexander built a house called 'Oak Hill', in Preston, in 1862, which was demolished in the 1960s. He died in 1871 and Elizabeth lived there until her death in 1922. Her son, William Joseph Clarke Brock, who married Granny Brock in 1886, continued to live there until his death in 1934. Oak Hill was sold in 1935 and Granny Brock went to live at 16 Roberts Street, Essendon.[321] On the death of Granny Brock, it became the home of Helen Souter, née Gamble, Jean's older sister, until her death in 2009. Granny Brock's only surviving child, May Isobel, married Desmond Gamble in 1915 and they purchased land in Greenvale, in 1921, the year Jean Gamble was born. They named it 'Brocklands', after the Brock family.[322]

By 1949, however, Granny Brock didn't have much left except her snobbery. She disapproved of the match her granddaughter, Jean Gamble, was making. The Simmies were city people, with new money (Jock Simmie wasn't shy of splashing it around) and they consumed alcohol, a practice frowned upon given Granny Brock's Methodist upbringing.[323] Richard Simmie relates that on his parents' wedding day, 5 March 1949, Jean's grandmother, Granny Brock refused to attend the wedding and would not allow May, Jean's mother to attend either. Bill, Jean's eldest brother, gave her away because Desmond, Jean's father had died in 1942. Jean contributed £50 pounds to the cost of her own wedding. Ivy Simmie made Jean's wedding dress, as well as finishing off her own outfit on the morning of the wedding.[324]

Granny Brock died a little over 3 months later. Jean never spoke fondly of her grandmother. Kath Foale, née Souter, Jean's niece, aged 9 at the wedding date, was being looked after by her grandmother and great grandmother on the day of the wedding and remembers very clearly the distress May suffered at not being present at her daughter's wedding. Kath later formed the opinion that Granny Brock was in awe of her granddaughter, Jean, because she was so capable and thus was intimidated by her.[325] Kath also heard that when Bessie had married William Brock, in 1886, Bessie wasn't considered a good match for William. They married three days after the birth of their first child, Constance, who died in 1914 from appendicitis. Many people note that the most strident snobs have themselves come from humble beginnings.

Jean's mother May started to make amends to their relationship after the birth of John and Jean's first son **Peter John Simmie** on 21 April 1950. However, this was cut short by the death of Jean's mother in August 1950. Jean felt the loss of her parents keenly but was especially hit hard with the sudden death of John's mother Ivy with whom she had become very close—as compared to her father-in-law, Jock Simmie. By 1952, Jean was very much alone without the older generation to support and help her as the family grew to three boys by 1954 (Peter, **Philip Edward Simmie**, born 10 April 1952 and **Richard James Simmie**, born 16 October 1954).[326] Richard Simmie recalls:

> Jock demanded a lot of John's time, actually seven days a week, so Jean was left mostly to herself to raise the children and deal with a husband who was hardly around and when he was, their relationship was tense to say the least. I grew up in what seemed like an environment of constant arguing. Despite taking on more of the farm work and responsibility, John was still expected to stoke the AGA stove for his father twice a day. Our father wasn't around very much because he was constantly working.[327]

In 1952, not long before the death of Ivy Simmie, the International Harvester company magazine *Expanding Horizons*, extolled the virtues

Three generations of the Simmie family at Harpsdale, 1952: Jock Simmie (standing), Ivy Simmie (seated right), Jean Simmie (seated middle), John Simmie (seated left), Joyce Simmie (seated on ground) and son Peter Simmie.
(*Expanding Horizons*, 1952)

of 'the Australian farm family' and featured the Simmies at Harpsdale:

> The farm family is historically one of society's strongest pillars. Food for human consumption, fibre for clothing and feed for our animals is produced from the soil by farmers and their families working together. The power and capacity of modern farm machines have broadened the horizons of farm families by providing more time for leisure and self-improvement—by ensuring greater productivity and profit from their efforts.[328]

By this time of his life, with Simmie & Co well established and his DH Stud well on the way to be a leader in the industry, Jock lived very well. As he put on more weight, his clothes were all tailored, by Henry Bucks, in later life, as well as other tailors such as by Keith Parlon, Ladies & Gents High Class Tailor for English dinner suits and dress coats for example. Although rarely seen without a pipe in hand, he also liked his cigars—from G A Carter & Son, in North Melbourne (100 cost £4.15.0).

Christmas time was always a highlight of the year. Jock bought bulk supplies of tinned fruits and salmon which were handed out to all those at the Christmas day celebration. He also bought sherry, port and other alcohol for the guests to share. As the family expanded so did the Christmas celebrations and Jock was always remembered for his generosity. Christmas day drinks were always served at the bar, nibbles provided by Dorrie Howe; Jean Simmie cooked the pork and made the plum pudding, Joyce Simmie the turkey and Great Western champagne was served at lunch, the only time champagne was ever consumed during the year.[329]

Cars also featured prominently in the family, another sign of the well-off status of the family. Jock Simmie drove a 1940 Oldsmobile (plate BX 653) right through to 1952. Ivy drove a 1937 Vauxhall (plate DX 86755) but in February 1950, Jock bought her a new Humber Snipe Saloon. After Ivy's death Jock used this car himself until 1956 when he replaced it with a Chevrolet sedan which he bought and drove down from Esmond's Motors, in Canberra where he was a director. The 1949 Humber Snipe Saloon challenged Ivy Simmie. According to anecdotes passed down in the Simmie family:

> Ivy wasn't very tall, and no-one knew how she managed to drive the car. She didn't like changing gears so if starting from a standstill

going downhill, she would put the car in second or even third gear, and off she would go. John Simmie related how the car would shudder and shake and as if it was a miracle, go forwards, rarely stalling.[330]

The year before another link with the past went with the death of **John Ford Montgomery** on 6 August 1951 at 1 Kororoit Street, Sunshine, aged 89. He was buried in Echuca. His first marriage to Lillian Edgell had lasted 22 years and resulted in seven children. His second to Janet Simmie (née Aberline) had lasted 47 years. John Montgomery had been a stalwart father and provider to his extended family as well as devoted husband. Nonetheless his headstone in Echuca read 'Beloved husband of Lily' but no mention of Janet. Perhaps there was just too much information to put on the headstone. Of the six memorial notices in the *Sunshine Advocate* on 10 August, not one from the Simmie family. Only one notice on 7 August mentions the three stepsons at all and that is in the *Argus*.[331]

There is no real explanation for this as John Montgomery had been the stepfather of the three sons of James Simmie following his premature death and raised both them and his own children from his first marriage. This would have been a considerable burden on any family man in those days, let alone today. Less than three years later, on 19 March 1954, **Janet Montgomery** his wife and mother of Jock, George, and William Simmie, died at her home in Sunshine. Her memorial notice in the *Age* was an exact same notice as was issued for her late husband John in the *Argus*, three years before, with her name now inserted.[332]

Between these occurrences, on 7 February 1952, **Ivy Simmie** died from a heart attack.[333] With her sudden death, Jock was deeply upset and sat in his gardening shed, on the old redgum stump in the blacksmith shed, for days.[334] There is little doubt that Jock relied heavily on Ivy to sustain the home life and family throughout the years in Canberra. Later, when Jock was travelling back and forth to Canberra between 1931-1968 on Simmie & Co business and in Melbourne, while at the same time running his new stud farm at Harpsdale, Ivy maintained 'hearth and home'. Even when they moved to Harpsdale and Ivy lost house help and the other 'lifestyle' advantages of Brighton, she quickly adapted.

For example, Ivy would feed all the shearing team three meals a day for the duration of shearing, which usually lasted a couple of weeks. She still had her family and old retainer Willie McAuliffe

Mavis Millar, Richard Simmie, Philip Simmie, Joyce Gamble (F), Peter Simmie and Jean Simmie (back) at 'Cooinda', 1957-58 (RJ Simmie Collection)

to feed as well. The shearing team stayed in the billiards room, so she had to accommodate them as well.[335] Jock would not have been an easy man to live with, what with his war experience, being so involved with the business, Freemasons and all the clubs he belonged to, not to mention the farm. His drinking and constant pipe smoking may have suggested in retrospect that he was, in today's parlance, a very highly functioning substance abuser.[336] However, that was common among many of his generation, especially among those who had served in the front lines of the battlefields at Gallipoli and the Western Front.

Ivy was close to both her daughter-in-law Jean and her younger sister Dorrie. Ivy was well-off because of Jock's success in business and was able to be generous with her family, especially her less well-off sister Dorrie. Dorrie's husband Keith Howe was a floor manager at Joyce & Howe Shoes in Melbourne, a company started by his father and Dorrie and Ivy's father. Dorrie and Keith spent most weekends at Harpsdale, always helping in the garden. Jock also put in a tennis court, and they would hold tournaments especially Easter Saturday with a party to follow.[337]

In those days family gatherings were often set well in advance, but equally Harpsdale was often the scene of many impromptu social occasions with neighbours and friends as well. Ivy was also a very capable person and worked tirelessly in all that she did. Richard Simmie recalls: 'Ivy was always described in terms of warmth, love and respect. No one ever said a bad thing about her'.[338]

In time, Jock Simmie brought a new person into Harpsdale—Noelle June Stevenson (1921-1989). This was regarded as somewhat scandalous in the aftermath of Ivy's death, and no doubt led to some speculation in the family that Jock had known her for some time (there is no evidence of this, she was not living away—in Maribyrnong—from her father until 1954 according to electoral roll records). Jock had written his first will only five days after Ivy's death.

Later, in November 1964, Jock made a codicil to this 1952 will, where Noelle Stevenson is mentioned with a provision to be given £8/week for life; a rewrite of the will in 1966 repeats the codicil, but with the amount changed to $16/week for life and on her death, the money to go to his son John. Jock's wishes were not to be realised.[339] In February 1954, Jock's daughter Joyce Shirley Simmie married **Edward ('Ted') Alexander Clarke Gamble** (1919-2013), who was Jean Simmie's brother—the third of the four children of May and Desmond Gamble. Joyce and Ted subsequently had a daughter Kathryn Anne, who was born in December 1961, the last of Jock Simmie's grandchildren.[340]

It was perhaps no surprise then that in 1956, changes were afoot. By this time Jock Simmie was still heavily engaged in his own business (including with the Master Builders Association of Victoria) and private pursuits, while his son John's family was now complete. Harpsdale had been Jock and Ivy's retreat and haven, and now with Ivy gone the social life at Harpsdale would have largely died with her.[341]

In the circumstances, Jock's new companion could hardly have been a suitable replacement for Ivy.

Jock Simmie, always a keen horse racing enthusiast and a member of the Victorian Racing Club, spent more time at the Caulfield and Moonee Valley race tracks while also holding club memberships in a range of clubs in Canberra and Melbourne, including:

> Royal Canberra Golf Club
> Emerald Country Club
> Northern Suburban Club
> Returned Sailor's, Soldier's & Airman's Imperial League of Australia
> Brighton Yacht Club
> Oaklands Hunt Club
> Commonwealth Club
> Kingston Heath Golf Club.[342]

After Ivy's death, Jock always joined his son John's family at Belmont for the Sunday roast. Family lore has it that one Sunday Jock gave his daughter-in-law Jean £50 after a good day at the races. Jean used the money to buy a 3.5-foot round Victorian-era pedestal table, five chairs and a chiffonier. According to Richard Simmie, 'Jock would frequently remind her who really paid for them'. Later on Sundays, Joyce and Ted Gamble

'Kiloran', Mt. Martha 1960s
(RJ Simmie Collection)

At the beach. L to R: Jean Simmie, Mavis Millar, John Simmie under boat shed, Joyce Gamble neé Simmie, Edward 'Ted' Gamble, and three boys Richard, Philip and Peter. Joan Millar was taking the photograph.
(RJ Simmie Collection)

would call in at Belmont for afternoon tea and then go to Harpsdale to give Jock his dinner.[343]

So, in what may have been a master stroke for everyone, a holiday house (called 'Kiloran') was purchased on the Esplanade at Mt Martha, about 70 kilometres south east of Melbourne on the Mornington Peninsula, and just a short distance from the local beaches. The purchase included a beach bathing box. Kiloran, until its sale in 1970, remains a strong positive memory for all of those involved but especially the three sons of John Simmie. Peter Simmie, the eldest recalls: 'Getting up 5am of a morning and exploring the cliffs along the beach with my brother Philip. Our mother making sardine and tomato sandwiches for lunch on the beach. Going out fishing in the boat and nearly always getting the hand line tangled'.[344]

Richard Simmie's memories are acute. He recalls:

> It was to be the place of my best childhood memories as we would spend all of January each year. We stopped going in the late 1960s. Family friends, Mavis and Joan Millar would spend most of January with us. They

John ('Red Jack') Simmie at the BBQ, Mt Martha c1950s
(RJ Simmie Collection)

had a big dark blue Dodge car which we children would help them polish during the holidays. Jock allowed various cousins of his in Elmore and Bendigo to use the house throughout the year but Christmas was our time. Trips up to Arthur's Seat and taking the chair lift were great highlights in the Dodge.

The beach was great. We had a small clinker built dingy, named the Queen Mary, for our use as well as been taken out in a bigger boat to fish. I was always terrified out on the water as the boat use to leak. Due to sand getting caught in the boards as it dried out in the boat shed. As children we were not supposed to get into the boat when it was out of the water, but we couldn't resist. The leaking was minimal, more to do with my fears. I would be manning the bilge pump after the first hour or so on the water. The motor was frequently unreliable, and my father John had to row us back into shore on the odd occasion. Quite a feat when we would have often been a mile off shore. [345]

Richard continues:

There was no TV, only a basic wireless, so we had to entertain ourselves with board games, cards and late-night walks on the beach. It was a very simple life and remembered as being so much fun. We did eventually get a portable record player and there would have probably been a lot of singles, Beach Boys and the Beatles, and LP's of the Black and White Minstrels, Herb Elliot and the Tijuana Brass.

I spent a few weekends at Mt Martha in the Christmas of 1970-71 with my brothers and two of Philip's school friends, John and Ian. We were painting garage doors and so on, sprucing the place upon for sale. Six of us would pile into Peter's little 1968 Toyota Corolla and drive to the Portsea Pub. Robyn Abbey, Peter's girlfriend at the time (and later, his wife) would always be the designated driver somehow. She still is to this day.[346]

In 1959, **Mary Irons** (née **Simmie**), and aunt to Jock Simmie, died in Echuca aged 94. She had been born in 1864 and was the last of the first generation of Simmies in Victoria. Jock Simmie's son John was one of the pall bearers. John took over the care of Mary's dog, a cocker spaniel.[347]

The 1960s were to bring further major changes to Harpsdale and family life for the Simmies, but at least for a number of years life was very good. The farm was prospering, and John was increasingly in charge. It remained a predictable rural life with John taking delivery of sheep by rail in Craigieburn and droving them up Craigieburn Road to the farm.[348] With Dyson-Holland's sudden death in 1963, John had to step into the breach. Family holidays at Mt Martha continued in the summer holidays for John and his family.

For Jock's grandchildren, the fifties and sixties were fondly remembered. Peter Simmie, the eldest, recalls:

> Happy family times with brothers on the farm. My mother's cooking and love of the garden, planting different varieties of plants for different seasons. Looking after pet lambs. Riding our bikes to the small local school, Mickleham State School of 14 pupils. My parents went to the local dance and we three boys would sleep in the car, great fun. I loved shearing time, sweeping the floor and pressing the wool and learnt some new words from the shearers![349]

Philip Simmie recalled growing up at Belmont:

> I enjoyed my time living at Belmont. Loved exploring out doors and it was when I developed a great interest in cars. Our father bought us a go-kart, when I was about 12. Then we had a 1936 Oldsmobile and finally a 1946 Chevrolet. We had great fun driving them around the farm. I also loved shooting rabbits. My mother bought me a .22 rifle for my 14th birthday. Great times. We all learnt to drive at a very young age. Sometimes I would drive home from Mickleham State School, about 3 miles, and one time were pulled over by the police and mum was given a huge lecture by the policeman. He told my mother that I would become a delinquent. I was 11 years old at the time. That was the end of driving on the road.[350]

Then the school era began, and a long association with Haileybury College for all three boys. Although John Simmie had attended Scotch College like his cousins Roy and Jack, there had been a mix up in bookings and so no places there for the boys when it came time for secondary schooling. A family friend, Marge Redd, played bridge with the wife of the Headmaster of Haileybury College where her only child, Crombie, was a day boy. She got all three enrolled at Haileybury.[351] Peter started in 1962 and Philip in 1965. Richard commented later that 'I was like an only child, only having to deal with my brothers during school holidays'.

Peter Simmie had a mixed experience:

My experience at Haileybury was generally good for the first 3 years but as I got older I found the rules were the same for the older pupils as for the young. It was a huge challenge coming from such a small country school and at first I was homesick. I left Haileybury 1966 and went to Essendon Grammar where I completed year 11 and part year 12 subjects.[352]

Philip Simmie recalls that he was meant to go to boarding school at Haileybury College in 1963, but was not very happy about leaving home, so he was sent to Sunbury High School for a year. The following year he went to Haileybury and 'never looked back':

I never liked leaving home, so going to boarding school was the best thing ever for me. I developed a certain degree of independence and the ability to stand on my own two feet. Like most kids, I rebelled against all the discipline, but it taught me how to live with other people.

Peter was at Haileybury when I started. It was a great help having an older brother there. I was taken under the wings of some of his friends, so never felt completely alone while making friends from my own age group. I was a full-time boarder for five years. We only had Saturday leave, from 8am to 8pm, and one weekend leave per year plus normal school holidays. I would often go home for Saturday leave. I would catch the train from Hampton to Broadmeadows and my mother would pick me up. Then both my mother and father would drive me back to school.[353]

However, Philip didn't complete Year 12 in 1969 with a pass, due to, by his own admission, 'too many distractions and lack of commitment'.

Richard's experience was somewhat different. He remembered being greeted in his first year by a new teacher with "Not another Simmie", as the last of the brothers to attend—'somewhat demoralising and intimidating for a very quiet, shy and nerdy kid of 12'. Although Richard did well at the college, coming 4th overall in Year 11, the harsh drought through 1967-1968 threatened his last year as it impacted severely on finances at Harpsdale. John Simmie went to see the headmaster, David Bradshaw, and pleaded his case; school fees were reduced by two-thirds. Richard flourished. In his final year he became House Captain of Rendall, and finished 8th overall with such good results that, in a family first, he was accepted into the University of Melbourne to study medicine.

Into the late 1960s, Jock was still active in Simmie & Co in Canberra and in Melbourne and John would often pick him up from Essendon Airport on his return from Canberra; the boys remembered Jock would always have sweets for them. When the farm hand Rowan McClusky and his wife moved on in the mid-1960s, a series of house keepers were employed to look after Jock as his health deteriorated. Richard Simmie recalls:

> One of the housekeepers in particular, we called Auntie Lill (Muir). Jock [Simmie] had

John Ernest ('Jock') Simmie (1892-1968)
(RJ Simmie Collection)

budgies and Auntie Lill would teach them things like "Come on Jock, Butchie wants a beer". Jock drank a lot of beer, VB long necks, several per day.[354]

Remarkably, even though retired, Jock continued to travel to Canberra into 1968, before deteriorating health kept him close to Harpsdale and eventually into care. Architectural historian Ken Charlton remembers meeting Jock at the Simmie & Co office in Fyshwick in March 1968, just after the firm had won the contract to build Canberra's first Youth Hostel in O'Connor. Charlton recalled the occasion to Jock's grandson Richard Simmie:

> For Jock to be visiting Canberra when I dropped into the Simmie HQ was a stroke of luck. The meeting is etched in my memory, as I felt I was in the presence of a great man. I imagine he and his colleagues must have been keen to erect another prestige building, despite its modest size. Their price was so competitive the other tenders had no chance![355]

John Ernest 'Jock' Simmie died on 13 August 1968 in Melbourne and his ashes were added to Ivy Simmie's grave at Fawkner Cemetery.[356] He was listed in Australia's *Who's Who* which gave a potted summary of his official life in 1968:

> F.A.I.B., A.A.S.A., F.C.I.S.,F.A.C.A., Past president Master Builders' Assn., Breeder Dorset Horn Sheep: son of J. Simmie, Moama, N.S.W.; ed. Echuca State Sch.; Dir. Simmie & Co Pty. Ltd. Master Builders; Gov. Dir. Tomlins Simmie Pty. Ltd.; 2 yrs. 21 Bn. 1St A.I.F, Gallipoli & France, wounded Pozieres 1916; Pres. 21 Bn. Assn.; m. Apr. 2, 1920, Ivy, d. J. J. Joyce, 1 s. 1 d.; recreations, golf, racing; clubs, Canberra, Commonwealth (Canb.), R. S. L. (Caulfield), R.A.C.V., C.T.A., Kingston Heath Golf, Roy. Canberra Golf, V.R.C., M.V.R.C., address, Harpsdale, Yuroke, Vic., 3047.

Yet this summary is the barest of his life works as described in this history.

Harpsdale 1940—1968 145

JOHN ERNEST 'JOCK' SIMMIE
Family Tree

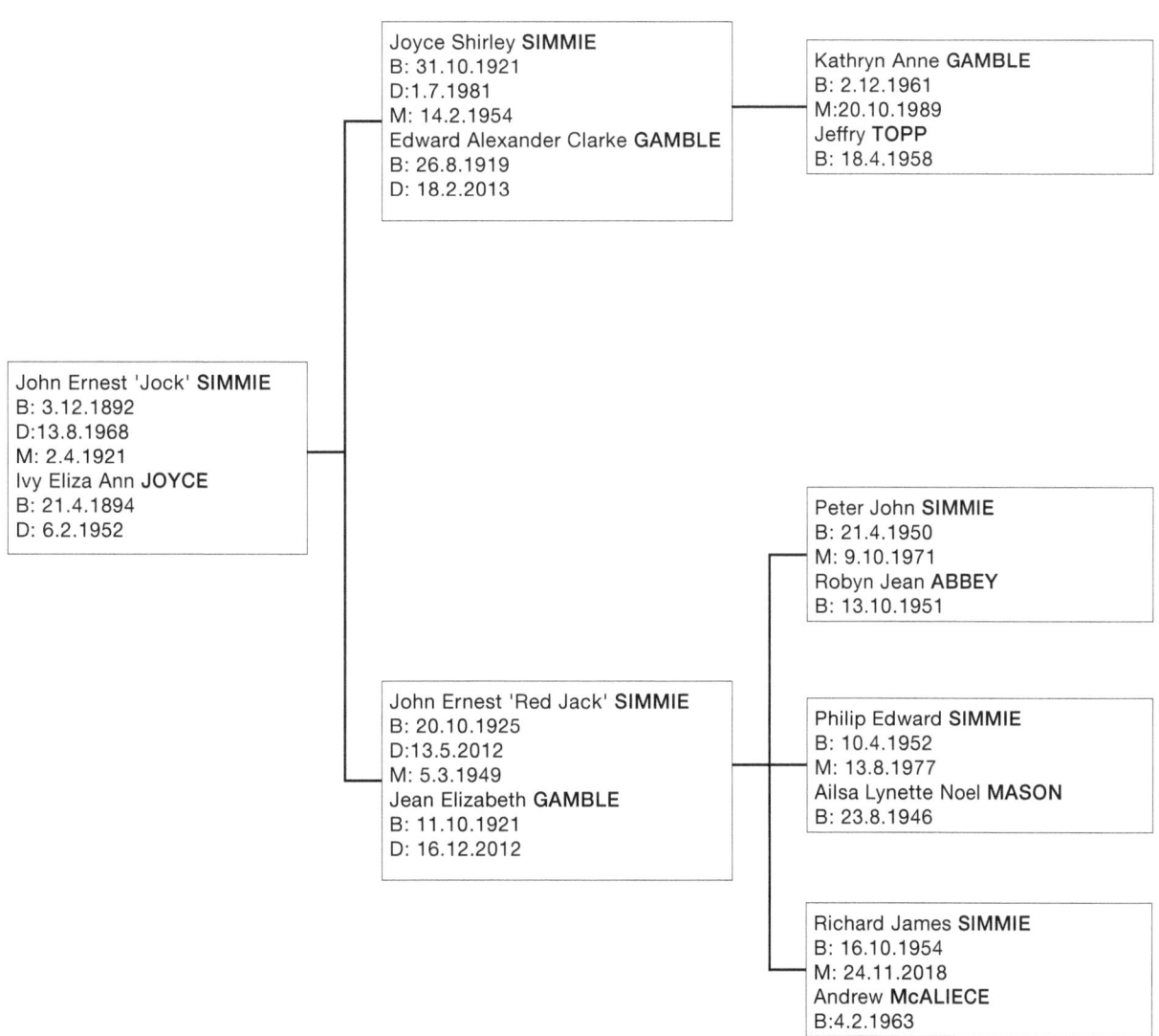

Chapter Five
Harpsdale 1969-2000

The death of Jock Simmie in 1968 was the end of an era and the formal passing of the family and property responsibilities to his son John Ernest Simmie. Of course, John Simmie had been working on the farm since leaving school in 1942 and learning about farming directly from the experienced Arthur Dyson-Holland, Jock Simmie's farm manager, as well as from his father, Jock Simmie. Working for the two older men was not without its difficulties for John Simmie. When he got a new Vauxhall car in 1963, it was a rare event—later he would often comment about how hard it was at the time to purchase new items such as a car or other things for the farm.[357]

By 1963 with the sudden death of Dyson-Holland, John moved into Dyson-Holland's role and managed Harpsdale and the Dorset Horn Stud but under Jock Simmie's watchful eye. The transitioning of power/control from Jock to John could be seen in the farm accounts:

> 1963 was the last year that Jock did the farm tax return in his usual manner—a folder full of receipts and invoices, hand written listings of expenses and income with totals.

1964/65—John introduces a ledger system for recording all expenses and income, in John's writing but Jock adds to it.

1965/66—Ledger is all in Jock's writing. He had made the transition to the new system.

1966/67 - Ledger is all in John's hand writing apart from the last entry which was in Jock's.

1967/68—Ledger is all in John's hand writing.[358]

Jock's Will of 1966 named his son John and daughter Joyce as Trustees. Joyce inherited Lot 5 in the Shire of Romsey, and the balance of the Estate went to his son John as a 'Life Tenant'. Now, however, John Simmie also had the immediate burden of private school fees for his children, the discovery that Jock's companion Noelle Stevenson had been left a life annuity in Jock's will, but worst of all were the death duties/probate, State and Federal, that amounted to $178,000 of the $438,000 Estate.[359] Even after liquidating all cash assets, selling the beach house at Mount Martha along with 31 acres of land, about $70,000 was still left to pay in 1970.

John by this stage had spent several thousand dollars in legal fees, a large sum for the day. Then there was also pressure from the Tax Department wanting to charge interest on the remaining debt and probably putting more pressure on liquidating assets which was contrary to Jock's will.[360] It wasn't until at least 1971, that John was finally finished with the probate. Several years of financial worry were compounded by the harsh drought of 1967-68. John Simmie's accountant, Phil Howard, who was very involved in the Estate affairs, encouraged him to borrow the money at the time to pay the Probate rather than liquidate all cash assets. Many years later he admitted to son Richard Simmie, "I regret not taking Phil Howard's advice about borrowing money".[361]

At Jock Simmie's death and following an inspection a description of Harpsdale in the Probate documents gave Harpsdale (including Belmont and Troodos) as a property consisting of about 1352 acres in a district annual average rainfall of 24 inches. The nearest school was Craigieburn, and it boasted a daily mail service. The report noted the country and soil as gently undulating land sloping down to a gully on the north western portion of the property:

> The soil is mostly volcanic with stoney outcrops evident on the rises and along the gully. Approximately 700 acres has

been cultivated and sown down in clovers and rye grass. The whole area has been top dressed periodically with good results. A sound, healthy property well suited for grazing and fattening both sheep and cattle. Some scouring [erosion] along the gully but this is being effectively dealt with under the supervision of the Soil Conservation Authority. It was adequately watered by four equipped bores, 18 dams of various capacities, and odd soaks in the gully. The property was conveniently sub-divided into 24 paddocks.

The fencing was in generally stock proof order and comprises mainly plain wire with some portions new and some portions requiring renovation. In terms of noxious weeds and vermin, the farm inspection noticed some areas of variegated and artichoke thistle and some horehound; rabbits were in evidence, but this pest is being kept well in check. The inspector noted in recent years the property had been running Crossbred ewes Corriedale wethers and beef breeders in addition to a small Dorset Horn Stud. He estimated the carrying capacity at 4,300 sheep or the equivalent in sheep and cattle. He valued the land at $233,765. [362]

The report also inspected and valued the 477 acres which Jock Simmie had bought near Deep Creek, which was to be Joyce Simmie's inheritance. The inspector noted that this land had been used almost exclusively for running fine, wooled wethers and could carry 1,075 sheep in normal seasons and was valued at $40,850. By 1972/73, however, John Simmie was finally and well and truly, his own man. In October that year he was reported in *Stock*

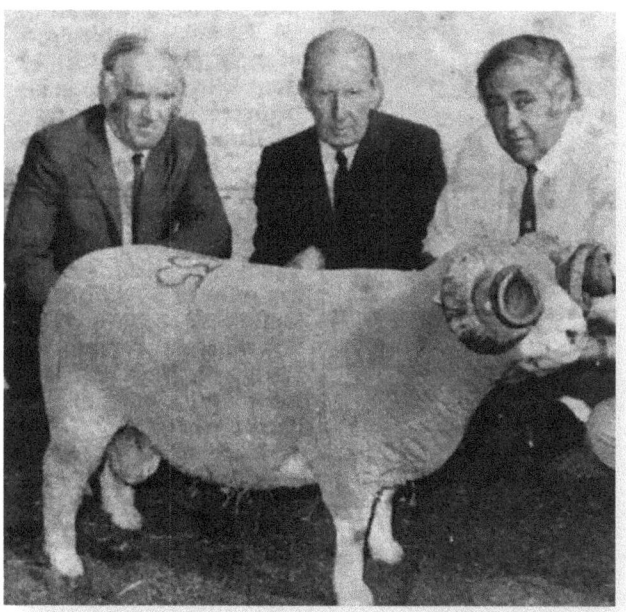

Top priced Dorset Horn ram and equal top ram at the SA Dorset Fair.
J E Simmie (L) with co-buyer W Martin (centre) and breeder L Hart (R)
(*Stock and Land*, 1971)

and Land as the co-buyer at the South Australian Dorset Fair of the top-priced Dorset Horn ram and equal top ram for $975.[363]

After Jock's death Harpsdale remained empty until February 1970 when John and Jean Simmie finally moved into the house from Belmont, where they had lived since 1949.[364] Jean Simmie was never fond of her late father-in-law, so to move into the big house took some convincing. After their move, Belmont became the residence for the farm hand. According to Richard Simmie, 'John couldn't tolerate working with people who did things to a lesser standard than he did'. John first employed an experienced New Zealander, who had highly trained sheep dogs. Unfortunately, it didn't last as his wife was homesick and they moved back to NZ.

Employed afterwards was one Keith Wilson, a World War Two veteran and his family and then Raymond Walter English, a 'stockman', who was the last person John employed in that capacity.[365] Philip Simmie recalls: 'Over the years drought made things very difficult and eventually forced [my father] to let go of farm labour. It was very tough to run the farm alone.' With Ray English's retirement in 1973, Philip Simmie, his second son and a qualified wool classer, came to work on the farm, as well as doing wool classing jobs in the district. Peter Simmie, the eldest son, recalls:

> I met my wife, Robyn [Abbey], in 1966 on the school bus when she was attending Penleigh Presbyterian Ladies College and I, Essendon Grammar. After leaving school she worked at Royal Insurance in the city. I also worked in Insurance at the same time. We got engaged in 1970 and married October 1971. Robyn also worked as veterinary nurse in Sunbury and 22 years at West Brunswick Clinic eventually as Practice Manager. We have two children, **Lisa** born 1974 and **Jarrod** born 1979.[366]

After their wedding Peter and Robyn Simmie moved into the cottage on the farm called Troodos, previously owned by Arthur Dyson-Holland. After the last farmhand departed, Peter and family moved into Belmont, with a few horses along with John Simmie's sheep for some years. Peter was not employed by his father except for hay carting contracts from time to time. Philip Simmie and family, now with **James** (b1979) and **Sarah** (b1981), would move to Queensland in 1988-89, but by 2001 when John Simmie himself retired, the farm was in a sad state of repairs.[367]

In December 1969, two painters were engaged to redecorate the interior of Harpsdale; they lived on site for 6 weeks doing all the work. Ivy Simmie had had the house decorated in cream—walls, woodwork and ceilings, with heavy venetian blinds and drapes on all windows. The carpet that was laid in 1941 was kept, but Jean Simmie engaged a company called Brighter Homes from Moonee Ponds for the window dressings (and spent $265.90 on five rooms). The venetian blinds were replaced with simple Holland blinds and there was extensive use of wallpaper, as is still seen to this day. All rooms except the sitting room, rear bedroom and office were done. John paid for the painters. Richard Simmie recalls:

> We moved into the big house in the first week of February 1970. I was actually allowed a weekend pass from boarding school to be present. A big deal in those days as we only ever had one weekend pass allowed per year.[368]

Meanwhile in order to pay the probate on Jock's estate, the holiday house on the Esplanade at Mt Martha, purchased in 1956, had to be sold in 1970. With the sale, an important part of the community life for three generations of the Simmie family went with it. It was sold for $16,000 of which

Gateway to Harpsdale, 1976
(State Library of Victoria)

half went to John's sister Joyce, as they were co-owners—but Joyce took no responsibility for paying any of the Probate. John Simmie was also forced to sell part of Belmont to meet probate—the property was reduced to about 160 acres [65 hectares]. Joyce also inherited 477 acres [193 hectares] in the Parish of Darraweit Guim in the Shire of Romsey, which Jock Simmie had bought in 1964. This land went to Joyce Gamble in July 1969. This was Joyce's inheritance, with any stock on it (950-odd wethers, value $9234, land value $40,800 at the time of Jock Simmie's death in 1968).[369]

At Harpsdale, further changes were made to the house over the first few years. The rear bedroom was done in 1972 to accommodate Richard Simmie when he started at Melbourne University in 1973 (the first in the extended family to ever attend university). His father spent weeks filling all the cracks especially in the ceiling, although John allowed Richard to choose the colours in the room. The sitting room was renovated in 1974 although the small office (now the study) was not refreshed until 2010. Jean Simmie was at first overwhelmed by the changes to her life, 'but after about two years, it was as if she had never lived anywhere else'.[370] It was about this time that Philip Simmie returned to the farm to work with his father on Harpsdale.

Meanwhile John Simmie's three sons had pursued their separate pathways in life, yet with Harpsdale and family (despite its ups and downs) as the point of reference and to which they would return throughout their lives.

Philip Simmie, on leaving school, spent two years at the Melbourne College of Textiles, a TAFE school in in Pascoe Vale, completing a Farm Management and Wool Classing Diploma, and in 1972, began working as a wool classer and shearing shed hand in the local area. After returning to Melbourne following a six-month break travelling interstate, Philip started working in the shearing sheds as a wool classer again, and in between shed jobs would help out on Harpsdale, initially living with John and Jean at the homestead. In 1975, Philip was invited to attend Derby Day at Flemington with his brother Peter and wife Robyn Simmie and a friend **Ailsa Mason**. Her parents had a horse stud which was diagonally opposite to Harpsdale, on Oaklands Road. Even though they lived so close to Harpsdale, Philip had never met Ailsa before then. Their common interest in horse racing started what was to become a lifetime partnership.

By 1976, finances were tight on the farm, due to low stock prices, so Philip went to work on a gas pipeline which started beside the West Gate Bridge and after that job, with Michelin Tyres. He moved in with Ailsa who at that time had a small unit in East Malvern. Finally, Philip returned to shearing shed work once again. He and Ailsa were married in August 1977. She had a 100-acre block of land, not far from Harpsdale, on which they built a house and had a small farm breeding a few thoroughbred horses and beef cattle. They moved there in early 1978, and Philip began working at Harpsdale again as well as on their own small farm.[371]

Peter Simmie also moved away from the farm after school, working for the State Savings Bank of Victoria then in various positions in the transport industry. He later became State manager for Toll Transport, a career of 25 years before retiring to Belmont where he and Robyn had lived since 1973. Peter recalls:

> We were lucky to have my parents living next door and even better when we had children. They were very supportive and the children [Lisa and Jarrod] loved walking or riding bikes to Harpsdale especially after Nanny had baked her chocolate slice. We had many happy dinners here at Belmont and at Harpsdale together. [372]

Belmont, c1970
(Courtesy Peter Simmie)

Availability of water was a constant factor in determining successful years, and especially to survive the drought years which came around regularly, such as 1967-68 and again several times through to the 21st century. In addition the household needed water for domestic use and for the garden. A bore had been sunk in the 1920s near the house which was a good producer but of water with a high saline content, to the point that watering in the summer resulted in garden leaves dying due to the heat and salty water. In 1982, Jean Simmie was supplied dam water for her garden rather than the bore water. The bore was dismantled and capped with a concrete plug.[373]

For primary production the property relied mostly on the dam in the centre of the property. From 1979 John Simmie replaced piping across the property with poly pipe, added new troughs, along with two 5,000 gallon water tanks. Water was pumped, initially by wind mill from the big dam which had been enlarged since the 1967-68 drought. John later replaced the windmill with a single cylinder diesel pump. With all the drought years of the early 2000s and into the 2010s (culminating in the Black Saturday bushfires which claimed 374 lives), the big dam was often so low on water it couldn't be used. As an interim solution

Peter Simmie plumbed in his bore at Belmont to the tank that fed the house garden and farm and allowed Richard to use it for stock.

In 2014 Richard added a 300,000-litre storage tank to help with the water supply for the garden (even decanting water from other tanks at the shearing shed, stables and work shop, when they were full). Finally in 2018, Peter Simmie had clean fill added to part of his property to the east of the big dam. It was an area that would flood with water but little of it would run off into the big dam. Once that work was done, however, the water from this area ran into the dam and now the dam became reliably half full, all of the time. In effect this finally provided the property with permanent water.

During the period when Jock Simmie was working with Dyson-Holland, from the 1940s into the 1960s, there was considerable investment in pasture improvements with perennial rye grass, clover and *Phalaris* grass, along with appropriate fertiliser.[374] By the early 1980s, John Simmie tried to do his own fertilising, but it was not a high priority and so the farm went for years with none. Yet the pastures remained in good condition, and effective weed control through spraying several times a year certainly contributed to that.[375]

The focus point of the property remained the homestead and the family life revolving around it. The exterior of Harpsdale was in desperate need of painting as it hadn't been done since 1954, the year Joyce Simmie married Edward Gamble and had her reception at Harpsdale, in a marquee on the south lawn. Richard Simmie had busied himself painting exterior windows and removing peeling paint on his holidays from school and then on weekends when he started at university. It was an interest which would flourish when Harpsdale needed real renovation in the years ahead. In 1974 Richard organised his parents' 25th wedding anniversary at Harpsdale with the help of his 'Auntie Joy' [Joyce Gamble], reinstating parties which had ceased after Ivy Simmie's early death in 1952.

Christmas was always at Harpsdale from 1941 until John Simmie's death in May 2012 except for two years, 1968 and 1969, when Joyce and Ted Gamble hosted Christmas at Cooinda as Harpsdale was still unoccupied at this time following Jock Simmie's death. John Simmie and his sister Joyce were close but not close to the point of ringing each other regularly for a chat. Joyce and Ted Gamble would always call in at Belmont on Sunday afternoon 'for a cuppa' before going to Jock Simmie at Harpsdale

Christmas at Harpsdale, 1983
Rear—Robyn Simmie, Jean Simmie, Ted Gamble, Dorrie Howe, Lisa Simmie, Ailsa Simmie with Sarah
Seated—Richard Simmie, Kate Gamble, Peter Simmie with Jarrod, Philip Simmie with James
Foreground—John Simmie with 'Sam', the family dog.
(RJ Simmie Collection)

John Simmie (R) sorting the wool clip at shearing 1986
(RJ Simmie Collection)

and giving him dinner. Jean Simmie and Joyce became good friends and Joyce would later always call in to Harpsdale to see Jean on her way back from town, at least twice a week.[376]

Joyce's unexpected diagnosis with cancer in late October 1980 led to her premature death in July 1981. She was sorely missed by Jean Simmie and other family members. Richard Simmie, who by this time was doing his training to become an anaesthetist at the Royal Melbourne Hospital dropped by to see her often in her last weeks, but her brother John, busy on the farm, unfortunately did not get to see her before she died. Joyce was admired as 'intelligent, sharp minded, a straight shooter and always up for a challenge in any conversation.' Her ashes were scattered at Cooinda, her marital home.[377]

Meanwhile life at Harpsdale went on. The Harpsdale Dorset Horn Stud was in existence until 1986 when John Simmie wound back very quickly on the DH ram and ewe production; it was subsequently sold. He kept a small flock of ewes to supply meat for domestic consumption until 1995 but he turned to Merino wether wool production until his retirement in 2001 with very mixed results.[378]

Extensions were made to the 1957 shearing shed built on site of the old one when John increased wool production with electricity and three new stands—electric shearing gear—still in use. The old shed had a motor-driven, belt shearing stand set up. The motor was later used as a garden feature. John had a good eye for sheep. He sold rams to many a local farmer and also further afield. One such buyer of a number of rams was Sir Robert Law-Smith in the late 70s and early 80s, who had a large property in the Macedon area.[379]

In 1989, Philip and Ailsa Simmie sold up their small property and moved to Queensland. There they bought a farm 45 km south west of Toowoomba and their children James and Sarah were weekly boarders in Toowoomba. It was a mixed farm, cropping and beef cattle.[380] Richard Simmie later commented:

> James and Sarah had a much better relationship with their grandparents from the times they visited them after they moved to Queensland. Jean and John drove up twice and stayed with them for 2 weeks each trip. Sarah and James got to see a side of John that we never saw, relaxed and on holidays. James in particular had a very robust personality which

Undated media image, 1990s, 'Recent Elders Clip of the Sale winner John Simmie, second from right, presented a high-quality consignment of 21.5-micron wool from his Harpsdale property at Yuroke. At right is John Nichol of Elders Kilmore and at left Elders technical officers based in Lara, Bob Plane and Bernie O'Brien
(RJ Simmie Collection)

also enabled him to absorb his grandfather's gruffness better than most in the family.[381]

Later Philip Simmie reflected on working with his father at Harpsdale:

Regarding the farming practices at Harpsdale, just about everything I learnt about farming I owe to my father. We were very similar in that I like doing things by myself and are bits of perfectionists. At the time there were many things that may have irritated me but as I get older, I can see that I am more and more like my father. The irritations were more superficial, like his lack of patience with the animals.

I suppose the biggest problem was his lack of willingness to employ people, especially the times that he could afford it. I do not think he was a lover of working with other people, mainly because of his lack of tolerance of people not doing things as well as himself or the way he wanted. Having said that, I think that we worked quite well together because of our similarities in the way we did things. I am the same. I can spend all day working on old cars by myself and are quite happy, but I am not running a farm.[382]

During these years Richard Simmie moved along a very different career path to his older brothers. He graduated from Melbourne University (Royal Melbourne Hospital—RMH) in December 1978 followed by a two-year residency at the RMH. He then entered the anaesthetic training program at the RMH for the next four years. Richard qualified as a Specialist Anaesthetist at the beginning of 1985 and worked as a staff anaesthetist at the RMH before organising a 12-month swap with two anaesthetists from the Southampton General Hospital in the UK. Travel followed and a return to Melbourne in late 1987. He then took up part time work at the RMH as a visiting Consultant until 2004 and also at the Royal Victorian Eye and Ear Hospital for 12 years as well. Between 2004 and 2015 Richard worked in private practice only. He retired in June 2015 after 37 years in medicine.[383]

In 1996 Peter Simmie, who had lived at Belmont since 1973, leased that part of Harpsdale from his father and later in 1996 established a shiraz and pinot noir vineyard from scratch after a trip to the Napa Valley in California. The vineyard was a success with a contract with Southcorp wines, but drought conditions made it difficult to continue producing premium wines and its last vintage was in 2008. Peter and Robyn then established a Red Angus stud in 2010 with ten heifers and a bull and the business continues today. During these years they also undertook extensive tree planting, fencing and laneway systems on the Belmont property along with house renovations.[384]

The marginal and drought years continued at Harpsdale. A snapshot of some Harpsdale farm records show the following entries, reflective of the tough business of farming during the nineties:

1990—High number deaths. Wet summer Feb rains. Wool rot, big fly problem. No jetting done. Pip, working dog died cancer 17.2.90. Wool co-op buying most wool at floor (860 clean). Fed Gov. drops floor price

Peter, Philip and Richard Simmie March 1989
(RJ Simmie Collection)

to 700 clean.[385]

1992—Very wet spring (92) & summer. Wool rot, very bad fly problems. Bad worm problems. Could not get jetting done. 455 died in 3 months, Jan to 1st week April 1993. Never had worse conditions.

1994—Indifferent year. Spring below normal rain, Autumn rain below average. June—stock in strong shorn condition.

1995—66 killed by dogs. Fed wheat 6 months. Drought broke in May, 95, to end of May. No feed, too cold for growth. No sunshine.

1996—80 sheep killed by dogs. Benara ewes with foot rot (clover Belmont paddock wet spring in 95). Late break from drought, turned cold, no feed. Wet late autumn into winter, paddocks turned to mud by stock. Cold, no sun or drying stock.[386]

1996—Winter of 96 very wet. Paddocks turned to mud by sheep from July through to end of September then stopped raining. Into drought. Very dry. Started hand feeding. Rain April 97. Stock fell in heap after shearing (stress). Lost 50+, recovered some energy by May.

John Simmie with 'Lance' c1992
(RJ Simmie Collection)

1997—Drought still feeding every second day. Benara foot rot. Couple of Benaras got through fence.[387]

1998/1999—Still drought. Stopped feeding as I reduced number & a little spring rain produced enough feed. Still no run of water. About 6 ft of water left. 7 sheep killed by dogs. 15 Nouranies short at shearing, stolen, same as last year. They were in 'Quell' paddock both times prior to shearing. Back boundary Mt Ridley Road. No run of water for nearly 2 years.[388]

Richard Simmie commented on the high sheep losses due to attacks by dogs:

> A property to the north, 'Tullock' was sold in the 1980's and subdivided into small lots, 10-20 acres. Hence there were a lot of city people who came to experience the country life style. There were several people who had not one but several dogs which were never restrained and left outdoors at night. When approached by my father, they never believed their dogs could do such a thing. 'Every morning when we get up, they are asleep at the back door'. They didn't seem to realise that as the owners went to sleep, the dogs congregated into packs and went hunting, hence the sheep losses. The neighbours soon learned that when their dogs didn't return, what had happened to them. The council was inept in dealing with the problem for many years, and it is legal to kill dogs that stray onto your property, so my father dealt with it.

A few years later, in 2001, John retired from farming. By then his health was poor but at 75 was still working. However by 2001 the farm (and the house) was in a poor state of maintenance. Jock Simmie's will had set up the land in a trust for his grandchildren—Peter, Philip and Richard. John Simmie was a 'tenant for life', which allowed him to sell the land and invest the capital and live off the interest.[389] In this respect John never 'owned' the farm. When John retired, he sold all the stock and leased the farm for a few years until he started to sell the land to fund his retirement. Some 800 acres was sold for this purpose, by selling the land that his children didn't want and so negotiations began around the future division of the estate. In order to sell the land, 5-6 km of fencing had to be done. Philip and Richard funded that and the Town Planning, surveying, fencing and Council Planning from June 2000 to October 2003. Altogether eight lots of land, starting in the northwest corner along Konagaderra Road were sold progressively through to 2006.[390]

As part of the agreement signed in 2001, Peter the eldest retained Belmont and some additional land—32 hectares to the east of the dam plus equal water rights with Richard to water Peter's vineyard. Phillip by this time had moved to Queensland so was paid out his share in cash, while Richard retained Harpsdale itself and the land around the dam, about 81 hectares all up—the minimum allowed under local planning laws. Richard agreed to keep their parents at Harpsdale for as long as possible, subject to mental and physical health.

Harpsdale—Repair and Restoration

After a very large storm which hit the property in December 1973 and caused quite a bit of damage, what insurance money was earmarked for house repairs was spent on the farm. By the mid-1980s there were recurring leaks from the slate roof which was in desperate need of repairs or replacing.

Richard Simmie, who has always had a deep affection for the house he spent so many years of his life in and around, started to gradually make repairs largely at his own expense from mid-1993.

The first thing done was to replace the finial above the veranda entrance to the house, which involved removal of veranda lace work for sand blasting and painting. In 1995 there were veranda repairs. In February 1996 a small section of the main hallway ceiling gave way, damaging the hall table that stood between the two doors of the sitting room. That was a simple insurance claim to repair both ceiling and hall table. By 1997 Richard had installed some basic watering systems for the garden and made up the Significant Tree label for the heritage Bhutan Cypress (*cupressus cashmeriana*), believed to be one of the original plantings by the Brodies in the 19th Century.

National Trust Register notice, Harpsdale
(RJ Simmie Collection)

Then, in April 1998, a large section of the dining room ceiling gave way damaging the table and one dining room chair. Jean Simmie had, only moments before, been sitting at that very spot. Fortuitously she got up and returned to the kitchen just before she heard the crash of the ceiling collapsing. The table and chair were repaired under insurance, but the ceiling repairs were declined. After a long battle with the insurance company, they finally agreed to do the repair works.

The slate roof was becoming a major issue. Richard engaged a conservation architect, Arthur Andronas, for opinions on the slate roof.[391] In the 1960s the roof over the master bedroom and the rear bedroom had been replaced with iron. On Andronas' advice, Richard had the whole roof removed and re-slated using all the original slate and some new slate which was used at the rear of the house. This major project was completed in February 1999.

To complement this work, in October that year, the kitchen chimneystack, from which the render had fallen off decades before, was completely rebuilt to match the original. It was rebuilt by hand, which in Richard's own words, was 'a truly great piece of craftsmanship'—it was finished in a different coloured render to show it had been restored. Installation of a hydronic heating system for the house, fired by a Parson wood-fired boiler to replace the expensive to run LPG boiler, was completed in 2002, along with a new garage door to replace the original wooden doors which had rotted away over the years. A garden designer was engaged to plan the new garden, but the plan was not suitable for dry conditions. [392]

Richard Simmie had already made his mark on Harpsdale, now he would begin the final chapter in the story of Harpsdale.

The old shearing shed motor turned into a garden feature
(RJ Simmie Collection)

Chapter Six
Harpsdale 2001- 2022

Farming Life

At this point in 2001 the farm was still leased, and Richard Simmie was working full time in medicine and had little spare time to start traditional farming. However, in order to get Primary Production status on the 200 acres of Harpsdale that would ultimately be his, he entered a contract with Woollybutt P/L to establish a tree plantation over 70 acres consisting of sugar, spotted and red iron bark gums, radiata pine and river sheoaks:

> I liked the idea of reforesting the very bare and stark landscape that I had grown up with. The early settlers were ruthless in how much they cleared. I was able to get a grant from the State Government to get a formal proposal. It is a very long-term investment, 30 plus years and I will not see the benefit of what I have had done but still take pleasure and pride in all the carbon that has been stored since its inception.[393]

Richard was always aware that a property of this size would never return a profit, let alone make ends meet. Owning Harpsdale was now a 'life style choice', but Richard had every intention of living the remainder of his life there as his father and grandfather had before him. He had already been planning to establish an olive tree grove of 1000 trees even before his father retired, and the main dam was enlarged to accommodate his water requirement as well as Peter's with the vineyard Peter had established on Belmont in 1996.

However, 2002 to 2008 saw repeated drought years with much pressure placed on the dwindling water supply despite the dam enlargement. There were several years when the dam was not providing any water to the farm. Richard abandoned his plans for the olive grove and had to rely on Peter's bore to supply the farm with water. By 2007 Richard purchased his first livestock—17 Black Angus weaners, to be fattened, a practice he continued thereafter, with the property maintaining between 10-20 head of cattle to the present day. In 2010 Richard also provided agistment of 200 Merino wethers to help with grass control in the tree plantation.

Following his father's death in 2012 Richard then purchased 30 Poll Dorset ewes with the aim of establishing a Stud. He soon realised the work involved to have a Registered Stud, as his grandfather had, was beyond his interests and capabilities. So, he contented himself with the breeding of lambs for the fat lamb market and the replacement of his breeding ewes. Rams were initially leased but later purchased by Richard for the mating season. The farm was once again running sheep—30 to 50 breeding ewes, and eventually two rams in addition to the cattle. In 2021, the big dam overflowed for the first time in over 20 years, another reminder of how challenging it was to farm this marginal land in the other years when water was scarce. The sale of all the remaining sheep in 2022 brought to an end the long saga of farming at Harpsdale. Farming continued with cattle and trees.

Family Life

In the meantime, family life continued at Harpsdale. Richard had grown up with a strong connection to and memories of the social activities at Harpsdale, especially when his grandmother was still alive. He was determined to recover and continue the long tradition of family celebrations, especially given his own creative skills. More than a decade earlier, in 1989, Richard had organised his parent's 40th wedding anniversary celebration at Harpsdale with original wedding guests and others. Another major celebration was in 1995, a surprise party for John Simmie's 70th, hosted by Richard and his partner **Andrew McAliece** (1963-), whom Richard had met in 1994.[394] In February

Restored pianola, 2004
(RJ Simmie Collection)

2003 Richard and Andrew hosted Andrew's 40th birthday party at Harpsdale with a 'Gone with the Wind' movie theme.[395]

In October 2004 came Richard's 50th birthday party. This night had an 'Opera Mania' theme, along with two opera singers, a baritone and soprano for the evening's entertainment. The highlight was the arrival of the restored pianola to accompany the singers. The Wertheim Pianola belonged to Ivy Simmie, and it was part of family sing-alongs over many years. However, by 2003, the player part wasn't working, and the woodwork (American burr walnut) was lifting in areas. It was sent off to be fully restored over 12 months and finally arrived back on the very day of the party. Other parties followed at Harpsdale over the years. In November 2006 a luncheon party was held for the 80th birthday of Andrew's aunt Anna Smyth, then on 24 November 2007, a Commitment Ceremony for Richard Simmie and Andrew. In 2009 came the 60th wedding anniversary for John and Jean Simmie, followed by Jean Simmie's 90th birthday party in 2011.

John Ernest Simmie, died at Brunswick Hospital on 13 May 2012. His funeral was held at Harpsdale, with family and friends. The eulogy was given by his youngest son, Richard, who said, *inter alia*:

> I have been fortunate to spend this recent time with him. I saw a side of him which I rarely saw throughout my life; a gentle, amusing and loving person. For most of my life he was often judgmental, critical, intolerant and unemotional in his dealings with his immediate family.... Not everyone saw this side of him.... Our friends speak with such fondness of their meetings with

him. Over the years, we had many parties at 'Harpsdale' and he loved being in the center of them. As he became more unwell, this fun loving side of his nature began to show more and more.[396]

John Simmie was buried at Bulla Cemetery in a family plot which had been purchased by Richard Simmie in the 1980s. When he died, he owned no stock, some physical assets and a relatively small amount of cash but he and Jean had retired well through the sale of land and the generosity of his children. Richard's mother, **Jean Simmie,** died not long after John, on 16 December 2012. Richard 's name then went on the title for the 'new' Harpsdale. Andrew McAliece gave the eulogy; his words included:

> I met Jean 18 years ago. From the very first she was open, friendly, welcoming and most important of all, accepting. I suspect, given the generation she came from, that may have been difficult. But perhaps I'm underestimating her. I feel it's a great testament to the love she had for her son.... Always accepting, always pleasant, always giving. There aren't many like Jean.[397]

Harpsdale continued to be the setting for the tradition of events and celebrations, for example cousin Kate Gamble's 50th birthday party in early February 2012, although she did all the organising. Even though the deaths of Richard's parents in such a short space of time in 2012 had cast a shadow over that year, life went on. In 2013 it was Andrew's 50th birthday, and the theme was 'Favourite movie or character'. Andrew came as Richard Gere from 'An Officer and a Gentleman' and Richard as Lucille Ball.[398] Then in 2014 Richard's nephew James Simmie, came down from Queensland to be married at Harpsdale. As Richard Simmie comments:

> Of John Simmie's four grandchildren, James Simmie had the best relationship with him. James seemed able to let John's most difficult and challenging character traits simply wash over him, rather than being affected by them. James chose to celebrate his wedding, both the ceremony and reception, at Harpsdale. John would have been so happy to have been present. James and his fiancé Emlyn stayed the week before the wedding at Harpsdale to prepare. After the Saturday wedding, there was a Sunday lunch party, given because so many guests had travelled from interstate. It was a further chance for the newlyweds to celebrate with their friends, before returning home to Queensland two days later.[399]

The themed celebrations continued with Richard Simmie's 60th birthday in October that year—'Come as your character of dubious integrity or victim of circumstance'—Richard Simmie as Sir John Kerr and Andrew as Whitney Houston. The following year, 2015, saw Joan Millar's 90th birthday and in 2016, a celebration of life for Mavis Millar, lifelong friend of Jean Simmie. They met at the Greenvale State school aged about 5 and remained firm friends for the next 86 years. Anna Smyth's 90th birthday was also at Harpsdale. Finally, with the change to legislation, awaited for so long, Richard and Andrew were married at Harpsdale in 2018—the following year was their 25th anniversary of knowing each other.[400]

Harpsdale—Repair and Restoration

Building on early restoration works undertaken by Richard Simmie before his father retired in 2001, early in 2003 discussions around the renovation of Harpsdale itself began. The old laundry, main bathroom and billiards room were in a sorry state of repairs. Richard set about designing the new laundry, bathroom and living room that would replace the old billiards room and open up the kitchen into a modern living space, thus bringing the house into the 21st Century. He engaged a local builder as it wasn't easy finding builders who were willing to travel even this short distance from Melbourne. Demolition of the billiards room started in December 2003 and the renovations started in earnest in March 2004. They took until December that year to complete, longer than it should have because the builder had chronic money problems. Richard Simmie recalls: 'When I kept paying him his progress payments, that money never went to the tradies working at Harpsdale but to tradies from previous jobs, so we had many a delay'.[401]

The new extension replaced the derelict billiards room with a large living space, connected to the kitchen with the added benefit of making the house far more comfortable and liveable for John and Jean in their later years. The billiards room was separated from the rear of the house by a courtyard, dated from the 1920s; the billiards table dated from 1918. The renovations included installing a second bathroom, replacing the existing laundry and the main bathroom. While this was underway there was landscaping of the immediate areas around the house and the first purchase of artwork for the garden—a birdbath by Folko Kooper Tasmania.[402]

The wedding arch feature at Harpsdale
(RJ Simmie Collection)

Further renovations, finally completed by May 2005, included reinstatement of the original driveway through the park after extensive damage to existing driveway following a 'weather event' of 186 mm rain in 32 hours. Next was to put in a swimming pool, which was completed in November 2006 in time for Anna Smyth's 80th birthday party poolside. That year windows were installed in the stables which started the conversion of the first floor into a flat, with Philip Simmie helping Richard to construct the staircase. In June 2006 a Wedding Arch feature was added to the garden.

In 2008, further work was undertaken. In June, repairs were made to the flooring of the central four rooms—new Baltic pine for the dining room and den and repairs to the remainder with old boards, which John Simmie paid for. In August, the 1941 carpet was replaced and in this case, Jean Simmie paid half of the outlay.[403] Jean was delighted to see her son, Richard, consolidating her lifetime of decorating Harpsdale. From 1971 until 2011, the exterior never had a completed paint finish. There were always sections of peeling paint. So in 2011 Richard Simmie engaged Michael Dempsey to restore the exterior of the house, as we see it today. It took him six months to complete, at a cost of $99,000. John Simmie contributed $49,000, 'the most he had ever contributed to any works on the house in his entire life'.[404]

Moving On—Sale of Harpsdale

In July 2018, Richard Simmie took a call from Oliver Kent, the Acquisition Manager of property development company Wolfdene.[405] Richard was curious to see what they would offer. After attaining a Private Ruling from the ATO regarding the Capital Gains Tax (CGT) implications of a sale, Richard's good record-keeping came in very useful. Having inherited the land through Jock Simmie's Trust, it was deemed a pre-1985 asset, consequently exempt from CGT. As noted earlier, Richard Simmie's original intention with regards to Harpsdale, was to live the rest of his life there, as his father did, and die there.

However, the first COVID-19 lockdown of 63 consecutive days in 2020, spent at Harpsdale, was the longest time Richard had spent there since his childhood. There were both good and bad memories. But he realised that he did not want to relive his parents' final years at Harpsdale. During this time he obtained legal opinions about the possibility of keeping six hectares of the property, that being the house and surrounding gardens, despite the minimum subdivision being 80 hectares. However this was not possible legally. Added to this was the question, was he enjoying the life of a sheep farmer? Also there was the very onerous task of maintenance of the land and the house and gardens. He also came to accept that nothing lasts forever. None of the next generation was interested and the National Trust was lukewarm at best with regards to acquiring the property. Richard finally accepted it was time to move on.

At the end of June 2020, Richard approached Wolfdene to further the discussion; a contract was quickly negotiated and signed on 31 July 2020.

Harpsdale 2022
(RJ Simmie Collection)

Although Richard has started to draw the curtains on the Simmie period at Harpsdale, he retained options to continue leasing the home itself for several years to come. In 2021, Richard stated he had no regrets about selling, a view that was reinforced after very challenging health issues in July and August of 2021. Recent years had taught him that life is always evolving and changing, including Simmie ownership of Harpsdale. He said, "It was time to move on". In 2026 the remaining property will pass to the new owners. What will become of Harpsdale itself is unknown, but 2025 is the 150th anniversary of its building; its history needs to be recorded.

Legacy

The story of the Simmie family connected to Harpsdale is not an unusual history in itself. Like other families which arrived in the mid-19th Century, they made a larger contribution than many to the development of their chosen colony, Victoria, and through Simmie & Co, to the development of the national capital, Canberra, as well. From humble beginnings in the northeast of Victoria, the dynamic interactions of marriage, birth and death led the family to the Sunshine Harvester factory in the early 20th Century, which gave the family stability—especially for the teenage brothers, Jock, Bill and George. All three enlisted when the Great War broke out; two served at Gallipoli and all three on the Western front. All were wounded, but all survived to return to a country forever changed by the casualties of that conflict and the impact of the Spanish Influenza pandemic.

Yet it was also a time of opportunity and for the entrepreneurial-minded, a good time to start new enterprises. In 1924, the three brothers formed a small building company Simmie & Co, in Melbourne. Jock Simmie, by now also a qualified accountant, identified another real opportunity for the fledgling company—the development of the National Capital. Immediately his veteran and Masonic connections propelled the company forward in Canberra where it won significant business through to the Great Depression of 1930-33. Iconic projects included the first retail centre in the Civic Centre, the Albert Hall, the Institute of Anatomy, and the Presbyterian Church of St Andrew. The Depression adversely affected business across the country; Jock moved his family back to Melbourne and his brother George left Simmie & Co to strike out on his own.

In Melbourne Simmie & Co had also done well from start-up, obtaining steady building work across the city constructing factories, apartments and residences, churches, and office buildings. The company was soon recognised as a leading building enterprise in Melbourne. Jock Simmie continued the Canberra business after 1931 and returned there every three weeks for the rest of his working life while also adding more of his time into the Melbourne end. World War Two accelerated business recovery and, in both Canberra, and Melbourne the company continued to grow. In Canberra the construction of the Australian War Memorial and the US Embassy (followed by others) showed Simmie & Co to be perhaps the most prominent builder in Canberra, and it would remain a leading company in that field until 1969. Similarly in Melbourne, Simmie & Co continued to be a force in the industry, securing among other projects the 1939-45 forecourt of the Shrine, and a wide range of other constructions right through to 1978. Both Jock and Bill Simmie were closely involved with the Master Builders Association and Jock was president in Victoria in 1956.

Jock Simmie had never forgotten his rural upbringing and in 1941, purchased Harpsdale near Craigieburn. It was to become the family seat until the present day. The district had been settled by early squatters, the Brodie family, in the mid-19th Century. The homestead itself was erected in 1875, designed by the architect John Augustus Bernard Koch, but with the demise of the Brodies in 1906 the house and land then passed through a series of owners until Jock Simmie purchased it in 1941. Jock did not work the land himself, employing Arthur Dyson-Holland, a nearby soldier settler, to manage the farm. Between Jock's business acumen and Dyson-Holland's practical farming experience a highly successful Dorset Horn Stud was established. Jock Simmie added to his holdings when he acquired Dyson-Holland's 'Troodos'. With Jock Simmie's death in 1968, his son John took over the farm and began a long period of mixed farming at the property, for the next 33 years until his retirement in 2001.

During this long period of occupation by the Simmies at Harpsdale, the cycle of births, deaths and marriages continued, contributing to both the family history and the characters and personalities within it. Jock Simmie was a somewhat distant father and grandfather, who gave most of his life to work and who relied heavily on his wife Ivy to manage the growing family as well as maintain 'hearth and home' at Harpsdale. It was perhaps no surprise and not unusual for his only son John to grow up under his somewhat formidable and successful father as equally, perhaps even more so, typical of his generation as emotionally distant and dedicated to work.

The premature death of John's sister Joyce in 1981 removed a positive influence. Without question, John Simmie and his wife Jean provided for their family of three boys (Peter, Philip and Richard) as they grew up, but they were mostly left to their own devices. All remember their lives in and around Harpsdale and the beach house at Mt Martha with fond recall. Unsurprisingly, while they all went on their separate pathways in life and despite the frictions at times within the family, Harpsdale remained the focal point of the family.

As John Simmie approached retirement, one thing was clear—Harpsdale was not big enough to sustain all three boys on the land. In the ensuing land settlement, the youngest son Richard took over Harpsdale itself. Smaller now than the original holdings due to land sales to fund John and Jean Simmie's retirement, and the land settlement between the sons, it remained an enduring symbol of the long history of land use and rural family life in the district. This was made even more the case through Richard Simmie's love and care for the homestead and surrounds.

Even as a young man at boarding school, Richard was fascinated by the homestead and his antecedents. The first of the family to go to university from where he developed a medical career of some 37 years, Richard nonetheless retained a keen interest in maintaining and restoring Harpsdale. On his own retirement, acknowledging that he would not be able to farm Harpsdale as his father and grandfather had before him, he continued the rural life of the farm while devoting himself to undoing years of neglect at the homestead itself. Ever engaged with family life Richard also reinstituted some of the large family celebrations and events he had experienced over his life at Harpsdale, supported by his husband Andrew.

So today, with the final sale of Harpsdale to occur in the very near future, the legacy of the Simmie family of Harpsdale and Simmie & Co will continue. It will continue through the many building projects of Simmie & Co in two cities, Canberra and Melbourne, from iconic public buildings in the national capital to heritage listed residences in both, in its contribution to the built landscape and civil society with schools, churches, civic centres, factories, offices and retail establishments.

The works of Simmie & Co are a testimonial to a company, formed by three veterans of World War One, which not only survived but prospered, and which provided livelihoods for hundreds of families over the life of the company. The conclusion of Harpsdale as a rural property will not detract from its own legacy of more than 150 years of agriculture and community life over successive generations, with the Simmie family extant for more than half of that time. Richard Simmie's collection of photographs, artefacts, ephemera, farm records, farm equipment and family heirlooms will continue that legacy as the R J Simmie Collection.

The history of this family, its building company, farmland and homestead is yet another story of Victoria, and to some extent, Canberra. From its arrival in Victoria from Scotland in 1852, the Simmie family across all of its branches, applied the famous Scottish traits of hard work, innovation, thrift and industry to build a better place for their families, their communities and their adopted new homeland. The Simmies of Simmie & Co and Harpsdale have made a notable contribution to the development mosaic of Victoria. Like all families, they have experienced good times and bad, times of war and poor economic times, the challenges of farming in the Australian environment, and the ups and downs of family life itself. Yet this is a very Australian story, and hopefully one that this history will help illuminate into future years.

JOHN ERNEST 'Red Jack' SIMMIE

Family Tree

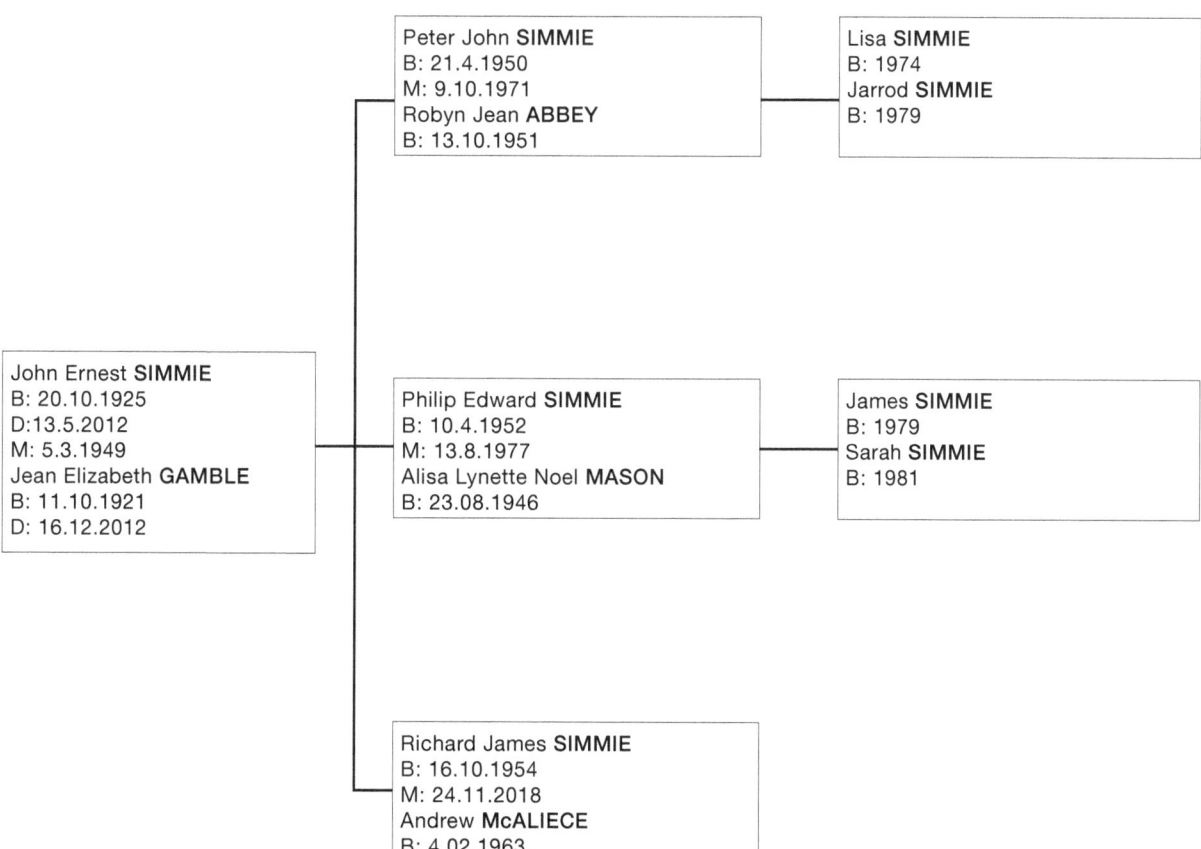

Annex A
Harpsdale & the Brodie Legacy to 1906

Located north of Melbourne on the Craigieburn Road West at Yuroke, Harpsdale had its colonial origins in the *Deep Creek* (or *Bulla Bulla*) pastoral run occupied by George Brodie and his brother Richard Brodie. Later subdivided and sold by the Crown from the 1840s, the Brodies purchased several portions of *Deep Creek* in the parishes of Yuroke, Bulla Bulla [from here simply referred to as Bulla] and Mickleham, part of which Richard Brodie later called 'Harpsdale'. More land was added by George Brodie after the death of Richard making a total of 1,764 acres. Two portions in Mickleham were excised from the Harpsdale estate in 1912, leaving 5 and 6 Mickleham and 18 Bulla. In 1921 200 acres of 18 Bulla was sold to the Crown under the Closer Settlement Act (Soldier Settlement), however this was re-acquired and returned to Harpsdale in 1965.

Prior to colonial settlement the Wurundjeri people of the Woiworung language group of the Kulin Nations occupied the district. Aboriginal Victoria has registered numerous sites of indigenous cultural significance in the district. In addition to the Deep Creek waterway (all waterways and 200 either side are registered sites), the online map shows several sites on the Victorian Aboriginal Heritage Register including one on Portion 18A Bulla (adjoining the Konagaderra Road) and several on Portions 7 and 8 Mickleham.

Harpsdale lies between the valleys of the Deep Creek (tributary of the Maribyrnong River) and Merri Creek (tributary of the Yarra River). Early plans show the surface geology and topography and hint at the vegetation of the general vicinity from the 1840s. A parish plan of Mickleham from 1856 shows the steep valley of the Deep Creek bordering Portions 7 and 8 in Mickleham on the west in addition to the unnamed creek which originates in Portion 6 and runs northwards to feed into Deep Creek.[406]

Geological Survey of Victoria Quarter Sheets 2NW and 7NE show the land at Bulla (Section 18) and Mickleham (Sections 6, 7 and 8) to be primarily volcanic with underlying Silurian sedimentary rocks.[407] The Upper Volcanic rocks of these basalt plains are typically basalt diorite, the Silurian rocks are sandy beds and slaty shales. The plans also indicate basalt depths of 10 feet east of Deep Creek, between 40 and 120 feet deep between Deep Creek and Emu Creek on the west and some granitic rocks are located at the southern end of Bulla and in Yuroke parishes. These maps suggest the soils of Harpsdale would have been mostly of a fertile basaltic (heavy reddish or black clays with thin loamy topsoils) and Ordovician (old, bleached clays) nature.[408]

In 1973 the Land Conservation Council reported on their Melbourne Study Area, with Harpsdale located in the 'Romsey Block' of the study area. The landscape was described as 'flat undulating basalt plains sloping gently from the north [which] have been almost completely developed for grazing. A number of volcanic cones give local relief while the few major streams are deeply entrenched. ... The only sizeable areas of public land support a range of open forest vegetation types.[409] In the same year the climate of the Romsey Block was recorded as:

> Average annual rainfall varied with elevation from about 600mm in the south to 1,000 mm at Macedon on the Divide, with winter maximum. The growing season near Melbourne typically lasts from March to January, with restricted growth during July. With increasing elevation, lower temperature restrict growth for longer periods (say from May to September) and at the highest point, Macedon, growth may cease during the coldest month, July.[410]

Early records of the diversity and distribution of natural vegetation of the district are rare but there are sources which show the types of plants and trees which would have been prevalent. David Kemp's 1842 map of Bulla parish, on which has been recorded the allotments sold and selected, shows landscape descriptions such as 'good forest land for sheep', 'thin forest land good pastures' and 'good soil thinly timbered'.[411] Surveyors often used trees to create benchmarks on their survey plans. In 1850 trees such as gum, box (Eucalypts) and Oak (she-oak) were recorded by a surveyor on the boundaries of Portions 5, 6, 7 and 8 of Mickleham parish.[412]

Similarly, in a plan of Bulla parish in 1852, a surveyor has recorded gum, box, she oaks and wattles (black and lightwood).[413] These may have been *Eucalyptus microcarpa* (Grey Box), *E. melliodora* (Yellow Box), *E. leucoxylon* (Yellow Gum), *E. camaldulensis* (River Red Gum) with *Allocasuarina verticillata* (Drooping She-oak), *Allocasuarina luehmannii* (Buloke), *Acacia melanoxylon* (Blackwood Wattle) and *Acacia dealbata* (Silver Wattle) all of which still survive in some pockets of Melbourne's basalt plains.[414]

Examining the remnant basalt plains flora which are known to exist it can be assumed that many of these would also have been present at Harpsdale at the time of colonial settlement. The Land Conservation Council recorded in 1973 that:

> ...public land near Oaklands carried woodlands of grey box (the nearest natural occurrence to Melbourne of this species) and river red gum grows along the Maribyrnong River and its tributaries, and an interesting development of yellow box grows on basalt between Jacksons and Emu creek north of Sunbury.[415]

Indigenous sources of food and fibre that grew in the district would have included Murrnong (yam daisies, *Microseris lanceolata*), Kangaroo grass (*Themeda triandra*), Flax-lily (*Dianella* sp.) Sweet Bursaria (Bursaria spinosa) and Greenhood orchids (*Pterostylis sp.*). It is highly likely that species such as Bluebells (*Wahlenbergia sp.*), Blue Devils (*Eryngium ovinum*), Tree Violet (*Melicytus dentatus*) and were also present.[416] Deep Creek and its tributaries would also have been a source of food in the form of fish, eels, yabbies and waterbirds.

Plants introduced through the process of European occupation have also made their impact on the landscape, especially those which became invasive and noxious weeds. The Romsey block of the Land Conservation Council's 1973 Melbourne Study area is made up of 37 land parishes. The most significant weed species recorded for this Romsey block (based on the number of land parishes within the block in which these weeds were recorded) were Bathurst Burr (20 parishes), Blackberry (27), Cape Broom (21), Flax-leaved Broom (35), Hawthorn (27), Horehound (21), Paterson's Curse (20), Sweet Briar (36), Saffron Thistle (27), Slender Thistle (33), Spear Thistle (35) and Variegated Thistle (36).[417]

Colonial Settlement and the Brodies

The good soils, fertile grasslands and fresh waterways which fed the traditional owners of the district, would also have been attractive to the early European settlers with their imported sheep and cattle. Pastoralists Fred Flintoff, Martin Batey and brothers Richard and George Sinclair Brodie held parts of what was known as the *Bulla-Bulla* and *Deep Creek* pastoral runs from 1836 onwards.[418] Flintoff and Batey had arrived in Victoria from Durham, England in 1841.[419] The Brodies had supposedly arrived in Victoria with sheep in May 1836 from Tasmania and by the time the runs were being subdivided they had established a homestead, sheep wash and cultivation areas adjoining Deep Creek and the north-eastern corner of what is now the township of Bulla.[420]

While Richard Brodie managed their station, George Brodie operated as an auctioneer in Melbourne.[421] From 1842 onwards the colonial government began selling and leasing out portions of Deep Creek, some of the auctions being held by George Brodie.[422] By 1849 the Brodie brothers leased 3,675 at Bulla, for which they had applied for a pre-emptive right and were required to pay 20 shillings [£1] per acre to purchase.[423] Richard Brodie, and brother James Sinclair Brodie, purchased Portions 11, 12 and 13 of nearby Yuroke, in 1847 and 1849 totalling over 2,300 acres, for about £2,345.[424] This Yuroke property was known as 'Dunhelen' by 1859, when occupied by John C Cochrane, and had a 'comfortable cottage' on it by 1865.[425] Portion 18 of Bulla was not sold to Richard Brodie until October 1851[426]

In May 1853 George and Richard Brodie also purchased Allotments A and B of Portion 20 in Bulla (total of 586 acres), and in October 1854 Richard purchased Allotment 1 of Section 24 (306 acres) of the same parish, all fronting the Emu Creek. The Government had advertised both allotments in Portion 20 would be sold at auction in October 1851, however they were withdrawn from sale, this being the location of the Brodie's homestead and sheep wash.[427].

In December 1852, Richard Brodie leased three allotments (total of 890 acres) to Charles Farro for five years for £400 per annum.[428] The terms of the lease required Farro, at his own cost to 'stump grub up and clear all tree stumps and roots from off all land that shall be brought under cultivation during the term', fill any holes created by such grubbing, 'plough, manure and cultivate' any cultivated land, spread any manure or compost produced, not remove any ornamental trees, or any trees other than for clearing a paddock for cultivation.

While it is unclear whether there was a house on the land, the lease states Farro also had use of the barn and stack yard for a period after his lease expired to enable him to, lay, thresh and dress his crops.[429] In March of 1857 Richard Brodie of Deep Creek sought tenders from fencers and stonewallers to erect 'about 3 ½ miles either Rail Fence or Stone Wall'.[430] The outcome of this advertisement, especially in terms of whether a stone or a rail fence resulted, is unknown, however this may give light to other information known about the property.

The *Argus* of 29 June 1864 includes an advertisement by Richard Brodie announcing the sale of 800 ewes, 'by M. McCaw and another ... at 'farm of Harpsdale (late Guests') ... on account of Mr. Thomas Brown, junior of Yaloak Vale'.[431] This is the first identifiable use of the name Harpsdale for Brodie's property. The notice implies that someone of the name Guest had occupied Harpsdale prior to this notice.

Richard Brodie was found dead in the Emu Creek in January 1872, with a death notice in the *Argus* stating he had died at Helensville.[432] His will, dated 2 November 1868, and probate file also describe him as being of Helensville, and not Harpsdale.[433] George Brodie did not inherit Harpsdale specifically and the title for the land was never transferred to George.[434] Throughout this period there is no identifiable description of the property to suggest whether there was any form of dwelling on the Harpsdale estate.

In January 1874 David Brodie (1835-1905), son of George, was recorded as being of Harpsdale.[435] David had married Fanny Kelly in Canada in 1871 and the couple arrived in Victoria in August 1873.[436] David's daughter Helen was born at Fitzroy in September 1873, while their next child, George Sinclair, was born at Harpsdale in February 1875, indicating the family moved to Harpsdale sometime between September 1873 and January 1874.[437] Architect J A B Koch advertised for tenders for building a residence for D Brodie of Harpsdale in September 1875. However, if David's son George was born at Harpsdale in February 1875, it does suggest an earlier residence was already there.[438] William McKenzie Brodie, David and Fanny's next child, was born at Harpsdale in December 1875.[439] Interestingly, a William Kelly had a son born 'at the residence of D. Brodie, Esq, Harpsdale' in April 1878, suggesting other members of Fanny's family were also residing on the estate.[440]

Throughout the rest of the 1870s and much of the 1880s, David Brodie is regularly selling sheep at markets, primarily whethers, lambs and ewes, but also cows and bullocks from Harpsdale.[441] The *Argus* of 1877 reveals that some of these sheep were cross-bred Lincolns.[442] Lincolns are an English long-wool breed which in Australia is typically cross-bred with Merinos to produce Corriedales, which give a 'fleece of excellent quality and produced first-class fat lambs'.[443] This suggests David was earning income from both the production of wool and meat. While there is no direct evidence from this period of any crops being grown on Harpsdale, there would have been a need to cultivate land to produce hay and crops such as oats for feeding sheep, cattle and horses.[444]

While David was occupying Harpsdale, it was the death of David Brodie's father, George Brodie, in September 1880 which triggered the gradual transfer of ownership to David.[445] In an inventory of George's Brodie's estate in 1881, Harpsdale of (1,541 acres) is valued at £10,301 being a large part of the total £50,351 worth of real estate. Harpsdale is described as being:

> ...all those pieces of land being Section Eighteen Parish of Bulla ... containing 640 acres, allotments 7 and 8 containing 658 acres [all valued at £7 per acre] Allotment 6 containing 243 acres [valued at £5 per acre] [with] improvements six roomed stone house and outhouses—shearing shed—sheep yards—two dams and fencing.[446]

Portion 5 Mickleham of 261 acres was not included under the description of Harpsdale, but was referred to as 'McHugh's Lot', valued at £5 per acre, making a total of £1,308, but it had no improvement other than a 'brush fence on the southern boundary'.⁴⁴⁷ In his will, George Brodie left his son David the Harpsdale property, however McHugh's lot formed part of his residuary estate that was to be divided up and various shares distributed to numerous family members, including further shares to his sons David Brodie and Richard Sinclair Brodie.

The 1883 mortgage coincides with an advertisement in the *Argus* in March 1883 by architect Koch for tenders for 'brick stabling at Harpsdale, Mickleham'.⁴⁴⁸ A further advertisement from Koch for 'additions to residence at Mickleham' in July 1883 has been attributed to Harpsdale, however the advertisement cited does not actually refer to Brodie or Harpsdale.⁴⁴⁹

In August 1885, David was elected as a councillor for the Shire of Broadmeadows for the first time when he stood unopposed for the Mickleham Ward.⁴⁵⁰ He was also made a magistrate for the Central Bailiwick in January 1887⁴⁵¹ In August 1888, and also in 1891, David was again elected unopposed to the Shire council.⁴⁵²

In June 1887 David Brodie advertised part (1,150 acres of 1,518) of Harpsdale for lease by auction, for five years commencing July 1. The estate agent described the land on offer as a:

...very desirable property is to be let for grazing purposes only, and is essentially suitable for a sheep depot, being within 15 miles of the Flemington yards. It is permanently watered by the Deep Creek to which it has a frontage of three miles, and it is all securely fenced and subdivided into three paddocks. The flats on the creek are very rich.⁴⁵³

Based on newspaper reports of livestock sales from October 1890 to January 1892, David

The bellows, in the stables at Harpsdale, believed to be the original machine installed after 1883 (RJ Simmie Collection)

had leased Harpsdale to Hewitt Henderson.[454] Henderson was a dairy farmer, based at Epping and most of the livestock being sold for him were calves, cows and bullocks. Assuming his lease of Harpsdale did commence on 1 July 1887 then Henderson was due to leave Harpsdale on 30 June 1892. Henderson died on 31 December 1892.[455]

The second half of the 1890s was a relatively quiet period for Harpsdale. Newspaper reports of the Oakland Hounds hunting parties running through Harpsdale began appearing in the newspapers in July 1894.[456] These articles usually recorded the various riders and their horses, and in June and July 1894 once such rider was a W. Brodie, or Mr. Brodie, sometimes on a horse named 'Harpsdale'.[457] This suggests the rider was David's son, William, who was a member of the Club and partly explains the permission given to the Club to ride through the property, however in 1894 the Master of the Club was Mr Alex McDougall of Warlaby, who was David Brodie's tenant.[458] McDougall's lease expired in 1895 however the runs by the club through Harpsdale continued.

Some evidence emerges of crops being grown on Harpsdale during the early 1900s. In June 1901 the Oaklands Hounds chased a hare through Mr. Brodie's crop however, 'with the assistance of the aforesaid crop and a stone wall, … it managed to escape.'[459] This report also confirms that there were stone walls on Harpsdale, potentially dating from Richard Brodie's requests for wallers in 1857 (see above). Similarly, another hare was chased in 1902 'diagonally through the large growing crop, … through the sheep paddock, and returned across the road to Mr. McRae's.'[460]

From the late 1880s through to 1903, the period was notable for the continuous mortgaging and repayment and re-mortgaging of Harpsdale by David Brodie as well as leasing of various portions of the property. There is little evidence for the purpose of these mortgages other than expenditure on improving the property itself, or David dealing with the consequences of the generally poor economic circumstances in Victoria emanating from the 1890s depression.[461] While no direct evidence of David owing money (other than the mortgages) or taking action against debtors during this period has been found to date, the funds may also have been used to support other family members.[462]

This apparent constant need for new finance finally resulted in an advertisement in late January 1904 for a clearing sale at Harpsdale, at which he offered for sale 'the whole of his dairy cattle, heavy and light horses, vehicles, farming implements' and three 'stacks oaten and wheaten hay' which is evidence of oat and wheat crops being sown.[463] In the meantime he advertised Harpsdale for lease by tender for four years commencing 1 March 1904, describing the property as 'containing 321 acres, well fenced and subdivided into 3 paddocks, large stone house, brick stables, wool shed, &c.'.[464] On March 14, David Brodie and William Henry Poole signed a lease for 323 acres of Harpsdale, 220 of which were cultivated.[465]

The lease included the Harpsdale 'Homestead Paddock with the farmhouse and other buildings', further described as being a 'stone dwelling house … of thirteen rooms … and all stables and other outbuildings.' Poole was not permitted to interfere with David's stacks of hay until 31 October 1904, was required to remove all briars, gorse, star thistles and 'all noxious weeds', 'comply with the provisions of The Thistle Act 1890', 'destroy all the rabbits and other vermin' and conform to 'the Vermin Destruction Act 1890'.[466] The regular fox and hare hunting trips through the property by the Oaklands Hounds were probably seen as a means by which any Harpsdale tenants were complying with the lease conditions, regardless of whether this was an effective means of control.

The results of Brodie's sale were reported to be: Cows in milk sold to £9 backward springers £6 10/ to £8/10; 2-year-old heifers at £5/10/: yearlings at £2/12/6; 2-year-old steers at £4/15/: draught horses, 10 geldings and mares sold from £25 to £41: buggy horses to £21. Implements—Winch £8/ 5: windmill and chaffcutter £17; D. F. ploughs, £4/5/ to £6/5; seed drills £5 and £5/10; lorry, £35; buggy, £15; hay drays £5 to £10/5/ and other implements and sundries at equally good price. Two stacks of hay, consisting of about 220 tons were not sold.[467]

The recording of the chaffcutter, ploughs, seed drills, hay drays and haystacks is further evidence of cultivation, cropping and harvesting occurring on Harpsdale at that time.

Less than a year after the sale and the signing of the lease, David Brodie died at his home in Brunswick on 6 January 1905, aged 69, having retired from farming.[468] He left a widow, Fanny and three sons and four daughters the eldest son being the Reverend G. S Brodie. An obituary described David as being 'an impartial justice of the peace, whose decisions always commanded respect', having a 'ready wit and pleasant ways', a pioneer and a true Scot.'[469]

The Brodie coat of arms remains in place at Harpsdale
(RJ Simmie Collection)

David had left his entire estate to his wife during her life or until she remarried, to ensure Fanny and the children were taken care of until the youngest child became an adult or any younger daughters were married.[470] Upon the death or marriage of Fanny the estate was to be sold and divided into the same number of shares as he had surviving children, and when each of those children either reached the age of 21, or if a daughter younger than this had married, they would then receive their respective share.

David's estate was assessed by his executors to consist of Portions 5, 6, 7 and 8 parish of Mickleham and 18 Bulla, a total of *1,764* acres 1 rood and 24 perches. On Portion 18 was erected a homestead which was a 'blue stone house slate roof known as 'Harpsdale' [containing] 12 rooms also stables woolshed and outhouses'. There was also a 5-roomed weather board house on Portion 7. The real estate was valued at £8 per acre or a total of £14,113-10-0. There was also 346 tons of hay stacked at the property in very poor condition and valued at £0-15-0 per ton (£259-10-0), rent owed by Mr Harvey Patterson (£106-0-0) and Mr Poole (£20-0-0), and David had a one-sixth interest in the sum of £10,000 (being £1,666) in the estate of his late father, but this was not payable; until the death of his widow (i.e., David's stepmother). The total estate was valued at £16,235, however David owed over £13,431, the majority of which was the mortgage with Jane Mein and other debts resulting from money David had borrowed, leaving a net estate value of only £2,804.

Having obtained a grant of probate, the executors applied in February 1907 to transfer all of David's real estate from the 'old' or 'General Law' titles system to a Torrens Title.[471] New titles for Harpsdale were issued on 6 July 1907, with all five Portions (5, 6, 7, 8 and 18) being transferred to a single new title covering 1,860 acres.[472]

Annex B
Harpsdale 1907-1940

While the ongoing leases at Harpsdale of Paterson's and Poole's expired in 1906 and 1908 respectively, in 1905 they had the Oakland Hounds running through Harpsdale chasing hares through the paddocks and crops.[473] By August 1907, Lewis Robertson was residing at Harpsdale when their son Struan celebrated his 21st first birthday on the property.[474] By June 1907 Robertson had taken a three-year lease for the homestead and land formerly leased to Poole.[475]

Yet only six months later, in December 1907, Mrs Robertson began advertising that a clearing sale would be held at Harpsdale, the property having been sold.[476] The notices describe a wide range of farming and household items offered for sale. There were:

> 6 cows in full profit, 9 forward and backward springers, 10 heifers, 18 months old; Ayrshire bull, 5 calves, buggy mare, 3 Berkshire sows, 6 young pigs, 20 pairs fowls, Massey-Harris reaper and binder (practically new), seed drill, set harrows, roller, hay rake, set of brass-mounted double harness, Sharples separator (30 gallons), 6 bags of oats, quantity of bags, and the whole of the NEW HOUSEHOLD FURNITURE of 10 ROOMS, consisting of carpets, linoleums, bedsteads, overmantels,

sideboard, extension dining table (10ft.), bookcase, duchesse pairs, suites of furniture, kitchen utensils, mangles, &c.[477]

The reaper and binder, the seed drill, harrows, roller and the hay rake would all have been used for cropping and haymaking. The separator, along with the cattle and specifically the Ayrshire bull, suggest dairying but perhaps only for domestic and local use. With Ayrshire cattle known to be 'reasonable large' milk volume producers, the highest recorded output being 8,277 litres over 300 days (i.e., 27.6 litres per day) the 30-gallon (113 litre) separator would have been able to handle the milk of at least 4 cows at a time.[478]

The advertisement also suggests the house on Harpsdale only had ten rooms, or the Robertsons were only occupying 10 of the 12 rooms mentioned in David Brodie's probate.[479]

In the meantime, Robert S. Anderson appears to have been occupying Harpsdale for several years when he offered crossbred and merino ewes, 'comeback' fat sheep, Merino wethers and crossbred and comeback wethers between 1908 and 1911.[480]

John Mills purchased Harpsdale in 1911.[481] Reported to have been a 'well known breeder of Clydesdale horses' and known to be a judge of horses at agricultural shows, Mills was also continuing the tradition of raising sheep on the property, demonstrated by his sale of 68 Lincoln rams in September 1912.[482] Earlier the same year, a newspaper report on a hunting trip by the Oaklands Hounds recounted that:

> Returning to the high grounds, another hare got up in St John Estate, and at once shot away north, on to Brookville, where it turned easterly, and, in its flight crossed the Oaklands road into Harpsdale. This property, however, is so protected by barb wires and crops that the master and field could not follow hounds at point of entry, but were forced to make a considerable detour, and, on reaching the pack, they were found at fault, and could not be got to speak to the line again.[483]

With previous hunting parties regularly running through Harpsdale, the appearance of the barbed wire suggests a change in ownership also resulted in a change of acceptance of the horses, hounds and humans charging through crops and over fences.

Mills did not keep Harpsdale for long. In early December 1918, a clearing sale for Harpsdale was advertised for 13 December, also announcing that Harpsdale had been sold.[484] The list of items for sale was long, and included livestock, implements, machinery, hay, vehicles and harnesses and sundries 'too numerous to mention'. The full advertised list consisted of:

SHEEP.-1400 SHEEP, including 500 Lincoln ewes, off shears, pure bred. 300 Lincoln lambs, not shorn, pure bred. 410 wethers and ewes, 2-tooth. 140 Lincoln rams, 2 and 4-tooth, pure bred. 50 fat wethers.

HORSES –94 HORSES, comprising Pure-bred Clydesdale mares some with foals at foot. Full pedigrees at sale. Heavy draught and useful farm colts and fillies. Good ponies and light horses.

IMPLEMENTS, MACHINERY, Etc. Stump-jump 4-furrow disc plough (Robinson). Stump-jump 3-furrow disc plough (McKay), light 3-furrow disc plough, 3-furrow mouldboard set plough (Robinson), strong single-furrow plough, garden plough, winnower, corn crusher, scoop, mud scoop, reaper and binder (Osborn); 15-hoe drill. Grass seeder attached (Massey Harris); 4 set Harrows, wooden roller, spring-tooth cultivator (McCormack), Buck scraper, hand seed sower, 2 land graders, mower, petrol engine (6 1/2 h.p.) wool press. Avery scales (10 cwt.), low down pump and several hand pumps, large cast-iron BOILER.

Hand truck, large and small sets blocks and pulleys, double action Trewhella jack, small jack, stump and stone lifter, stone sledge, 10 portable horse feeders, stack stage, large blacksmith's bellows', large anvil, vice, drill block, large quantity of useful blacksmith's tools and iron, set of taps and dies (screw to 3/4in.), emery grinder, 3 stack ladders, 2 pairs steps, set painter's trestles & planks, portable copper, wheelbarrow, grindstone, quantity inch and 3/8 inch piping, bends, elbows, taps, etc.; pipe-vice and cutter, pipe dies to 1in., 2 rolls barb wire, plain wire and wire netting, 10 sheets G. iron, also ridging and down piping; 700 droppers, 2 x 1 1/2 in., large quantity loops, 1000 STEEL DROPPERS, 250 old sleepers, iron tank (200 gal.), cask cement. 600 new bricks. Quantity sawn timber.

HAY. Etc. Stack hay, about 30 tons; 2 stacks straw, about 40 tons: 50 bags seed oats; also quantity empty oat and chaff bags, tarpaulins.

VEHICLES. HARNESS, Etc. Bow waggon, 4-horse, 4in. tyres; tip dray and frame. 4in. tyres; gig; 6-horse set pulleys and chains; 7 collars, hames and winkers: 4 cart saddles and breechings, 3 sets light harness, riding saddle, plough and leading chains and swingle bars, 10 horse rugs.[485]

The diversity of livestock reflects Mills' breeding Clydesdales and breeding and fattening Lincoln sheep. The machinery naturally comes from a period when agriculture still relied heavily upon the horse but had increasingly used horses to draw more complex machinery for the sowing, harvesting and processing of crops. Some of the farm machinery and equipment, such as the stump-jump ploughs and Trewhella jacks and grubbers (the Trewhella foundry at Trentham began in 1894 and closed in 1951), were designed to deal with Australian conditions.[486] The lack of any dairying stock and equipment also demonstrates that the brief period of dairying on Harpsdale had ceased. The *Herald* on 19 December 1918 announced that Harpsdale, of 1,161 acres, had been sold to Mr A. C. Wilson.[487] The supposed purchase price was £14,518.[488]

Arthur Chesney Wilson, originally from Gunbower (in Victoria, near the border of NSW and north-west of Echuca), also appears to have objected to unwelcome visitors to his new property in Bulla. In March 1919 he wrote to the secretary of the Bulla branch of the Farmers' Union supporting, both morally and financially, the need for farmers to band together 'to protect their land, stock, and themselves against all kinds of trespassers and abuse'.[489]

The issues which concerned the farmers were the 'week-enders, rabbiters, and poachers, the holiday-makers and the careless use of fire chaps', who either engaged in trespass, verbal abuse or accidentally caused fires which in turn damaged farms and their owners. As a result of the meeting held on 8 March 1919, at which representatives of the Victorian Farmers' Union, local fire brigades and local councils attended, the 'Property-owners' Defence Association' was formed to lobby various departments of the Victorian government to change laws to provide full protection to farmers against trespassers.[490]

Months earlier, when Wilson was paying attention to the trespassing problem, another major change was about to take place at Harpsdale. Following World War One, the Victorian Government passed the Discharged Soldier Settlement Act 1917 'for the settlement on the land of returned soldiers from World War One, under more liberal conditions than for closer settlement.'[491] The Closer Settlement Act 1904 itself 'gave the government the power to compulsorily acquire land from freeholders for subdivision and allocation as closer settlement blocks.'[492] A modern insight into these schemes reveals that:

> Closer settlement achieved limited success. Some areas were unsuitable for intensive cultivation, some blocks were too small, and some settlers were unsuited to the task of farming. The general reliance on government advances to settlers, combined with poor seasons and adverse economic conditions, resulted in the accumulation of large debts by settlers and the abandonment of many holdings. Several official inquiries into the effectiveness of closer and soldier settlement led to changes in administration, the easing of terms of occupation and the adjustment of liabilities.[493]

There was quite a process by which the government chose the location and quantity of land to acquire for this scheme, but the larger estates were generally targeted.[494] The Closer Settlement Board obviously came knocking on Wilson's door in early 1919 when Stanley Gordon Lording, an employee of Wilson, applied to occupy 200 acres of the Harpsdale estate. After protracted negotiations, and Lording agreeing to go ahead with the conditional purchase lease, Wilson sold the land to the Government for £11-10 per acre on 28 January 1921.[495] The land in question, which once more became Crown land, was on the south-west corner of Portion 18 Bulla and became known as Allotment 18A. The history of this portion of Harpsdale, also known as Troodos, is covered under a separate headingunder a separate heading in Annex C.

While in the process of negotiating the sale of Troodos, Wilson's attitude to the trespassing 'weekenders' did not waiver. In the Memorandum of Understanding between Wilson and Lording dated 9 April 1920, where it states: 'The Vendor further agrees to permit the agents surveyors or authorized representatives of the Board to have free access in and over the said land in all reasonable hours during the said one month', Wilson has written in 'with due notice on account of weekenders'.[496]

In late January 1921, Wilson began offering Harpsdale, now only 960 acres, for sale by auction in April.[497] Wilson was prepared to sell the property in either one lot or three consisting of 246 (Portion 5), 303 and 412 acres respectively, with the largest lot containing the homestead. The advertisements described the property as:

> There are 13 paddocks of from 4 to 334 acres, 3 dams, 3 tanks, 16 acres lucerne, 506 acres ready for plough, good woolshed, cement dip and yards, fencing mostly netted and barbed, good timber for fencing, shelter, and firewood; new bore (6in. cased), giving 270 to 280 gals. p.h. of practically fresh water, with new 14in. mill, pump, and tanks, commanding all the premises and garden; fine House (12 rooms), halls, and verandahs; hot and cold water and gas laid on, sewered, telephone.[498]

One of the requirements of Conditional Purchase Leases was that the occupant had to reside on the allotment for at least 8 months so each year. With there being no house on Troodos, Lording was permitted to continue to live at Harpsdale, so Wilson's 1921 sale notices therefore prompted some concern from the Closer Settlement Board in May 1921.[499] The Board's inspector replied on May 14 that 'Wilson is the owner of Harpsdale & Lording is a foreman there; the property is not sold a good offer being refused & Lording is still residing there.'[500]

In late 1924 Wilson finally sold Harpsdale.[501] After a clearing sale in October, Wilson moved to Keilor, along with Stanley and Beatrice Lording of who had cancelled their occupation of Allotment 18A.[502] Wilson died at Arundel aged 82 in 1935.[503] Prior to Wilson's death, in 1930 part of Portion 6 had been excised to the Country Roads Board to permit a realignment of the Konagaderra Road.[504]

The purchaser of Harpsdale from Wilson was James Ferguson, however the title was not updated until 1932 and his name does not actually appear on the title.[505] James Ferguson married Linda May Pratt in 1924 and by 1925 they were residing at Harpsdale.[506] In 1926 a daughter was born to the couple at Moreland and the family were still residing at Harpsdale in 1927, but appear to have left the district soon after.[507]

In November 1932 the title to the remainder of Harpsdale was transferred in its entirety to stock and station agents William Edward Brock Macleod (1/2 share), Archibald Norman Macarthur (1/4 share) and James Anthony Webster (1/4 share) as tenants in common.[508] Macarthur and Macleod were one of the stock agents which occupants and owners of Harpsdale regularly used to sell their livestock.[509] Whether the new owners were

Ferguson's executors, his business associates or his mortgagees is unclear.

Macarthur and Macleod Pty Ltd was registered as a company in Victoria in 1929 with capital of £75,000 in £1 shares. The directors were William Edward Brock Macleod, Frederick Gilder, Archibald Norman Macarthur, and James Anthony Webster.[510] On the date the title for Harpsdale was transferred to the new owners, they mortgaged the property to Phillip Lewis Aitken and James Ford Strachan, solicitors and partners in the law firm Aitken Walker and Strachan.[511] This mortgage was repaid in 1937.

Dunvegan Castle in the Isle of Skye in Scotland is the ancestral home of the Macleod family.[512] The formation of Macarthur and Macleod Pty Ltd in Victoria in 1929 roughly coincides with mention of the Dunvegan Pastoral Company in association with Harpsdale from March 1928 until 1937 when Harpsdale was sold once more.[513] In fact W E B MacLeod was stated to be the 'governing director' of the Company in 1928.[514] The discrepancy in the dates between Dunvegan occupying the farm in 1928 and the transfer of title to them in 1932 indicates the property was being purchased from the previous owner privately (i.e. payments made by the purchaser directly to the owner and not via a mortgage) and it took until 1937 for this to be completed.

A detailed exposé of Harpsdale under the ownership of Dunvegan Pastoral Company was published in the *Australasian* in 1928. The article described the 'substantial stone and brick' homestead with numerous outbuildings located on an elevated portion of the property with a 'comprehensive panoramic view'.[515] Three underground water tanks collected rainwater, from which water was pumped into a 15,000-gallon header tank. An 'energetic and progressive policy of development' had been initiated for the 1,000-acre property which was divided into 20 fields devoted primarily to sheep and agriculture.[516] John Mills had supposedly determined that much of the farm should be 'broken up' for cultivation, and Macleod's plans for the property followed this belief. In 1927 117 acres had been sown to wheat, 50 acres to Algerian Oats and 80 to Japanese millet.

The term 'Algerian Oats' dates to a variety used in Australia, including Victoria, by the 1880s, other contemporary varieties being Tartarian, Polish and Calcutta.[517] Originating in the Mediterranean, this form of oats was the subject of a breeding and crop experimenting program in Australia in the early twentieth-century to create an 'Australian Algerian' variety by 1918 that was notably rust-resistant.[518] Most oat varieties had been grown for grain production for livestock (and human) food, but varieties like Algerian were also deemed to be valuable for the strength of their straw for hay.[519]

Millet in various forms was typically a seed and fodder crop, with the straw of some species being a material additionally used to make straw brooms.[520] Japan Millet (or Pearl or Egyptian Millet), *Pencillaria spicata*, in use in Victoria by 1878, was shown to thrive in warm weather but frost prevented the seed from ripening. Japanese Millet (or Japanese Barnyard Millet or Barnyard Grass), *Panicum crus-galli*, was trialled in Australia from the 1890s for a summer green fodder crop and silage production.[521] Given the problems with seed ripening in the first species in cold climates, it is most likely Harpsdale was using the second species of millet.

In addition to wheat, oats and millet, there was also 1,500 merino wethers and lambs on Harpsdale for fattening in 1928.[522] Comebacks and Lincolns were also raised on the property during Dunvegan's ownership.[523] Water was said to be 'abundant' from a 370-foot-deep bore pumping into a 7,000 gallon tank and distributed to the 'garden, orchard, and to about six of the fields' and supplementing the house. Paddocks away from this reticulated system had dams, one of which was described as 'a lake.'[524] The pastures themselves had a strong population of indigenous grasses interspersed with clovers. Some topdressing with superphosphate was also being trialled.

By 1928 the decline in use of horses, which were fed with oat crops, prompted a replacement of oat crops with wheat. Wheat had supposedly been abandoned for oats in the early years of colonial settlement due to wet weather, but the trials at Harpsdale in the 1920s to produce wheat for flour, in what appeared to be dryer years, were quite successful. The soil at Harpsdale was, however, deemed to be depleted of fertility and a sequence of crop rotations, topdressing and establishment of clover was planned to restore the land. In 17 acres of the 117 acres sown to wheat, the *Currawa* variety of wheat was being trialled, a successful variety known for its drought tolerance.[525]

Harpsdale also played a role in 1928 in some experiments by Sir Edward Mitchell in transporting sheep on a six-wheeled Thornycroft motor-lorry chassis specifically adapted for the purpose.[526] Assisting Mitchell was Arthur Holland (*sic,* see

Troodos, below), who 'had a long experience among sheep, and in the Harpsdale woolshed, lent by Mr. W. E. D. Macleod, a series of experiments were, carried out' with some sheep also provided by Macleod.[527] Mitchell's motive was to facilitate the transportation of sheep, without undue stress or physical impact, from drought-stricken areas for agistment or permit them to arrive in better condition at livestock markets. In a trial run, merino wethers were loaded at Harpsdale, 'carried 300, miles to Bindi Station:

> ...on a very hot day, the heat being increased by a following north wind and sometimes bush fires on both sides of the road, but they remained cool and contented underneath the canvas. They were unloaded at Bairnsdale at night and reloaded there in the morning. ... On the return journey 42 fat come-back whethers [sic] were loaded off grass at Bindi Station, averaging over 130 1b live weight, and 18 fat lambs were loaded at Tongio, 10 miles nearer Melbourne, averaging about 80lb. live weight. These weights were too great to enable the third tier to be loaded without serious overloading for the Tambo Valley Road. The sheep were run right through to the Newmarket yards without stopping in about 20 hours from the place where the lambs were loaded. All were unloaded at Newmarket, and next day they were sold at a late sale in a falling market at good prices.[528]

Mitchell applied for a patent for this invention in 1928.[529]

By 1936 some fat cows and calves were being raised at Harpsdale though they had not replaced the sheep.[530] The following year, the mortgage on Harpsdale was discharged, resulting from the sale of the property to Reginald William Stringer.[531] With Stringer's occupation of Harpsdale, the Oaklands Hounds were once more reported, in June 1938, to be chasing hares through the paddocks of the property however, based on newspaper reports of their antics, this appears to have been one of the last occasions this occurred.[532] In September 1939, Stringer offered Harpsdale for sale, a 954-acre 'highly improved property ... ideal for fat lamb raising, wool growing and general farming purposes. The brick residence, with all modern conveniences and complete out-buildings, are both substantial and in good order.[533] There were no bids for the properties.[534] However, in early 1940, John Ernest 'Jock' Simmie purchased Harpsdale, supposedly at £12 per acre*, a caveat being put on the title in March 1941, and the title being transferred in January 1944.[535]

Annex C
Troodos, Arthur Dyson-Holland & Harpsdale

The Public Record Office Victoria's *Lands Guide* details the process by which World War One veterans could be eligible to occupy land under the Closer Settlement Schemes.[536] A Qualification Certificate was required that demonstrated 'extensive proof of pervious farming experience ... together with a reference from the applicant's local repatriation committee and others, and the applicant had to submit to an oral examination by the committee.'[537]

In May 1919, Stanley Gordon Lording, an employee of Arthur Chesney Wilson of Harpsdale, applied to the Closer Settlement Board for a Qualification Certificate.[538] Lording had served with the 4th Field Artillery Brigade, for 3 years, partly as a gunner in France, and was discharged in May 1919 as medically unfit having been gassed. He provided a reference from a farmer who wrote that he had 'known the bearer S. G. Lording for a number of years, and can recommend his as being capable of managing any farm work he might be asked to do on a farm both dairying or agricultural (sic) work'.[539] Wilson of Harpsdale also acted as referee, writing that

Sir, I have known Mr Lording for over 8 years. For four years, and up to the time of his going to the front, Mr Lording under my personal direction and supervision was managing and working a farm of 200 acres; 30 of which was crop, 50 lucerne. He ploughed, put in, irrigated, cut and stacked, or pressed the produce year by year. Also he managed 30 dairy cows with the necessary pigs etc., and 20 to 40 mixed cattle.....

Mr Lording is capable now of taking on any such management on his own, or any other man's account. He is not afraid for work. I give this with great confidence and pleasure.[540]

The secretary of the shire of Rochester also recommended Lording to the Soldiers Land Repatriation Committee in June 1919 as a suitable applicant for land.

At the time of his application, Lording was married with one child. His wife owned a cottage and a few acres and Lording was originally considering running the farm on a share basis with Wilson to be a partner, however further certification would be required for Wilson so the application for 200 acres at Mickleham for mixed farming went through under his own name.[541] Wilson offered to sell the land to the Crown for £12 per acre, and, as shown above, the negotiations were protracted with Lording having to wait until January 1921 before he could legally occupy the land.

An assessment of the suitability of the land for farming made in December 1919 reported that the country was gently undulating, with grey loamy and black soil, metal roads. 110 acres was cultivated to oats (Wilson had no knowledge of previous yields) and 80% of the land was deemed cultivable. The Water supply was a dam and tank, rainfall being typically 23 to 25 inches [575-626 mm]. The land's carrying capacity was deemed to be 2½ or 3½ sheep per acre but there was no knowledge of how many cows could be kept for dairying. The land was best suited for oats, perhaps dairying with rape, millet and maize. Some timber on the land was Box but chiefly Gum suitable for buildings and fencing. There were 30 to 80 head of cattle on the property.[542]

In January 1920 the Board was informed that Wilson's offer of £20 per acre had expired—a reassessment of Lording's application in January 1920 recommended that land be purchased, but only at £10-10-0 per acre considering the quality of the soil on that part of Harpsdale was 'below a fair medium average quality of volcanic' soil. The Bulla Shire Council did, however, recommend the purchase price of £12 per acre.[543] Lording's certificate of Qualification was issued in March 1920.[544]

Wilson rejected the Board's offer in March 1920 and the Board decided to take no further action however Lording wrote to the Board asking for a fresh application.[545] The Board still refused to increase its offer for the land. The assessor deemed the southern third of the land on offer to be 'timbered with gum and the surface crab-holey [gilgaeid soil]. The value of the timber would pay for the clearing, after which the land could be ploughed and levelled for cropping.'[546] About forty chains of fencing was also require on the northern boundary. As Lording's employer, Wilson was 'prepared to stick to the applicant from time to time and see him through' which the assessor believed 'he would do as they have been trusted employees and he is a man of means' and a bachelor. The Lordings would continue to live with Wilson. Wilson accepted the Board's offer of £11-10-0 per acre in June 1920 and in June and September Wilson and Lording signed the relevant agreements for purchase.[547] From this time the land was known as Allotment 18A.

The next requirement was for Lording to apply for a Conditional Purchase Lease to occupy the land while he gradually made down payments to purchase the land. One of the conditions was that leaseholders were required to reside on the land for at least eight months of each year. In Lording's case he would be required to make half-yearly instalments of £70-13-0 with a total purchase price of £2,358-10-6. As time progressed, Lording became very keen to occupy the land to permit him to sow a crop and feed his sheep off the grass that was otherwise going to waste, so he simply wrote to the Board in December 1920 that he had taken matters into his own hands and taken possession of the land and purchased a hundred sheep.[548]

Lording signed a Memorandum of Agreement to purchase the land, with Wilson acting as witness, in early April 1921.[549] A few weeks later the Board's Chief Inspector was notified that Wilson had advertised Harpsdale for sale and questioned whether Lording was still residing with Wilson, noting there was no house on Allotment 18A.[550] The Board were assured that Lording, Wilson's foreman, was still at Harpsdale and Wilson had refused a good offer for Harpsdale, leaving the property unsold.

With his first purchased instalment payment due, Lording wrote to the Board in October as follows:

> I am in receipt of pass book showing my first payment on above land as £70-13-0 plus interest £74-3-6. At present I am not able to make the payment my last years crop of 50 acres—a very fine one—was—nearly two-thirds of it anyway—invaded by caterpillars; which you should understand, for a first year, is a pretty severe setback! Otherwise, instead of the appeal made below you would be receiving a cheque.
>
> I would refer you to Para 4 of Discharged S. S. Acts (Vic) and request that I be allowed the option of two years at least free of payments & interest. This I do not wish, by a good many years, to be 37 ¼ years acquiring the freehold. If possible and with a good season, I will bring all payments up to date next year.
>
> Please let me know how the half-yearly instalment of £70-13-0 is arrived at, and what my annual instalment must be to avoid interest, and whether you are prepared to receive an amount on account.[551]

On 20 January 1923, Lording was once more handed a lease and given ten days to sign and return it.[552] Lording once more refused.[553] Lording's occupancy of 18A was officially cancelled on 20 February and published in the *Victoria Government Gazette* the following day.[554] Lording now began to dispute the amount the Board wanted him to pay for his period of occupation of 18A. On 27 February Lording wrote to the Board:

> Sir, I have yours of the 21st Inst, in which the Board claims £295-0-4 in payments for my occupancy of the land referred to therein. My passbook clearly states that the amount due to the 25th July 1922 is £74-3-6—being first half-yearly instalment—the second instalment then must be also approx. £74-3-6 due on the 25th Jan 1923—making a total of approximately £148-7-90. Please advise me as to the correctness of any calculations. The Act provides that no instalment shall be payable the first year and I have not signed any lease with the Board. My letter of the 7th Oct last, your reply to which I urgently waited for was never sent to me—please refer to same. Earlier my letter of 6th June also urgent the Board chose to ignore, beyond threatening to terminate my occupancy of

the land. Seemingly I am to buy the property, accept all the conditions without question and remain in ignorance of much that it is my right to have clearly explained. These & others points which I will not innumerate make it impossible for me to undertake to work to pay off the dues, interest etc upon the land which I hoped to purchase from the Board.[555]

Lording, now of Keilor, wrote to the board seeking an appointment, stating he would only speak with the Chief of the Board.[556] From Lording's perspective this meeting was very fruitful. Not only did the Chief appear to show Lording some respect and compassion (which really was what the whole Soldier Settlement Scheme was meant to be about) but an agreement was also reached that Lording would settle the matter with a payment of £20.[557]

Lording's letter of thanks to the Chief also showed the impact of the whole matter on his outlook on life:

Dear Sir, enclosed with this please find statement of my affairs which I hope you will find quite in accord with your commands at our talk this afternoon. May I again express how grateful I feel towards you for your generous treatment of my indebtedness to the Board. With that debt lifted from me I feel now that I can push along and hope that one day I shall be able to tell that success has come my way. To have been received by you as was my pleasure today is something that will always be remembered.[558]

The 'statement of my affairs' Lording included with this letter outlined a returned soldier who was finding life quite difficult:

Sir, In respect of the above Boards claim of £295 from me for use & occupation of Crown Allotment 18A Bulla, I beg to state that I am not in a position to meet any such account. I have neither land, house or furniture, but work for wages at the rate of £1 per week as my upkeep. The most money I could possibly raise would be about £140 including my war gratuity. I'm being asked to submit an offer towards settlement being(?) I say £20—and hope that will go towards settling a matter which unhappily is a great worry to me. In a previous letter I advised the Board that during my occupation of the land in questions I had the misfortune to have my first crop invaded by caterpillars and I shall be glad to hear from the Board that under these circumstances the matter will be closed & thus allow me to face the future more happily.[559]

A man of his word, Lording paid the £20 on 19 August 1925 and his association with 18A ended.[560]

As soon as 18A was repossessed by the Board, they set about finding a new occupant for the land. The land was formally advertised in the *Victoria Government Gazette* as an allotment for Discharged Soldiers four days later.[561] By now the Board had John Thomas Chiller of Cundare North, near Colac who quickly made an application for a lease of the land.[562] Chiller who had been trying unsuccessfully for four years to run a dairying operation on 76 acres of Soldier Settlement at Cundare North, had a qualification in Dairying, was aged 32, a farm labourer before the war and had a wife and mother to support.[563]

Chiller believed part of the problem at Cundare was the lack of water, so, having visited 18A and satisfied he could make a living on it, he was keen to relocate and try again running a mixed farming operation. He requested that the Board build a four-roomed house on the allotment, and permit him an advance to purchase milking cows, for which he would be liable, with interest, through his instalment payments.[564] Chiller would build the cow sheds and outbuildings and erect fences. At the time of application Chiller had assets consisting of 16 cows, two horses, 11 other livestock, 8 poddies (calves) and farm implements to a total value of £100 but acknowledged that the Board owned the stock and implements.[565]

A permit to occupy the land was forwarded to Chiller on 15 May and a Conditional Purchase Lease approved on 13 March 1925.[566] By July 1927 the improvements to the land included a house which had cost £343 and an advance of £381 had been made for materials, however Chiller, like Lording, had experienced problems making a living from the 200-acre block.[567] Following another revaluation, the land and original fencing was deemed to be worth £2,358 (100 acres at £13 per acre and 100 acres at £10-10 per acre), and with the improvements the whole property was now valued at £3,083.[568] A cow shed (£40), machinery shed & feed room (£35), men's hut (£20), fowl house (£5) were further improvement added during Chiller's tenure, however the amount of £237 expended on boring and casing to find a water supply on the block was not included as it was unsuccessful.[569]

The inspector's report recorded that of the 200 acres, 150 was cultivable, while the remaining 50 was pasture land. He thought the land could carry 1.5 sheep per acre and was best suited to mixed farming. The land was fairly level throughout, two paddocks on the north end of about 50 acres each had been cultivated, the soil being dark loam, while the south end was 'crab-holey & fairly rough but could be broken down, this portion is timbered with large red gum trees.'[570] Chiller, had however worked up a considerable debt with the board in the form of advances for horses, disc plough and chains, a wagon, water tanks, building materials, fencing wire and the water boring attempt, totalling over £532, which, when added to the £371 worth of liabilities transferred from the Cundare block was unsustainable.[571] Chiller's lease of Allotment 18A was declared void on 24 August 1927 for 'non-payment of instalments' and readvertised a week later as open for occupation under a Conditional Purchase Lease with half-yearly instalments of £72-15-0, the purchase of any of the improvements was to be paid for in addition to this.[572] The next person the Board found to gamble on the allotment was Arthur Kirke Dyson-Holland of Moonee Ponds.[573]

Dyson-Holland was born in Tasmania in 1894 to George Harold Wollaston Dyson-Holland, a bank manager, and his wife Lillias Frances Macarthur.[574] The family later moved to Queensland. After his father died in 1914, Arthur enlisted in World War One in Queensland in June 1917 where he was working at a station overseer.[575] He served in France before returning to Australia in 1919, the same year his mother remarried to William Edward Brock Macleod, Macleod being the partner in Macarthur and Macleod stock agents.[576]

Perhaps with the business acumen and support of his extended family, Dyson-Holland was quick to state that he 'considered that the land was too highly valued by £2 per acre and would not lodge an application at the Board's price. He said that he would communicate with the Board on the subject of revaluation.'[577] A revaluation took place on 21 October 1927 where the valuer increased the value of the best 100 acres from £13 per acre to £13-10, reduced the value of the other 100 acres of 'stony and crab-holey' land down from £10-10 per acre to £9-10 (total of £2,300) and, with the improvements of £517, the whole property was valued at £2,817.

The Board resolved on 21 October 1927 to make the property available for a capital value of £2,482 for land and part of improvements (i.e., everything but the house); the balance of improvements (the house) of £335 was to be treated as an additional advance.[578] With these changes approved, the allotment was readvertised as available on 2 November and Dyson-Holland applied for a Conditional Purchase Lease the following day.[579]

Arthur Kirke Dyson Holland was aged 33, single, and while his stepfather William Macleod had agreed to furnish him with assets and act as guarantee for his endeavour, he requested the Board assist him in making improvements. While stating he currently had no occupation, he had 17 years of experience on the land and referred to himself as a station manager. He did not hold any land, had never been insolvent, had not previously applied for Closer Settlement allotment, and had £215 in assets (£15 cash in hand and £200 invested in a business) with no liabilities. He intended to use the land for cropping and grazing stock, was prepared to make his home on 18A but asked the Board to erect two additional rooms on the house for use as a kitchen and a bathroom and install three additional water tanks to ensure he had an adequate water supply.

Aware that there was a limit of £625 on the value of advances he could receive, he stated he would pay cash for the existing improvements. Macleod agreed that he would 'finance me [Arthur] in the undertaking and has given me cheques for £156 to pay deposit on land and value of assets taken over' which Arthur then paid for.[580] Dyson-Holland was sent his permit for occupancy on 24 February 1928 and, having signed a Conditional Purchase Lease (which required 72 half-yearly instalments of £72-3) on 7 November 1927 and paid his deposit, he settled in on 18A Bulla which by May 1928 he was calling *Troodos*.[581] Arthur had married Leila Nelson-Slee in Burwood, NSW in 1928.[582] The financial strains on the new settlers began to show early on and he was in arrears with his instalments by May 1930.[583] By May 1931, Dyson-Holland reported that 'since being on the Block I have put over £1000 of my own private money into the place. And put over £500 worth of improvements in as well'.[584] A son, Kirke, was born to the couple in 1932 which would have further complicated the financial position.[585]

An annual return for June 1933 shows Dyson-Holland had harvested 106 tons of hay, 46 of which he used on the farm for horses and cows. Of the remainder he figured he would need to use some for fallowing and cows.[586] He sold oat straw to Dunvegan Pastoral Company for £25, £23 of which

Harvesting at Harpsdale 1929 with a Robinson header
(RJ Simmie Collection)

Harvesting at Harpsdale January 1929
(RJ Simmie Collection)

were spent on superphosphate for the crops. His oat crop yielded 100 bags of cleaned grain half of which he held for seed, the remainder he sold to Robertson Pty Ltd to which he was in debt. The chaff cutting cost him £19 for 46 tons.

His wheat crop produced 100 bags, of which he sold 42, 35 of which earned £14 which he used to pay part of the £44 owing for harvesting and thrashing wages. The remaining seven bags were used to pay the chaff cutter his wages. Eighteen bags of wheat were kept for sowing a 'shandy' crop, 12 were sown for grain, and 10 were kept for fowl feed.[587] He still expected to be in debt with Robertson after the wheat sale. In November 1933 he sold 20 tons of his hay for a total of £52-10 but had to include £2-10 of his own money to send the total amount he owed the Commission, as one of the buyers (Mr S Heritage) had not paid Dyson Holland all he owed.[588]

In April 1934 Dyson-Holland appealed to the Board to assist him in buying the four tons of superphosphate he needed for sowing his crops. He was attempting to diversify into dairying and knew that would need more building materials, but he was hoping to save up enough to purchase them before the inspector visited. There were already signs of a drought, Dyson-Holland noting in a letter that 'the country here has gone to pieces the last month, hardly any feed, no grass at any rate, we need rain badly. Too many north winds about. Am hoping the Milk Board will be of some benefit to the producers. We need all the help we can get.'[589]

Throughout 1931 to 1935 Dyson-Holland was regularly selling hay and bags of oats to make payments off his lease on Allotment 18A as well as selling hay for his own revenue.[590] He was also paying for crop insurance, manure, and freight. In January 1934, the Board agreed to write off £123 of the £294 worth of instalments still owing.[591] The drought conditions continued into 1936. In January of that year Dyson-Holland wrote:

> So far I have not been able to dispose of my straw as the mills have been closed & they are not buying yet. But hope the price increases before I sell it. My harvest this year has been the worst since I have been on the Block. The 30 acres I resowed was a complete washout. I did not cut a blade from it. That was the experience of a good many farmers in this District. My complete Harvest amounts to 30 tons of Hay from 70 acres. This won't see me through the year so I will be forced to buy later on. However, I live in the hopes of paying my commitment somehow or paying

most of it. I have sown 7 acres of maize but up to date it has not been successful. It was in just a bit late, I think. Anyway, I hope to get some oats in early & so save buying too much chaff.[592]

The mill he was hoping to sell his straw to was a paper mill, mainly because rain had damaged the straw and that was about the only option he had for earning any income from it. But useful rain was still eluding the district in March 1936 and things did not improve.[593]

By April 1936, 185 of the 200 acres of land was cultivable, the balance being too stony for anything but grazing. There was 'artificial' pasture in 15 acres, 35 of native grasses and 70 acres in fallow which was then sown to oats. Of this oat crop, 30 acres were resown, but it was a total failure, as was the experiment of sowing eight acres of maize, due to lack of rain and all he got was 20 tons of hay. Dyson Holland's dairy herd had increased to 31 from 24, 22 of which were being milked, which yielded about £19 per cow per annum. There were also seven horses and 96 sheep (including 76 Dorset Horn ewes and 42 lambs) which produced 106 lambs. Even after selling 60 lambs, he still owed Macarthur and Macleod £375, had an outstanding loan of £400 at 5% interest, a bank overdraft of £250 and owed rates of £24.[594] An April 1936 financial statement shows that for the 1934-35 financial year he earned £481 from sale of cream & milk, £19 from selling eggs and £104 in salary from outside work.

He had undertaken 53 acres of stone and stump clearing and 20 acres of clearing trees. By this time, he was married with two children, a son and daughter, but they were too young to help on the farm. He employed a man halftime and had a girl working in the house due to his wife being in ill health. Dyson-Holland was, in the eyes of the inspector, working the block to full advantage and was managing his parent's property adjoining (i.e., Harpsdale being run by Dunvegan) for which he received £2 per week, all he earned went into Allotment 18A.[595] A bout of influenza in April 1936 had prevented him from making a further payment and while some rain arrived the weather was too cold for the vegetation to grow much in response and be of benefit to the cows. He anticipated a 'cold winter & a lean one where I am concerned, having to buy chaff & bran & pollard to feed them.'[596]

By October 1936 Dyson-Holland had lost his milk contract because he refused to accept a price lower than that fixed by the Milk Board (which, he thought, 80% of dairy farmers were already doing), and while resorting to selling cream at a return of approximately £5-3-0 per fortnight, intended to cease dairying. Instead, he intended to 'sow down more land with pasture & grasses & run sheep on the property'. He was also trying to sell straw to meet his instalments and when he succeeded in doing so in December, by the time he paid for associated cartage and rail freight he had only £13-10-0 to pay to the Commission.[597]

By May 1937 the farm was described as 'bleak and exposed & at present bare of cattle feed. Not suitable for dairying'.[598] 'Abnormal' rains in January 1937 damaged his hay and the Board were seeking news in February that he had sold the hay so he would be able to make a payment, but the hay remained unsold in late March and the dry weather persisted.[599] Dyson-Holland was hoping to maximise any proceeds from the sale of the hay, and as the drought continued, he remained hopeful this would happen. The hay was still not sold in mid-May, but he hoped to have done so by the end of June.[600]

This however prompted the Board to take a deep look into Dyson-Holland's finances in June 1937 and were somewhat shocked at the position he was in.[601] He had external debts of £1087-0-0, guaranteed by his stepfather but for which he held no security. There was also a private loan of £400-0-0 to his step-aunt Christina Elizabeth Turner, nèe Macleod of Essendon, also with no security, and a stock mortgage of £246-0-0 with Macarthur and McLeod for cattle and sheep.[602] He had also taken out a loan of £127-0-0 against his Life Insurance Policy, owed a further £36-0-0 for council rates and £28-0-0 in sundries and was in arrears with his instalments to the extent of £141 with another instalment almost due.

The Board, having advised Dyson-Holland to interview his creditors, informed him they would not be prepared to write down his debts if it looked like his overall efforts towards owning the property would prove to be futile.[603] Dyson-Holland agreed to take action, stated his intention to sell all the cattle on the property (to reduce his debt) and replace them with sheep and felt assured that his relatives would assist him. Macleod assured the Chairman of the Board that between himself and his sister (Christina Turner) they could make arrangements to secure Holland's position. The Chairman agreed to defer the matter, pending a revaluation of block, but if the Board was not satisfied with the arrangements, they would reconsider Dyson-Holland's occupation of the land.[604]

In August 1937, the Board wrote off another £16 of Dyson-Holland's instalment debt.[605] By October 1937, 26 tons of hay had been sold for £96-3-10, the extended drought making the expected proceeds sent to the Board smaller due to Dyson Holland using some of the remainder to feed his livestock. When the Board queried the tally of the quantity of hay available, it was pointed out that the hay was lighter than anticipated, also noting that he had been unable 'to sell the stock and plant as proposed' so his debts with the Board as of 30 June 1937 remained at £127.[606] The dairy herd was to be sold through Macarthur and Macleod who would get the proceeds and in the meantime Dyson-Holland had purchased 80 ewes with lambs to ultimately get the proceeds from the lambs and the wool. He was also doing wool classing work for neighbouring farms for living expenses.[607]

The drought continued unabated. In February 1939 Dyson-Holland had been unable to sell his sheep and had been carting water to them for two months. Heatwaves had stopped his hens from laying eggs and that source of income dried up, resulting in his extended family buying food for him and his family.[608] A lack of capital in April that year prevented him from improving his pasture and increasing his poultry flock.[609] He had 185 wethers, 24 lambs and 19 ewes and owed Macarthur and Macleod £200 on them which is all they were worth. For the first time, a comment in the extensive file on the allotment reveals that the inspector recognised that the block is too small for him to make a living, and he could not improve his pastures to increase his carrying capacity.[610]

Dyson-Holland could not pay his September 1939 instalment but hoped to sell his lambs and the wool to cover the payment.[611] The wool remained unsold in April 1940, but he eventually received his wool cheque by the middle of the year.[612] At that time his wife had been in hospital for a month, and he had been unable to get to Melbourne to pay his instalment and by May he informed the Board that he had sold his sheep at a loss due to the low market prices.[613]

Although not immediately evident his luck was about to turn with the purchase of Harpsdale in January 1941 by Jock Simmie, also a World War One veteran and a director of Simmie & Co, with its building operations in Canberra and Melbourne. Dyson-Holland became the farm manager for the new owner Jock Simmie, for wages of £5 per week.[614] It was the start of a long and mutually agreeable relationship between Dyson-Holland and Jock Simmie and his family, which lasted for more than 20 years.

By this time, Dyson-Holland had renegotiated his lease to reduce the instalments by extending the purchase period. The new lease, dated 1 March 1939, with a debt of £1005-3-0 of 78 half-yearly instalments of only £26-7-7 over 39½ years, would have seen him making his final payment in September 1978.[615] Despite the reduced instalments, Dyson-Holland had not paid his September 1941 instalment by October.[616] The inspector noted that he thought Dyson-Holland would sell the allotment to his employer, Simmie, who had approached Dyson-Holland on the subject, and the inspector thought this was a wise move.[617] Dyson-Holland paid his September 1941 instalment in February 1942, just before the March 1942 instalment was due.[618]

The inspector's assessment on the allotment of July 1942 seemed more upbeat, with a report that it was a 'good prospect', Dyson-Holland was a 'good settler' who had 300 ewes at present lambing.[619] In September 1946 however, there was no stock, it being out on agistment, no plant and 270 fowls on the land.[620] Dyson-Holland was still working as manager for Harpsdale. The stock were frequently 'on agistment' over the next few years, during which time he remained employed by Simmie.[621] In August 1947 the inspector noted that Dyson-Holland took 'particular interest' in controlling vermin and noxious weeds.[622]

Then, with little explanation as to the source of the funds, Dyson-Holland sent the Board a cheque for £778-5-3 on 30 March 1955, this being the balance owing on the property.[623] The Board of Land and Works approved the issue of a Crown Grant for the land in June.[624] The grant was issued on 16 June 1955, and Troodos once more became privately-owned land.[625] Jock Simmie's interest in purchasing the land remained, not least to 're-unite' Troodos with the rest of Harpsdale, but that would take another decade, the death of Dyson-Holland and a Supreme Court case.

Endnotes

1. Hamblin, M., *A Family History of Cornelia Creek Run & the Simmies,* South Melbourne, 2020. The Simmie name derives from Simon and means son of Simon, part of Clan Fraser, Perthshire Region, Scotland.

2. *ibid,* pp213-246 and https://www.parliament.vic.gov.au/component/fabrik/details/24/842. George Simmie became owner of the Cornelia Creek Run and a Member of the Victorian Legislative Council. When he died in 1906 his nephew John Simmie (1860-1950)—son of his older brother John—was the executor of his will.

3. The fourth was also William James ('Bill') Simmie (1899-1958). He later became involved in the flour mill business in Bendigo, called Tomlins, Simmie & Co established by his uncle, John Simmie, in 1912. At the time, living in Elmore, John Simmie was a grain merchant and president of the Huntly Shire Council.

4. Hamblin, M., *op.cit.,* p248.

5. Marriage Certificate 5818/1889, J Simmie and J Aberline, Births, Deaths & Marriages (BDM) NSW.

6. *Sydney Mail & New South Wales Advertiser,* 11 April 1891, p840.

7   See, Hamblin, M, *op.cit.*, pp111-114 for details of George Simmie's businesses and land purchases. The Cornelia Creek Station alone at George Simmie's death in 1906 was over 37,000 acres in area (almost 15,000 hectares) and had a wool shed with 25 shearer's stands. George Simmie as a contractor was heavily engaged in the Bendigo-to Echuca construction. See also Coulson, H., *Echuca-Moama Murray River Neighbours,* McCabe Prints: Wangaratta, 2009.

8   *Riverine Herald,* 5 March 1897, p2.

9   *New South Wales Government Gazette,* No165, 8 March 1895, p1.

10 Hamblin, M, *op.cit.*, pp257-264. Millewa Lodge 1059 English Constitution (EC) was (re-established) at Echuca in September 1879 with the first Lodge master installed 30/10/79. 'Re-established' because it was originally established in 1863 as the Echuca Lodge of Advancement EC but seems to have gone into abeyance some years later. The lodge then became Millewa Lodge 47 (Victorian Constitution) in late 1889 when the English, Scottish and Irish Constitutions lodges amalgamated under the United Grand Lodge of Victoria.

11 *Riverine Herald,* op.cit., p2. Death Certificate 1897/001873, James Simmie, BDM NSW.

12 *Elmore Standard,* 12 March 1897, p2.

13 Will, James Simmie, dated 18 November 1896 and *Advocate,* 31 July 1897, p17.

14 *Riverine Herald,* 7 April 1897, p2. The first verses of the hymn 'Abide with Me' by Scottish Anglican Henry Francis Lyte (1793-1847). The hymn is also sung at closing of a Masonic Lodge in English Constitution masonry, to which Millewa Lodge belonged.

15 *Bendigo Advertiser,* 1 March 1897, p3.

16 *Elmore Standard,* 23 July 1897, p2.

17 Hamblin, M, *op.cit.*, p249 and *Leader,* 9 November 1901, p43.

18 Probate William James Simmie, PROV.

19 Victorian Electoral Roll, Division of Echuca 1905. The children were William John, Amelia May Emily Selina, Lillian Maud, Albert Reid, Christina Violet and Elsie Gladys. Birth Certificate, Eric Ford Aberline Montgomery, 1906, Victoria Births, Deaths, Marriages.

20 *Age,* 25 October 1901. Holt's agency seemed to have been a well-run organization, and he was able to supply clergy of different denominations, so that the address (and possibly the witnesses) are the only clue to Holt's Agency. The use of

an agency may simply have meant a desire for privacy, or perhaps no particular allegiance to a denomination. Holt had a group of ministers of different denominations who were glad to make an extra income and appear to have been available "on call" though the "Free Christian Church". It does not seem to have had a church of its own in Melbourne as such. http://roosen.com.au/Background/Free_Christian_Church.html.

21   Eric Montgomery also became a carpenter by trade.

22   Foskett, A., Johnstone, P. & Andrew, D., *On Solid Foundations, Canberra Tradesmen's Union Club*, Canberra, 2001, p140.

23   https://en.wikipedia.org/wiki/Sunshine,_Victoria and https://en.wikipedia.org/wiki/Hugh_Victor_McKay. The population of the shire by 1921 was 4,431 residents, doubling since 1911 and compared to just 250 in 1901. https://www.ayton.id.au/gary/History/H_Aust_Vic_Sunshine.htm.

24   Ford, O., *Harvester Town: The making of Sunshine 1890-1925*, S&DHS, 2001, p141.

25   *ibid.,* p150.

26   Victorian Electoral Rolls; Ford, O., *op.cit.,* pp100-102.

27   Victorian Electoral Rolls; Victorian Register of Deaths, John Ford Montgomery, Entry 8961, 8 August 1951.

28   Hamblin, M., *A Family History of the Cornelia Creek & the Simmies, South Melbourne 2020,* pp288-289.

29   *Argus, 14* June 1916, p10.

30   https://collections.museumsvictoria.com.au/articles/12510; Ford, O., *op.cit.,* p170. A R Montgomery was allocated to the 4th Field Artillery Battery along with George Simmie. Both went to Gallipoli, but Montgomery was initially a problem soldier, suffering periods of detention in Egypt and then imprisoned for two years with hard labour 'for violence against his superior officers' in 1915. His sentence was suspended when he was sent to active duty in France, where he served out the rest of the war without further issues. He returned to his old job at McKay's Harvester Works and moved into John and Janet Montgomery's Ridley Street home while they were temporarily in Melbourne in the late 1920s. B2455, Albert Reid Montgomery, NAA and Victorian Electoral Rolls.

31   The 2nd FA Brigade was one of three artillery brigades raised to support the 2nd Infantry Brigade in 1st Division; it drew soldiers mainly

from Victoria. The brigade consisted of three FA batteries, of which the 4th FAB was one. The batteries were equipped with 18 pounder field guns.

32   AIF unit war diaries, Headquarters, 2nd Australian Field Artillery Brigade, AWM4 13/30/5—April 1915.

33   'Drivers' rode the left horse of the two x two horse teams pulling one gun and its limber.

34   4th FAB as part of the 1st Division's artillery and was in action from the start of the battle from 31 July 1917; George Simmie was wounded just three days later. Although his wounds were described as gunshot wounds, it is more likely that they were shrapnel wounds from German counter-battery fire. The 2nd Australian FA Brigade incurred the heaviest artillery casualties of all the Australian artillery units in France, suffering a total of 231 deaths and 1,036 casualties. Horner, D., *The Gunners: a history of Australian Artillery*, Allen & Underwood, 1995, p188.

35   B2455, 960 George Herbert Simmie, National Archives of Australia (NAA).

36   Syphilis was treated primarily with an arsenic based drug called Novarsenobillon which carried significant side-effects. This class of drugs were replaced by penicillin but not until the 1940s.

37   B2455, 972 John Ernest Simmie, NAA. Note that although Jock's service number was close to that of George, numbers were allocated within units not sequentially in the AIF as a whole.

38   See https://military.wikia.org/wiki/HMT_Southland, About 40 men perished but over 1400 survived.

39   AIF unit war diaries, 21st Infantry Battalion, AWM4 23/38/11—July 1916.

40   AIF unit war diaries, Headquarters, 2nd Australian Field Artillery Brigade, AWM4 13/30/5—July 1916.

41   AIF unit war diaries, 24th Infantry Battalion, AWM4 23/41/30—March 1918.

42   The 24th's Lieutenant George Ingram won a Victoria Cross in that fight.

43   By 1926, it was the Commonwealth Audit Office at Findon House, 350 Flinders Lane, and headed in Victoria by Chief Auditor R Reeves. Dates of service in the office—Statement of Service, Richard Harold Reeves, Chief Auditor Victoria to JE Simmie, 26 October 1926, RJ Simmie Collection.

44 Foskett, A., Johnstone, P. & Andrew, D., *op.cit.,* p140.

45 Certificate of Appreciation, RSSILA Sunshine to JE Simmie 1919, RJ Simmie Collection.

46 Foskett, A., Johnstone, P. & Andrew, D., *op.cit.,* p.140. Colonel 'Lang' was in fact Henry H Ling, who had been transferred to the Audit Office from the NSW Postal Service in 1904 and headed the office in South Australia until World War One broke out. He then headed the Finance Department for Army in Victoria Barracks, Melbourne. There he was given an entirely notional military rank of Major and then 'promoted' to Lieutenant-Colonel in 1917, becoming the Commonwealth Inspector of Military Accounts. After involvement in several important auditing inquiries and commissions, in 1926 Ling went to Rabaul with the post-war Australian administration as Colonel Ling.

47 Victoria Electoral Roll 1922, Australian Electoral Commission. Later the Commonwealth Audit Office; in 1919 it was working from Victoria Barracks Melbourne.

48 *Argus, 1*0 August 1922, p1.

49 *Argus,* 19 February 1923, p10.

50 Joyce married Edward Gamble on 14 February 1954; their daughter Kathryn Anne was born in 1961.

51 A2487/ 1921/18257—Application for Assistance—GH Simmie, NAA.

52 VPRS 13033/P2 Unit120, Item 100532, and VPRS932/P1, Unit 225, Item 10053, PROV.

53 *Age,* 5 July 1924, p8.

54 *Building,* Vol 35, No205, 12 September 1924, p39.

55 *Building, 1*2 May 1928, p151; Argus, 7 September 1928, p9 and *Herald,* 10 September 1928, p1.

56 *Argus,* 21 July 1924, p20. Bill Simmie became a partner on 14 August 1924. VPRS932/P1, Unit 225, Item 10053, PROV

57 Statement of Service, RH Reeves, Chief Auditor Victoria to JE Simmie, 26 October 1926, RJ Simmie Collection.

58 *Argus,* 21 July 1924, p20. Jock Simmie replaced D B Hedderwick and also his cousin Bruce Pitcairn Hedderwick (of the legal firm) as directors—they had both died.

59 VPRS932/P1, Unit 225, Item 10053, PROV

60 *ibid* and *Herald,* 16 October 1931, p17. Bill Simmie's son Roy, worked at Colonial Spark Plug Co for 12 to 18 months, as a young man, c1938. Roy would have gained early employment there

60. through his uncle George, an investor and director at the company. RJ Simmie to author, 11 June 2021.

61. *Age,* 21 October 1921, p12. George's Probate of 1944 listed 5,362 shares in the Colonial Spark Plug P/L valued at 15/- per share. VPRS 7591/P2, Unit 1283, Item 365/719.

62. *Herald,* 26 December 1931, p7.

63. A627, 5467/1931—Application for Letters Patent for an invention by Arthur Edward Geere and George Herbert Simmie—Improvements in Spark Plugs, NAA.

64. *Record,* 17 September 1932, p8.

65. R J Simmie to author, 24 May 2021.

66. Of interest in the Richard Simmie Collection is an invitation to that opening for J J Joyce. John James Joyce was Jock's father-in-law, and the invitation may have been obtained by Jock Simmie for his wife Ivy. Joyce was very involved with the Victorian Football League. He played for Britannia in the 1880's which later became part of Collingwood. He was made an Honorary Life Member in 1921. Invitation and Simmie Family History Notes, R J Simmie Collection.

67. Wigmore, L., *The Long View: a history of Canberra, Australia's national capital,* FW Cheshire, 1963, p120.

68. *Canberra Times,* 4 November 1926, p8.

69. *Canberra Times,* 18 November 1926, p9.

70. Freeman, P., *Thoroughly Modern: The Life and Times of Moir + Sutherland Architects,* Uro Publications 2021, pp41 & 97.

71. Bendigo, Victoria born, Oliphant served with the engineers on the Western Front, and was wounded in action in 1918. B2455, Oliphant, Kenneth Henry Bell, NAA.

72. *Canberra Times,* 27 July 1965, p34.

73. https://en.wikipedia.org/wiki/Harold_Edward_Elliott

74. Freeman, P., *op.cit., p79.* The Hotel Canberra was not licensed to serve alcohol until 1928 (which is why it was initially called a 'hostel'), owing to Minister for Home Affairs King O'Malley's decision to keep Canberra free of alcohol as it was being constructed. https://en.wikipedia.org/wiki/Hotel_Canberra. That must have been tough for the builders, but no doubt led to the rapid rise in pubs in Queanbeyan just over the border in NSW.

75. https://www.architecture.com.au/wp-content/uploads/r015_albert_hall_rstca.pdf

76. *Canberra Times,* 12 March 1928, p4.

77 *Canberra Times,* 26 August 1927, p2.

78 *Canberra Times,* 17 August 1928, p5.

79 *Canberra Times,* 22 November 1927, p1. In 1933 it became the Royal Canberra Golf Club.

80 *Canberra Times,* 22 August 1928, p4. The Red Hill residence was for James Carrington Brackenreg and his wife Helen. Branckenreg was a lands officer who had been living in Acton—but had obviously been promoted in public service ranks to justify moving to the higher end suburb of Red Hill.

81 In 1927 only 545b houses had been authorised for building and as of 30 June that year only 239 had been completed, the remainder were under construction. *The Master Builders that built Canberra: 100 years of building in the nation's capital, Canberra* MBA ACT, 2013, p102.

82 B2455, Cahill, A J, National Archives of Australia.

83 Public works were approved by the Parliamentary Public Works Committee.

84 *Canberra Times,* 22 August 1928, p4.

85 *Argus,* 6 February 1929, p1.

86 *Canberra Times,* 11 April 1929, p1. See Freeman, P., *op.cit.*, pp87-91. For details of the contract see CT86/1, 408, IOA erection...NAA.

87 *Building,* Vol44, No260, 12 April 1929, p48. Professor McKenzie was the first Director of the Institute.

88 *Canberra Times,* 18 May 1929, p1.

89 A292, C11 PT 2, IOA—contract...NAA.

90 https://www.architecture.com.au/wp-content/uploads/r022_screensound_australia_rstca.pdf. Moir moved to Canberra with his first wife Nance Aubrey 1927 to take up a position in the recently created Architects' Department of the Federal Capital Commission (FCC), itself only created in 1925. Freeman, P., *op.cit.,* pp73 & 78.

91 *Canberra Times,* 14 May 1929, p4 and 5 November 1954, p8—Esmond died in 1954 and had disposed of his final interests in the company in 1940.

92 UGLNSW record, 14 August 1929, RJ Simmie Collection.

93 *Canberra Times,* 9 August 1929, p1.

94 *Canberra Times,* 24 December 1929, p1 and 26 December 1929, p4.

95 Overall, J., *Canberra: Yesterday, Today & Tomorrow,* FCPA, 1995, p24.

96 Eight architects were given notice, including M J Moir, who laboured for the dole before accepting employment as manager of the Capitol Theatre in

Manuka and setting up a private practice in 1932. Freeman, P., *op.cit.*, pp103-106.

97 *Canberra Times,* 15 February 1930, p2.

98 Freeman, P., *op.cit.,* p102.

99 TM Shakespeare founded *The Canberra Times* in 1926. He was a friend of M J Moir.

100 Supreme Grand Chapter of Royal Arch Masons of NSW record; RJ Simmie Collection.

101 *Canberra Times,* 24 December 1931, p2.

102 *Canberra Times,* 28 November 1931, p3.

103 When Jock and Ivy Simmie moved to 'Harpsdale' in 1941, Jack Joyce went to live with his daughter Dorrie and husband Keith Howe at 12 Burnside Avenue, Canterbury until his death on 20 January 1945. His funeral 'was very well attended', the mourners including the well-known John Wren of Collingwood—bookmaker, boxing and wrestling promoter, Irish nationalist, land speculator, newspaper owner, racecourse and racehorse owner, soldier, pro-conscriptionist and theatre owner. R J Simmie to author, 7 June 2021. For details of Wren, see https://en.wikipedia.org/wiki/John_Wren.

104 Erskine House is the oldest and largest surviving guest house in Victoria. Now a resort hotel.

105 *Age,* 1 January 1940, p3.

106 Section 55, Parish of Meangora, County of St Vincent. His fellow applicants included Hubert John Denholm, a works inspector and World War One veteran; Thomas Henry Trevillian, an engineer; and John Samuel Crapp, a contractor. *Canberra Times,* 20 October 1932 p4 and *Australian Electoral Rolls* 1931.

107 *Canberra Times,* 5 May 1933 p1 and 26 May 1933, p6.

108 The contract was let through and in association with Sydney architects Emil L Sodersteen and John Crust. *Building,* Vol53, No318, 12 February 1934, p11.

109 *Canberra Times,* 9 February 1934, p1, 16 February 1934, p3 and 22 February 1934, p2.

110 *Canberra Times,* 22 February 1934, p2.

111 *Canberra Times,* 18 April 1934, p1. 22 February 1934, p2.

112 Unknown news clipping, 'Thomas Borrowman was Building Pioneer', c27 May 1957, in the RJ Simmie Collection.

113 *Canberra Times,* 31 August 1934, p4.

114 Foskett, A., Johnstone, P, and Andrew, D., *On Solid Foundations—the Building and Construction of the Nation's Capital 1020-1950,* Canberra

115 *Canberra Times,* 2 July 1935 p3 and 24 September 1935, p5.

116 Amongst the first films to be screened at the Civic Theatre were Grace Moore in *Love Me "Forever"*; Fred Astaire and Ginger Rogers in Top Hat; Merle Oberon, Frederick Marsh and Herbert Marshall in *The Dark Angel*; Charles Laughton and Clarke Gable in *Mutiny on the Bounty*; Ronald Colman in *The Man Who Broke the Bank at Monte Carlo*; and Jessie Matthews in *Just a Girl.*

117 *Canberra Times,* 6 July 1935, p3. When Jock was at the movies at the Capitol Theatre that December his car was stolen (it was later recovered). It was telling that it was described as 'an old Chevrolet'. New models had not yet arrived after the Depression. H E Jones was a senior security and intelligence officer who moved to Canberra in 1927; he continued in that role until 1944. See Templeton, J., 'Jones, Harold Edward (1878-1965' in *Australian Dictionary of Biography, Vol9,* MUP, 1983, pp512-513.

118 *Canberra Times,* 6 March 1936, p4. The Simmie Bowl continued to be presented annually for many years to come.

119 *Canberra Times,* 25 September 1937, p2.

120 Lodge 519 surrendered its warrant in 1988. The Remembrance Mark Lodge 133 most probably held its meetings in the new Masonic Temple completed in Barton in 1936—M J Moir and K Oliphant were the architects. Jock Simmie would have been at the dedication ceremony of the temple along with fellow Freemasons Moir, Oliphant, and Shakespeare. Freeman, P., *op.cit.,* p133-134. Masonic jewels in R J Simmie Collection.

121 *Canberra Times, 29* May 1936, p2 and 6 November 1936, p5. RMC had been re-located to NSW during the Depression and returned to Duntroon in early 1937. https://www.architecture.com.au/wp-content/uploads/r055g_parade_ground_and_associated_buildings_group.pdf

122 https://www.architecture.com.au/wp-content/uploads/r102_house_at_3_wilmot_crescent_forrest_rstca.pdf. W H B Dickson was also the president of the Canberra Chamber of Commerce, and a director of the Capitol Theatre in Manuka where M J Moir was the manager. Dickson was struck off the roll of solicitors in 1940 following 'serious misconduct'. Freeman, P., *op.cit., pp134-137 and Canberra Times,* 7 June 1940, p2.

123 *Canberra Times,* 10 July 1937, p2.

124 *Canberra Times,* 25 June 1938, p6. Evans and family actually lived at the Manuka service station. Freeman, P., *op.cit.,* pp146-148.

125 *Canberra Times,* 28 August 1937, p2. Subscribers included Latham Withall, the company secretary, had worked for the Department of Defence in the Geelong Woollen Clothing Mill before World War One. He served in England during the war and then with the Australian Ordnance Corps. B2455 Withall, Latham, NAA. Dudley Lalor was a builder's foreman and presumably worked for Simmie & Co, while Gwilym Thomas Evans, had enlisted for the 1st AIF but rejected on medical grounds. MT1486/1, Evans, Gwilym Thomas, NAA.

126 *Canberra Times,* 14 September 1937, p4.

127 Foley, J, Pyke, 'Sir Louis Frederick (1907-1988)' in *Australian Dictionary of Biography*, 2012.

128 J Simmie to Secretary, Department of the Interior, 2 May 1935, NAA CRS A292/1, in McKernan, M., *Here Is Their Spirit,* UQP, 1991, p.148.

129 *Canberra Times,* 21 October 1937, p4.

130 Australian War Memorial, RSTCA R016, RSTCA—ACT, 1984.

131 *Building,* Vol67, No401, 24 January 1941, p69.

132 McKernan, M., *op.cit.,* p166.

133 *ibid.*

134 *Canberra Times,* 9 July 1938, p2 and 2 February 1939, p4.

135 *Canberra Times,* 9 May 1939, p3. Westridge was renamed Yarralumla in 1955. Construction, 28 June 1939, p9.

136 A432, 1940/651—Simmie & Co—Failure... NAA. The relevant legal requirements were in the Companies Ordinance 1931-1936 and the Companies (Amendment) Act 1906.

137 *Canberra Times,* 17 April 1940, p5.

138 *Canberra Times,* 10 November 1939, p6 and 5 January 1940, p1.

139 *Canberra Times, 1 March 1975,* p24. Chandler was a linotype operator and his wife Elizabeth, a hairdresser at the time, but could still afford the house, reflecting the egalitarianism in Canberra at that time. The Chandlers later went into the jewellery business. Raggatt at that time was Director, Mineral Resources Survey—years later he would become the Secretary, Commonwealth Department of National Development. See Freeman, P., *op.cit.*, pp195-197.

140 Moir's first wife had died in late 1929. He remarried in 1932 and his wife Heather joined his practice.

141 Heritage (Decision about Registration of the Blandforida 4 Housing Precinct Forrest) Notice 2007 (No 1), 1 March 2007.

142 *Age,* 10 January 1933, p11.

143 *Age,* 2 July 1930, p14.

144 *Age,* 8 July 1930, p10.

145 *Herald,* 1 October 1931, p22.

146 https://www.stmonicasparish.com.au/history-of-st-monicas.html

147 *Building*, 24 July 1939, p33.

148 *Age,* 11 January 1936, p15.

149 20th Century Buildings Register RAIA Vic Register 08.

150 *Decoration & Glass, January* 1938, pp25-27.

151 *Argus,* 20 December 1937, p1. Keith Howe of Joyce & Howe shoes, a business associate.

152 *Age,* 21 July 1938, p10.

153 *Argus,* 14 June 1939, p11,

154 The Alfred Lawrence & Co. factory made food essences and food colourings.

155 *Age,* 20 August 1940, p2.

156 *Age*, 24 February 1940, p18. Patrick Joseph O'Connor (1901-1959) entered the Victorian Railways Architects Office as an articled pupil. He studied architecture at night classes conducted at the Working Men's College and after gaining experience in the Railways Department, he set up in practice as an architect in Collins Street in 1926. He took James Thomas Brophy into partnership in 1946, after which the practice was known as O'Connor & Brophy. P.J. O'Connor specialised in ecclesiastical and liquor industry work, and designed many Catholic churches, convents, presbyteries, and schools in Victoria. Information in the Hermes heritage database entry for St Patrick's Catholic Presbytery, Camperdown, from John O'Connor, the son of P J O'Connor.

157 *Sunshine Advocate,* 31 January 1941, p2.

158 Letter from Alf Lloyd to Mrs Meehan 3 July 2001. The images and detail about Edward and Alf Lloyd courtesy of Shaun Crosby, of My Lady's Church Sunshine history group. Alf Lloyd later became a director of Simmie & Co

159 *Melton Express,* 27 July 1940, p3 and *Bacchus Marsh Express,* 24 August 1940, p3.

160 *Construction,* 10 May 1945, p10. The Department of the Interior was created in April 1939. Among its diverse portfolio of responsibilities was the

Australian War Memorial, and execution of Commonwealth engineering projects in the States.

161 *Age*, 10 September 1947, p14.

162 *Advocate*, 11 March 1954, p22.

163 *Age*, 5 September 1946, p1. While the Second World War was followed by an unprecedented demand for housing in and around Melbourne, residential expansion was hampered by a shortage of materials and labour, and a size limit (1,250 square feet) in force since 1940. Until these restrictions were relaxed in the early 1950s, numerous attempts were made by government departments, organisations, companies and even individuals to solve the housing crisis: Prefabrication was seen as an ideal solution… The Housing Commission had far more success with factory-made concrete dwellings….. prefabrication still managed to attract a stigma that 'made it a dirty word in Victoria before the 1950s were out'. Survey of Post-War Built Heritage in Victoria: Stage One Volume 1: Contextual Overview, Methodology, Lists & Appendices Prepared for Heritage Victoria October 2008 p22 and Lewis, M., *The Portable Building*, p33.09.

164 Foley, J, Pyke, 'Sir Louis Frederick (1907-1988)' in *Australian Dictionary of Biography*, 2012. Pyke had served in Army Service Corps during World War Two. The War Service Homes Division of the then Department of Works and Housing, which provided prefabricated homes to war veterans would have also been a natural business target of Pyke-Simmie.

165 R Simmie to author 23 and 25 May 2021. Pyke-Simmie also had a trading company—Simmie Homes. Simmie Homes closed on 17 June 1955, but Pyke-Simmie continued until 27 April 1967, just before Jock Simmie's death the following year.

166 Later Sir Andrew Bruce Small—see https://adb.anu.edu.au/biography/small-sir-andrew-bruce-11714.

167 B884/S111558 and A435 1945/4/4997 Muhlstein Ernest. See also Dictionary of Unsung Architects, Ernest E Milton (1893-1968), http://www.builtheritage.com.au/dua_milston.html.

168 *Wodonga & Towong Sentinel*, 22 February 1952, p1. Simmie & Co beat out Lodge Bros. which almost certainly tendered for the work as well. Lodge Bros were commissioned to build the Shrine of Remembrance in the late 1920s, and early 1930s. In 1947, Lodge Bros were manufacturing a further stage at the Shrine of Remembrance, that being

the carving and fixing of the bluestone servicemen on the top of the 1939-1945 War Memorial at the Eternal Flame. https://www.lodgebros.com.au/project/melbourne-shrine/

169 *Construction,* 7 July 1954, p7.

170 Kate Gamble to R J Simmie, 2 July 2021.

171 Keast, W R H., *A History of the Master Builders Association of Victoria,* MBAV, 1994, pp51, 54, 64, 69, 74, 143, 150, 153.

172 *Age,* 24 January 1955, p1.

173 See https://forgottenaustralianactresses.com/category/cowper-murphy-appleford/ and *Age,* 22 October 1955, p30.

174 *Age, 17* May 1955, p12, and 26 January 1956, p12. There is some unproven but entirely plausible speculation within the family that it was Wren, a Catholic, who also made the connections for Simmie & Co to build Catholic churches in Melbourne.

175 Summary of Grounds, R., Mockridge, J., Murphy, J., Pearce, P F., and Simpson, R., Specifications and Correspondence relating to the Hotham Gardens or Arden Street flat development, North Melbourne, State Library of Victoria, based on Survey of Post-War Built Heritage in Victoria: Stage One, Heritage Victoria, 2008.

176 Proximity to the rail line, and the port, resulted in a large number of rail related industries setting up in Spotswood and nearby Newport. One such business was the Semaphore Iron Works which was established in Spotswood 1878 and manufactured railway signals and equipment for the Victorian network. It was later known as McKenzie and Holland. See 'Spotswood & South Kingsville Profile', Hobsons Bay City Council, 2011.

177 *Canberra Times,* 23 January 1942, p4. The foundation stone for the Ambassador's Residence was laid jointly by the Australian Prime Minister (John Curtin), Senator Collings and America's Minister, Nelson T. Johnson, on 4 July 1942. Wartime shortages lengthened the construction time, but the building was occupied by Christmas, 1943. https://au.usembassy.gov/embassy-consulates/canberra/ambassadors-residence/

178 Freeman, P., *op.cit., p205.*

179 USA Chancery, Residence and Precinct, R068, RSTCA-ACT, 1984

180 *Canberra Times,* 15 April 1943, p3.

181 *Construction,* 30 September 1942, p7; *Canberra Times,* 24 September 1943, p2 and 24 November 1943, p8, *Construction,* 17 May 1944 p9 and

Canberra Times 8 September 1944, p2, 6 October 1944, p3, 19 December 1944, p2 and 22 December 1944, p2.

182 *The Master Builders that built Canberra: 100 years of building in the nation's capital,* Canberra MBA ACT, 2013, p104. The fact that decades later some of these were still in use may have given rise to the expression 'It's a social blunder to live in Narrabundah'.

183 *Canberra Times,* 19 October 1945, p2 and 2 April 1946, p2.

184 *Canberra Times,* 18 April 1946, p4.

185 *Construction,* 27 November 1946, p14.

186 This was the first residence built at former sheep station 'Weetangera' which was to become Belconnen—but Oliphant never lived there, disliking it and regarding it as beyond their budget. He and his wife moved instead near the ANU campus at Acton, but the ANU was obliged to build the house anyway. Freeman, P., op.cit., p218-221 and email, P Freeman to author, 4 July 2021. For Oliphant, see https://en.wikipedia.org/wiki/Mark_Oliphant.

187 UGLV Record, 15 April 1947, R J Simmie Collection.

188 *Canberra Times,* 19 January 1951, p3, 2 April 1951, p3, 8 February 1952, p5 and 1 April 1952, p4. The Federal Capital Territory became the Australian Capital territory—ACT—in 1938.

189 *Canberra Times,* 24 April 1953, p3.

190 *Canberra Times,* 12 June 1953, p4 and 3 December 1954, p2.

191 *Construction,* 15 December 1954, p2.

192 *Canberra Times,* 11 January 1954, p2.

193 *Canberra Times,* 1 May 1954, p5.

194 *Construction,* 15 December 1954, p2.

195 *Canberra Times,* 18 October 1954, p2. Moir's wife Heather Sutherland was killed in a car accident in Canberra in 1953. Moir remarried, to Delitia Harrington, in 1955.

196 Barrow, G; *Canberra's Embassies,* ANU Press, 1978, p72.

197 *Canberra Times,* 1 April 1955, p2 and 25 February 19157, p3.

198 *Canberra Times,* 14 April 1956, p2. The union was described by the *Canberra Times* in 1957 as 'one of the most militant elements in the building trades' group of unions'. *Canberra Times, 3* September 1957, p9. Patrick Martin 'Pat' Clancy (1919 –1987) was an Australian trade unionist

and Communist.

199 *Canberra Times,* 19 January 1956, p2, 20 January 1956, p2, 7 March 1956, p2 and *Canberra Times,* 21 April 1956, p2.

200 *Canberra Times,* 23 January 1956, p2.

201 *Canberra Times,* 16 October 1956, p8.

202 *On Solid Foundations—the building and construction of the nation's capital 1920 to 1950,* Canberra Tradesmen's Union Club, August 2001, p140.

203 https://www.dfat.gov.au/publications/countries-economies-and-regions/60th-anniversary-australia-malaysia/60-years-australia-in-malaysia/introduction.html; *Canberra Times,* 23 September 1959, p14. The new practice was named in 1956 and renamed again as Moir & Slater in 1959 when Ward retired.

204 Freeman, P., *op.cit.,* pp288-289. *Canberra Times,* 7 February 1963, p7; 14 June 1963, p30 and 16 November 1963, p2.

205 *Canberra Times,* 2 September 1957, p6; 26 August 1960, p23; 8 October 1960, p2; 4 January 1961, p12; and 21 November 1961, p12.

206 R J Simmie to author, 18 July 2021.

207 *Canberra Times,* 15 March 1957, p10 and 28 July 1961, p15. The founder of Esmond's Motors, John Esmond, died in late 1954. *Canberra Times,* 5 November 1954, p8. By 1958 Canberra's population had reached 39,000.

208 Agreement, J E Simmie, and E G Stubington, 2 June 1955 and Esmond's Motors Statements of Accounts 30 June 1956, R J Simmie Collection. Jock Simmie purchased his Victorian property from 1940.

209 Freeman, P., *op.cit.,* pp291-292.

210 *Canberra Times,* 14 April 1962, p20.

211 *Canberra Times,* 7 July 1962, p13.

212 *Canberra Times,* 17 July 1962, p3, 4 August 1962, p3 and 18 January 1963, p14.

213 Named after Robert Gordon Menzies (1894-1970), 12th Prime Minister of Australia. See RSTCA R056—https://www.architecture.com.au/wp-content/uploads/r056_rg_menzies_building_rstca.pdf.

214 RJ Simmie to author, 7 June 2021.

215 Freeman, P., *op.cit.,* p292.

216 *Canberra Times,* 9 June 1964, p23.

217 See https://adb.anu.edu.au/biography/shakespeare-thomas-mitchell-8393. Shakespeare's son, Arthur, was also a member (1945-1955) of

218   *Canberra Times,* 19 June 1964, p19 and *Canberra Times,* 31 July 1964, p7.

219   *Red Hill Outlook,* No.8, Canberra Grammar School, December 1965. The design architect Roy Simpson, who had earlier designed the block which completed the north side of the school quad. Speech by P J McKeown, Headmaster, 3 October 1965.

220   *Canberra Times,* 14 March 1968, p13.

221   *Canberra Times,* 28 June 1969, p8.

222   William was also shown as a director of Builders Steel Forms Ltd. Annual Return Simmie & Co, 14 January 1960, RJ Simmie Collection.

223   VPRS932/P1, Unit 225, Item 10053. The legal firm Hedderwick Fookes & Alston still represented the company.

224   $40,000 went missing. The missing money was never found. One possibility is that Jock Simmie loaned it to someone without any paper trail, but he would have had to give it in the form of a cheque and there are no bank records for such an amount being deposited or withdrawn. R J Simmie to author, 7 June 2021.

225   R J Simmie to author, 24 May 2021. **Roy William Simmie** (1920-2004) attended Scotch College from 1934–37. He was a member of the 1937 athletics team. Roy served in the AIF from 1942–43 as a private in the 1 Tank Transporter Coy, AASC, then served in the RAAF from 1943–45, being a leading aircraftman in the 5 Service Flying Training School when demobilised. Roy married Nova Marie Roberts in 1947. They had a son and a daughter. Nova died in 1998. Roy's brother, Jack (died 1994) attended Scotch, as did his cousin John, and grandsons Ashley and Andrew Ball. https://www.scotch.vic.edu.au/greatscot/2005maygs/46obit.html

226   R J Simmie to author 18 July 2021. In 1933, the Spicer Shoe Company factory in Clifton Hill was acquired by Joyce and Howe Pty Ltd; by 1941 the factory had joint occupants, Joyce & Howe P/L, boot manufacturers, and Marshall shoes (1938) P/L, shoe manufacturers. Raworth, B., *Analysis on the building stock on the land known as 169 Noone Street, Clifton Hill etc.*, Report to the City of Yarra, September 2005.

227   R Simmie to author 6 June 2021. John James Joyce was a World War One veteran B2455, Joyce, John James 34112, NAA.

228   R Simmie to author 6 June 2021

229 RJ Simmie to author, 30 May 2021.Letters Flo Simmie to Jock Simmie, 21 January 1959 and reply 9 February 1959, R J Simmie Collection.

230 Letters, St Alban's Vestry to Anglican Diocese, 25 February and 29 March 1958; Letter from Prahran Council to Widdows and Simmie & Co 29 November 1962—Diocese Archives.

231 Widdows was born and died England but worked most of his life in Australia. In that time, he designed more than thirty Anglican churches, which makes him second only to Louis Williams in terms of ecclesiastical output. For eight years until 1966 he was in partnership with David Caldwell. https://heretoday.blog/tag/wystan-widdows/. Architectural Plans: Church of St Alban Armadale: Tower: Sketch Plan B, V2955, 14 November 1957, Wystan Widdows—Diocese Archives.

232 *Age,* 30 June 1962 and Letter, Vestry St Albans to Diocese 12 July 1962..

233 Letter, Widdows to St Albans Vestry, 9 May 1963—Diocese Archives. The architects and the Vestry were still arguing over final costs months after the completion of the project.

234 *Age,* 30 September 1963, p14 and *Messenger,* No 3060, October 1963, p146. Dr Woods was later knighted.

235 Simmie & Co Melbourne employee records, R J Simmie Collection.

236 R Simmie to author, 4 June 2021.

237 The architects were Romberg & Boyd. Robyn Boyd CBE (1919-1971) was perhaps Australia's most influential architect at the time.

238 *Building & Construction,* 12 February 1974, p4 and *Victorian Government Gazette* 44, 22 May 1974, p1711.

239 Interview with Ian Eilenberg by author 1 July 2022.

240 Willis, J, 'Health and Children' in Lewi, H & Goad, P., *Australia Modern,* Thames & Hudson, 2019, p8.

241 Heritage Council Victoria Determination 22 May 2020, and Booker, C., 'Brutalist Footscray 'bunker' built by mysterious architect wins heritage protection', *Age*, 23 May 2020 in https://www.theage.com.au/national/victoria/html. The hospital was closed in 1995.

242 VPRS932/P1/225/10053, PROV.

243 RJ Simmie to author, 19 June 2021.

244 '519 Mount Alexander Road, Moonee Ponds Statement of Significance', Moonee Valley Planning Scheme, MVCC May 2019; 'Moonee Valley Thematic Environmental History', for the City of

Moonee Valley, Living Histories 2012 and Steele, D., 'A Prominent Australian Builder & His Contribution to the Neighbourhood Character of 519 Mount Alexander Road', Moonee Ponds, 20 July 2012.

245 RJ Simmie to author 17 June 2021.

246 VPRS932/P1/225/10053, PROV.

247 Simmie Family History Notes, RJ Simmie Collection 2021. Norman Leslie Gallagher (1931–1999) was a controversial trade unionist, https://en.wikipedia.org/wiki/Norm_Gallagher—cite_note-abc.net.au-3 and Maoist who led the militant Builders Labourers Federation as Federal Secretary and as Victorian State Secretary. See https://en.wikipedia.org/wiki/Norm_Gallagher.

248 VPRS932/P1/225/10053, PROV.

249 *ibid.*

250 *Age,* 4 January 1978 p9 and 9 March 1978, p3. Jennings Industries had been awarded over $6 million in non-tender contracts.

251 *Age,* 24 June 1978, p43.

252 RJ Simmie to author 17 June 2021.

253 *Age,* 1 January 1940, p3.

254 VPRS932/P1/225/10053, PROV, item dated 31 October 1941.

255 For a history of Troodos, see Annex C.

256 VPRS932/P1/225/10053, PROV, items dated 29 January 1941 and 24 May 1941.

257 *ibid.,* leases Volume 1106 Folio 221068 and Volume 1160 Folio 231940.

258 *ibid.,* item dated 19 August 1940.

259 *ibid.,* item dated 3 October 1941.

260 *ibid.,* item dated 31 October 1941.

261 *ibid.,* item dated 2 February 1942.

262 R J Simmie to author, 26 June 2021.

263 *ibid.,* item dated 17 July 1942.

264 *ibid.,* item dated 24 September 1946.

265 *ibid.,* item dated 5 August 1947, 12 October 1949, 7 September 1950, 23 January 1952, 9 September 1952, and 19 November 1952.

266 *ibid.,* item dated 5 August 1947.

267 *ibid.,* item dated 30 March 1955.

268 PROV, VPRS 5714/P0, Unit 776, Item 356/12, items dated 15 April 1955, 9 May 1955, 16 May 1955, 28 May 1955, 10 June 1966, 18 June 1955.

269 *Victorian Certificate of Title*, Volume 8085 Folio 444.

270 Another story passed down in the Simmie family related how Leila Dyson–Holland, whilst

shopping in a bakery in Puckle Street, Moonee Ponds, was telling the lady behind the counter about her large rose garden on her farm. She didn't realize Ivy was behind her and heard everything. Ivy stepped forward and said "Mrs Dyson- Holland's husband is the farm Manager on my husband's property, Harpsdale" leaving it quite clear about whose rose garden she was talking about. The house at Troodos was a small weatherboard house constructed in about 1923/24 with no reliable water for anything but a basic garden. R J Simmie to author 30 May 2021.

271 Winneke was knighted in 1957 and became Chief Justice of the Victorian Supreme Court in 1964. He was later the first Australian Governor of Victoria. See Charles Francis, 'Winneke, Henry Christian (1874–1943)', in *Australian Dictionary of Biography*, Volume 12, Melbourne University Press, 1990.

272 Supreme Court of Victoria, VPRS 267/P0005, 1964/4597.

273 George Howard Earp (1892- 1951). He was a pioneer in pasture improvement work in northeast of Victoria. Born in New Zealand and came to Australia as a child. Educated at Melbourne Grammar then studied architecture. Enlisted in WW1, served with 5th Battalion of the AIF at Gallipoli and France. Purchased 'Athlea' in 1923 and established his Dorset Horn Stud in 1927.

274 Harpsdale Dorset Horn Stud Book, R J Simmie Collection. The Newbold Dorset Horn Stud was registered in October 1917 by William J. Dawkins. He bred the first Poll Dorsets in the world in 1937. He was a Founding Member of the Australian Poll Dorset Association, one of the most influential sheep flocks in the history of the Australian prime lamb industry. The Poll Dorset breed was established by using a Corriedale ram mated to a pure-bred Dorset Horn ewe. The progeny—'good polled ewe lamb' was then mated to a Newbold Dorset Horn ram in 1940. Progeny—polled ram lamb. Dawkins was later awarded an OBE for his services to the industry.

275 R J Simmie Collection.

276 The separator is still held by the R J Simmie Collection.

277 In 1948 for example, farm records show 20 DH rams to Ballarat by train for £4-0-9.

278 R J Simmie Collection records.

279 R J Simmie Collection. The Newmarket Saleyards reached an annual world record of sales in 1944

of over 6.5 million sheep. https://collections.museumsvictoria.com.au/articles/4573. In 1953 a single day record of sales at Newmarket was reached. More than 150,000 sheep were sold requiring more than 1,000 railway trucks and over 300 'motor transports. https://collections.museumsvictoria.com.au/articles/4573, quoting Vincent, K., *On the Fall of the Hammer: A personal history of Newmarket saleyards,* SLV 1992.

280   R J Simmie notes to author, 25 August 2021.

281   R J Simmie to author, 26 June 2021.

282   Wm. McAuliffe lived on site. His bedroom was a fibrocement room in the garden (where the present orchard is) and he was fed by Ivy. He ate in the kitchen whilst the family ate in the vestibule. He would bathe once a week, in the bath installed in the laundry for this purpose. It was described as a big occasion with Wm. getting very concerned about his privacy. R J Simmie to author, 26 June 2021. Wm. McAuliffe is most likely William Samuel McAuliffe, who came from a farming family near Bendigo and was a farm labourer all of his life. He started working at Harpsdale in 1942 and died in 1958. He did not serve in World War One. Australian Electoral Rolls 1913-1954; Ancestry.com.au.

283   The Lloyd family may have been the same family from which Alfred Lloyd, noted as a foreman on Simmie projects in 1942 and who later became a company director of Simmie & Co in the 1960s.

284   Some of these original traps remain in the R J Simmie Collection.

285   R J Simmie to author, 26 June 2021.

286   R J Simmie Collection records.

287   R J Simmie notes to author, 25 August 2021.

288   *The Australian Farm & Home,* 1 January 1951, p29.

289   *ibid.*

290   *Age,* 8 November 1955, p7. The Comeback is a type of domestic sheep originating in Australia. This type of sheep results from crossbreds produced by British Longwool sheep and Merinos being mated back to Merinos. This cross is made to achieve a finer, better style of wool. The Comeback sheep are raised for meat and their fine wool. https://en.wikipedia.org/wiki/Comeback_sheep

291   R J Simmie to author, 23 May 2021.

292   R J Simmie Collection records.

293   *Age,* 24 November 1956, p9.

294   R J Simmie to author, 26 June 2021.

295   R J Simmie Collection records.

296 *ibid.*

297 *Canberra Times,* 29 April 1957, p8.

298 R J Simmie to author, 26 June 2021. In 1947 the Melbourne-Adelaide single return airfare was= £23.8.0. By 1959, it was down to £9.9.0.

299 *Age* 21 October 1960, p3.

300 R J Simmie to author, 26 June 2021.

301 *Age,* 20 June 1961, p5.

302 A reminiscence of Ian Gamble, Ted Gamble's nephew. R J Simmie to author, 23 May 2021

303 R J Simmie to author, 26 June 2021.

304 https://collections.museumsvictoria.com.au/articles/4573.

305 R J Simmie to author, 30 May 2021.

306 R J Simmie to author, 26 June 2021. Excerpts from family friend Joan Millar's diary noted dances or parties at Harpsdale every month or two through 1942 and 1943. Even in 1948 comes the notation 'very good party at Simmies'. Simmie History Notes, R J Simmie Collection.

307 R J Simmie to author, 30 May 2021.

308 Simmie History Notes, R J Simmie Collection.

309 During World War Two, the arrival of US forces in Melbourne and the location of US General Douglas MacArthur's headquarters meant a number of Melbourne schools had buildings requisitioned by the military. For example, the military used Wesley College and Melbourne Grammar—The Master- General of the Ordnance Branch of Land Headquarters relocated from Wesley College to Albert Park Barracks in January 1944. The Deaf, Dumb and Blind Institute building, Melbourne Boy's High School at South Yarra and Merton Hall were gradually able to reoccupy their schools as well. See https://www.ozatwar.com/locations/albertparkbarracks.htm

310 R J Simmie to author, 24 July 2021.

311 *Argus,* 28 September 1939, p2.

312 Dunhelen—this Yuroke property was known as Dunhelen by 1859 when Richard Brodie owned it. It had a 'comfortable cottage' on it by 1865, predating Harpsdale. The Websters moved there in 1935 and left in around 1985. Joan Millar turned 96 in 2021. Mavis Millar and Jean Gamble had been friends since childhood. R J Simmie to author, 17 July 2021.

313 R J Simmie to author, 26 June 2021.

314 The motorcycle cost between £130-160, about a year's worth of wages for young John Simmie. R J Simmie to author, 26 June 2021.

315 Senator Webster was able to assist John Simmie in 1968 following Jock Simmie's death, when the probate debt repayment schedule with the Government became an issue. R J Simmie to author, 17 July 2021.

316 The car had a gas producer on the back during the war.

317 RJ Simmie to author, 22 May 2021.

318 Penleigh Girls College was originally established in 1871 in Moonee Ponds. It amalgamated with Essendon Grammar School in 1977 to become Penleigh and Essendon Grammar School (PEGS).

319 RJ Simmie to author 25 August 2021.

320 RJ Simmie to author 25 August 2021.

321 R J Simmie to author, 14 October 2021.

322 Desmond Gamble's older brother, William, went to Dookie College in 1886 when it opened. He was 17. He was an outstanding student winning many prizes. After Dookie, he went to the Boer war (1899), was wounded and repatriated. Post war he went to work for the department of Agriculture as a demonstrator in farming methods. In 1907 he was promoted to farm manager of Dookie and in 1916 made Principal of Dookie, a role he held until 1922. He was the first of only two graduates to hold the position of Principal.

323 R J Simmie to author, 17 July 2021.

324 R J Simmie to author, 9 February 2022.

325 R J Simmie to author, 17 July 2021.

326 *ibid.*

327 *ibid.* Ivy Simmie cooked mostly on the AGA stove, fuelled by coke, but in 1950 she bought an electric stove that was placed in the laundry as did Jean Simmie in later years. Aga is an acronym for aktiebolaget gas-accumulator, the name of a Swedish company that invented a system of storage for the acetylene gas used in lighthouses. Aga stoves have been sold since 1929.

328 *Expanding Horizons, International Harvester magazine,* 1952, p29.

329 R J Simmie to author, 25 August 2021.

330 R J Simmie to author, 30 May 2021.

331 *Sunshine Advocate,* 10 August 1951, p8 and the Argus, 7 August 1951, p12.

332 *Age,* 20 March 1954, p19.

333 Ivy Simmie and daughter Joyce Gamble were to embark on a tour to the UK and Europe for 8 months in March 1952, but Ivy died less than 4 weeks before departure. Dorrie, Ivy's sister, stepped in and accompanied Joyce on this holiday.

Jock never left Australia after returning from the war. Neither did Jean or John Simmie.

334   R J Simmie to author, 30 May 1921.

335   *ibid.*

336   RJ Simmie to author, 7 June 2021.

337   R J Simmie to author, 26 June 2021

338   R J Simmie to author, 30 May 2021.

339   Noelle Stevenson never received the money as there was no cash left in Jock Simmie's Estate when he died in 1968 to create a moiety to pay her. R J Simmie to author, 7 June 2021.

340   Simmie Family History notes, R J Simmie Collection.

341   In a sign of the times, and Simmie prosperity, Harpsdale saw its first television, an Astor, purchased in October 1953 for £219-9-0. Jock Simmie enjoyed watching the wrestling matches.

342   R J Simmie notes to author, 25 August 2021.

343   R J Simmie notes to author, 25 August 2021. Joyce was also supposed to do house cleaning for her father, but it wasn't done very thoroughly. Periodically, professional cleaners were brought in to give the house a good clean.

344   Peter Simmie to author, 11 October 2021.

345   The bigger boat was 16 or 18 foot long and built by Eric Montgomery. After Mt Martha was sold, the boat sat in a shed at the farm until John found someone to buy it in the 1980's. Eric Ford Montgomery was initially a carpenter and around 1949, a builder, including of boats. He married Veronica Frances Pope in 1926 but divorced in December 1945. He remarried to Dorothy May Kelly a month later in January 1946 and moved to Sydney. Australian Electoral Rolls 1928-1972. According to R J Simmie, he bought a boat building business in Sydney but did not keep in contact with the extended family in Victoria. His wife Dorothy died in 1963 and Eric was noted at Scotland Island at Pittwater north of Sydney in 1977, with a possible daughter Ivy Grace Montgomery living nearby in Mosman. Australian Electoral records 1930-1980.

346   R J Simmie to author, 16 July 2021.

347   Simmie History Notes, R J Simmie Collection.

348   R J Simmie to author, 16 July 2021.

349   Peter Simmie to author, 11 October 2021.

350   Philip Simmie to author, 6 September 2021.

351   R J Simmie to author, 15 September 2021.

352   Peter Simmie to author, 11 October 2021.

353   Philip Simmie to author, 6 September 2021.

354 R J Simmie to author, 26 June 2021.

355 Ken Charlton to Richard Simmie 22 November 2022.

356 Jock's name was only added to the tombstone in 2012 by grandson Peter. John Simmie had not got around to doing it before he died himself. R J Simmie to author, 8 September 2021.

357 In 1967, John Simmie got another new car, a Rambler American 440, white with red interior, comfortable, quick but shocking brakes and handling. R J Simmie to author, 26 August 2021.

358 John continued recording farm expenditure and income in the ledger system until 2003/04. Richard Simmie recorded 2004/05 in the ledger system for the last time. RJ Simmie to author, 25 August 2021.

359 In his Codicil to the 1952 Will dated 28 November 1964, Noelle Stevenson is to be given £8/week for life. Jock rewrote his will on the 10 August 1968, /1966. Again, she is mentioned, same address and now to receive $16/week for life and on her death, the money to go to John. However, she never received a cent as there was no cash left in the Estate to create a moiety to pay her.

360 At this point John Simmie called upon the best man at his wedding, now Senator James Webster, to intercede with the Tax Department, which he did. RJ Simmie to author, 26 August 2021.

361 Phil Howard became one of John Simmie's close friends; he died in 1993, an event recorded in the farm records. R Simmie to author, 7 June 2021.

362 Jock Simmie Probate document dated 13 October 1968.

363 *Stock and Land,* 28 October 1971, p12.

364 Richard Simmie recollects that a party had been held there in late 1968 for Peter Simmie's 18th: "It was such a wild party that my parents vowed never to hold one again". RJ Simmie to Author 25 August 2021.

365 Ray English gave his home address as Belmont, Yuroke in1972. Australian Electoral Rolls, 1972—Ancestry.com.au.

366 Peter Simmie to author, 11 October 2021.

367 R J Simmie to author, 26 June 2021.

368 RJ Simmie to author 25 August 2021.

369 Joyce later sold this land in 1981 for about $77,000. After Joyce's death in 1981 her probate showed the sale had not gone been completed and there was money owing to the estate. Her probate was granted to her brother John who sold it to Peter Hoban in November 1985.

370 R J Simmie to author, 25 August 2021.

371 Philip Simmie to author, 6 & 14 September 2021.

372 Peter Simmie to author, 11 October 2021.

373 It was tested in 2003 and found to be dry; deeper drilling was expensive and not justified. Belmont also had a bore which is still producing.

374 *Phalaris* can become dominant and needs to be controlled by grazing or it can become a troublesome weed.

375 Farmers of the era often conducted herbicide spraying from an open tractor without personal protection; John Simmie was no exception. This long-term exposure may well have contributed to John Simmie's ill health in later years of his life.

376 R J Simmie to author, 8 September 2021.

377 RJ Simmie to author, 25 August 2021.

378 Extensions were made to the 1957 shearing shed built on site of the old one when John increased wool production with electricity and new 3 stands—electric shearing gear—still in use. The old shed had a motor driven belt shearing stand set up. Old motor is now used as a garden feature.

379 Law-Smith's daughter married Rupert Clarke in 1977. Lady Clarke years later remembered the Simmie name and described Harpsdale very well. She had visited the property, with her father, when he was looking at DH rams. R J Simmie to author, 8 September 2021.

380 Philip Simmie to author, 6 September 2021. Philip and family moved to 'Felton Homestead', out of Pittsworth, Darling Downs. The old Queenslander homestead had been the home of James Tyson, a pastoral pioneer of the late 1800's; the home was built in 1870. Unfortunately it was destroyed by fire in 2013.

381 R J Simmie to author, 8 September 2021.

382 Philip Simmie to author, 6 September 2021.

383 R J Simmie to author, 15 September 2021.

384 Peter Simmie to author, 11 October 2021.

385 The Wool Floor Price was abolished in 1991. The replacement dog, Lance, cost $1200.

386 Probably Merino ewes bought from the Benara Pastoral Company near Jerilderie in NSW.

387 The fencing had not been maintained for some time.

388 'Nouranies' may refer to sheep bought from Nowranie Pastoral Company near Oaklands, NSW and also near Jerilderie. The Quell paddock refers to a relatively isolated paddock at bottom side of the property adjoining Mount Ridley Road, making it easier to steal sheep. The origin of

the name of the paddock is unknown.

389 Jock Simmie did this to avoid Death Duties. Ironically Death Duties were abolished in the early 1970s.

390 Konagaderra Road was the western boundary of Harpsdale and Troodos. The NW corner of the property had land that was used as a road, which changed its course over the years.

391 Andronas Conservation Architecture P/L, an award-winning architectural practice specialising in architectural design and conservation.

392 'The first garden design was very twee, too many English box hedges, too English in style and not at all suitable for the harsh environment at Harpsdale. After 2012, a landscape architect, Kate Patterson, was engaged to do a garden plan incorporating the existing garden, and a key feature was to be as drought tolerant as possible. The drought in the early 2000's showed how critical this was. During this period nearly all the elm trees were lost to the dry; they had been there since 1875. Her design and ideas were fully implemented.' R J Simmie to author, 15 September 2021.

393 R J Simmie to author, 15 September 2021.

Richard had initially intended to plant a 1,000-tree olive grove but a series of dry years in the early 2000s made that project unfeasible. R J Simmie to author, 9 September 2021. Woolybutt P/L is a Victorian timber and forestry company and part of the Support Activities for Forestry Industry.

394 Andrew McAliece is a dentist who has owned his own practice for more than 25 years.

395 For the party, Andrew went as 'big Sam' and Richard as 'Scarlet'. Richard remembered 'going to the bathroom to get changed, I passed my father in the main hallway, in my work clothes, and one hour later passed him again, fully attired in my costume as Scarlet and he just smiled at me. A great night had by all.' RJ Simmie to author, 8 September 2021.

396 Eulogy, John Ernest Simmie, 2012, R J Simmie Collection.

397 Eulogy, Jean Simmie 2012, R J Simmie Collection.

398 Picking up his mother's prowess as a seamstress, Richard had learned how to make his own costumes.

399 R J Simmie to author, 15 September 2021.

400 The same Celebrant was engaged for the funerals of John and Jean Simmie, and she went on to

marry James Simmie in 2014 and then Richard and Andrew in 2018. R J Simmie to author, 8 September 2021.

401 Notes, RJ Simmie to author, 25 August 2021.

402 Folko Cooper and his partner Maureen Craig create garden sculpture and water features.

403 R J Simmie to author, 25 September 2021.

404 Michael Dempsey was an Irishman who had a Master's degree in Conservation from York University, UK. R J Simmie to author, 25 September 2021.

405 Wolfdene develops new communities and townhouse projects throughout Melbourne's growth corridors.

406 Surveyor General's Office, Victoria, *Parish of Mickleham in the County of Bourke [cartographic material]*, 1856, State Library of Victoria [SLV].

407 Geological Survey of Victoria, *Parts of Parishes of Bolinda, Mickleham, Kalkallo, Wollert, Yuroke, Bulla Bulla [cartographic material]*, No2, NW Melbourne: Geological Survey Office, 1860; *Geological Survey of Victoria, Parts of Parishes of Buttlejorrk, Bollinda, Mickleham, Bulla Bulla, and Holden [cartographic material]* No7, NE Melbourne: Geological Survey Office, 18600

408 Bull, M., 'Soils of Melbourne' in *Flora of Melbourne* (4th ed.), Hyland House, Victoria, 2014, pp36-41.

409 Land Conservation Council, Victoria, *Report on the Melbourne study area,* The Council, Melbourne, 1973, p273.

410 *ibid.*

411 PROV, VPRS 8168/P2, Unit 6409, Item *Sydney B26—Parish of Bulla-Bulla,* David Malcolm Kemp, 1840.

412 PROV, VPRS 16306/P1, Unit 11098, Putaway Plan M 113—*Parish of Mickleham*—Compilation, 1850.

413 PROV, VPRS 8168/P2, Unit 1490, Item Featr551—*Plan of the Portions Marked in the Parish of Bulla-Bulla,* Henry B Foot, Assistant Surveyor, 1852.

414 Bull, M., *op cit.*

415 Land Conservation Council, Victoria. *Report on the Melbourne study area.* The Council, Melbourne, 1973, p277.

416 *ibid.*

417 Land Conservation Council, Victoria. *Report on the Melbourne study area.* The Council, Melbourne, 1973: Appendix 4, 442-4.

418 Billis, R V. and A. S. Kenyon, A S., *Pastoral Pioneers*

of Port Phillip, Macmillan & Co., Melbourne, 1932, pp12, 21, 161, 171 and PROV, VPRS 5359, Pastoral Run Papers, Jacket 320, Run 327 Deep Creek and Jacket 233, Run 166 Bulla Bulla.

419 PROV, VPRS 14, Register of Assisted Immigrants from the United Kingdom Unit 2 Page 311, Fergusson, arrived January 1841; *Bacchus Marsh Express,* 19 November 1892, p3.

420 PROV, VPRS 5359, Pastoral Run Papers, Jacket 233, Run 166 Bulla Bulla—letter to the Colonial Secretary from G S & R Brodie, 20 May 1852 and PROV, VPRS 8168, Unit 1490 Historic Plan Collection, Featr551 Emu Creek, 1852.

421 *Bacchus Marsh Express,* 19 November 1892, p3.

422 *Port Phillip Patriot and Melbourne Advertiser,* 8 September 1842, p4.

423 *Argus,* 19 June 1849, p1.

424 *Port Phillip Gazette and Settler's Journal,* 11 December 1847, p2 and 26 June 1849, p1; *Argus,* 29 June 1849, p2; *Yuroke: County of Burke, Parish Plan Y74(4),* Melbourne, Department of Lands and Survey, 1965. James Brodie's purchase—*NSW Government Gazette,* 1 January 1850, p5. James died in 1858.

425 *Argus,* 31 August 1859, p8; *Bell's Life in Victoria and Sporting Chronicle,* 24 September 1859, p4; and the *Argus,* 3 October 1865, p8.

426 *Victoria Government Gazette,* 1 October 1851, p584; *Argus,* 18 October 1851, p2—which records that W A'Beckett purchased Portion 18, however the parish plan of Bulla shows Brodie's name on it. See: Bulla Bulla: County of Burke, Parish Plan B522(6), Melbourne, Department of Crown Lands and Survey, 1972.

427 *Argus,* 18 October 1851, p2; PROV, VPRS 5359, Pastoral Run Papers, Jacket 233, Run 166 Bulla Bulla, letters to the Colonial Secretary from G. S. & R. Brodie, dated 9 January 1852 and 20 May 1852. While the sale date for these is May 1853, by April 1855 the Brodies were yet to receive their Crown grants for Portion 20.

428 PROV, VPRS 460, P0, Unit 35781 Application File AP 35781, lease dated 31 December 1852.

429 *ibid.*

430 *Argus,* 10 March 1857, p7.

431 *Argus,* 29 June 1864, p2.

432 Victorian Death Index, registration number 3096 of 1872; PROV, VPRS 24/P0, Unit 267, Item 1871/1 Male, inquest of Richard Brodie; *Argus,* 22 January 1872, p4.

433 PROV, VPRS 7591/P2, Unit 5, Item 9/625, will

of Richard Brodie; PROV, VPRS 28/P2, Unit 6, Item 9/624 probate of Richard Brodie.

434 George Brodie had left for England in 1851.

435 *Argus,* 13 January 1874, p3; Victorian Death Index, registration number 759 of 1905.

436 *Argus,* 4 August 1873, p4.

437 *Argus,* 2 September 1873, p4; Victorian Birth Index, registration number 15763 of 1873; *Argus,* 1 March 1875, p1; Victorian Birth Index, registration number 891 of 1875.

438 *Argus,* 18 September 1875, p3.

439 *Australasian,* 16 December 1876, p25; Victorian Birth Index, registration number 880 of 1877.

440 *Argus,* 5 April 1878, p1; Victorian Birth Index, registration number 7164 of 1878 for Kelley, father William Beatte Kelley.

441 *Argus,* 30 November 1874, p3 and 24 May 1876, p3 and 29 December 1876, p2.

442 *Argus,* 14 June 1877, p3.

443 *British Sheep Breeds: Their Wool and its Uses,* British Wool Marketing Board, Yorkshire, 1984, p47.

444 While both Richard and George Brodies' probates do show some livestock as part of their personal estate, any fodder, or crops on the ground they owned are not recorded and must therefore have been included in the valuation of the real estate.

445 PROV, VPRS 28/P2, Unit 112, Item 21/585, probate of George S Brodie.

446 PROV, VPRS 28/P2, Unit 112, Item 21/585, probate of George S Brodie; note the 1875 tender called for a brick house. Note that nearby Helensville of 853 acres (Bulla parish Allotments 1 and 2 of Portion 24 plus 193 or 185 acres of Portion 14 (originally 502 acres)) and Katesville of 586 acres (Allotments A and B of Portion 20 Bulla) were left for the benefit of his daughter Helen Sinclair Brodie. The Five Mile Station at Bolinda (1,255 acres) and New Grove (Portion 17 of 632 acres in parish of Mickleham) was left to his daughter Catherine McKenzie Scott.

447 PROV, VPRS 28/P2, Unit 112, Item 21/585, probate of George S Brodie.

448 *Argus,* 30 March 1883, p2.

449 *Argus,* 12 July 1883, p3. *David Moloney & Vicki Johnson, City of Hume: Heritage Study of the former Shire of Bulla District,* 1998: Place No. 203. 1883 additions to the house were the master bedroom, NW corner and two more rooms in SW corner. These were added in triple, not the bluestone

rubble the rest of the house was built with, hence the reason it was rendered. Email, R J Simmie to author, 18 July 2021.

450   *Age,* 4 August 1885, p7.

451   *Victoria Government Gazette,* 28 January 1887, p177.

452   *Argus,* 10 August 1888 p9 and *Age,* 6 August 1891, p7.

453   *Argus,* 15 June 1887, p3.

454   *Australasian,* 18 October 1890, p27; *Weekly Times,* 26 December 1891, p22; *Australasian,* 30 January 1892, p27.

455   PROV, VPRS 28/P2, Unit 370, Item 53/142; *Argus,* 1 March 1893, p5.

456   *Sportsman,* 17 July 1894, p4.

457   *Sportsman,* 12 June 1894, p5; Sportsman, 10 July 1894, p5.

458   *Sportsman,* 24 July 1894, p7; *Sportsman,* 11 September 1894, p3; *Sunbury News,* 28 July 1900, p3.

459   *Australasian,* 29 June 1901, p20.

460   *Australasian,* 9 August 1902, p23.

461   As documented in Cannon, M., *The Land Boomers, Carlton:* Melbourne University Press, 1966.

462   Based on online searches in Trove digital newspapers and a search of the PROV catalogue.

463   *Age,* 28 January 1904, p2; *Argus,* 22 February 1904, p2.

464   *Age,* 13 February 1904, p3.

465   PROV, VPRS 460, P0, Unit 35781 Application File AP 35781, lease dated 14 March 1904.

466   *ibid.*

467   *Argus,* 25 February 1904, p8; *Weekly Times,* 27 February 1904, p26. A springer is a cow or heifer close to calving.

468   Victorian Death Index, registration number 759 of 1905; *Sunbury News,* 14 January 1905, p4.

469   *Sunbury News,* 14 January 1905, p4.

470   PROV, VPRS 28/P2, Unit 709, Item 93/341 and PROV, VPRS 28/P0, Unit 1208, Item 93/341, Probate of David Brodie; PROV, VPRS 7591/P2, Unit 371, Item 93/341, Will of David Brodie.

471   PROV, VPRS 460, P0, Unit 35781 Application File AP 35781, application dated 7 February 1906.

472   PROV, VPRS 460, P0, Unit 35781 Application File AP 35781; Victorian Certificate of Title, Volume 3211, Folio 642113 dated 6 July 1907.

473   *Australasian,* 29 July 1905, p20; *Australasian,* 3 June 1905, p20.

474 *Sunbury News,* 3 August 1907, p3; Victorian Birth Index, registration number 19312 of 1886 spelt as Struan Robertson, son of Lewis Robertson and Ann Wilkie.

475 VPRS 12024/P1, Unit 74, Item 1690 Matter of the Estate settled by David Brodie deceased, PROV.

476 *Age,* 21 December 1907, p2; *Argus,* 4 January 1908, p2.

477 *Argus,* 4 January 1908, p2. A 'backward springer' is a cow in the first 4-5 months of gestation, a 'forward springer' being a cow more than 5 months pregnant.

478 *National Farmers' Federation Australian Agricultural Year Book 1986,* Melbourne: Publishing and Marketing Australia, 1985, p165.

479 If Harpsdale had been sold, then the title was not updated until 1912 after David's executors repaid the outstanding mortgage. The timing of the actual sale in 1912 is probably not coincidental. David Charles Brodie, David and Fanny's youngest child was born in 1890, and thus turned 21 in 1911. *Argus,* 30 April 1890, p1; Victorian Birth Index, registration number 20462 of 1890 David Charles Brodie. Noting that Fanny Brodie did not remarry, and died in 1933, David Brodie's estate was broken up and sold from 1912 after David Charles 'came of age'. Victorian Death Index, registration number 1919 of 1933.

480 *Leader,* 11 April 1908, p37; *Weekly Times,* 27 March 1909, p34; *Weekly Times,* 6 August 1910, p33; *Weekly Times,* 14 January 1911.

481 Victorian Certificate of Title, Volume 3711 Folios 742096

482 *Australasian,* 24 March 1928, p44; *Horsham Times, 26* September 1919, p4; *Australasian,* 28 September 1912, p20.

483 *Australasian,* 9 August 1913, p23.

484 *Stock and Land,* 3 December 1918, p2.

485 *Flemington Spectator,* 5 December 1918, p2.

486 Federation University Australia. 'Trewhella Foundry'. https://bih.federation.edu.au/index.php/Trewhella_Foundry, 15 November 2016.

487 *Herald,* 19 December 1918, p18.

488 PROV, VPRS 5714/P0, Unit 776, Item 356/12.

489 *Farmers' Advocate,* 14 March 1919, p3.

490 *Argus,* 11 March 1919, p4.

491 Nelson, P., and Alves, L., *Lands Guide: A Guide to finding records of Crown land.* Melbourne: Public Record Office Victoria, 2009, p57.

492 Nelson, P., and Alves, L., *op.cit.,* p56.

493 Nelson, P., and Alves, L., *op.cit.*, p285.

494 See Garden, D., *Victoria A History,* Melbourne: Nelson, 1984 and for examples in the western district of Victoria, refer to Zachariah, R., *The Vanished Land, South Australia:* Wakefield Press, 2017.

495 PROV, VPRS 5714/P0, Unit 776, Item 356/12; Certificate of Title Volume 3711 Folio 742096.

496 PROV, VPRS 5714/P0, Unit 776, Item 356/12.

497 *Australasian,* 29 January 1921, p48; *Australasian,* 5 March 1921, p42.

498 *Australasian,* 5 March 1921, p42.

499 PROV, VPRS 5714/P0, Unit 776, Item 356/12.

500 *ibid.*

501 *Argus,* 11 October 1924, p26.

502 *Age,* 27 September 1924 p12; 1925 Corio (Sunbury) Electoral Roll, Australian Electoral Commission (per Ancestry.com), listed as Wilson, Arthur Clercing (sic), 'Arundel', Keilor, grazier. Same entry appears in 1926 (with the Lordings), 1928, 1931 and 1934.

503 *Herald,* 5 January 1935, p5; Victorian Death Index, registration number 307 of 1935 as Arthur Chestnay (sic) Wilson.

504 Certificate of Title, Volume 4660 Folio 931823, dated 20 June 1930, transferred to Volume 5678 Folio 1135581.

505 *Argus,* 11 October 1924, p26., Certificate of Title, Volume 4660 Folio 931823, dated 20 June 1930, transferred to Volume 5678 Folio 1135581.

506 Victorian Marriage Index, registration number 1221 of 1924; 1925 Corio (Wallan Wallan) Electoral Roll, Australian Electoral Commission (per Ancestry.com).

507 1926 Corio (Wallan Wallan) Electoral Roll (per Ancestry.com), 1927 Corio (Broadmeadows) Electoral Roll, Australian Electoral Commission (per Ancestry.com); *Argus, 3 May 1926, p1.*

508 Certificate of Title, Volume 4660 Folio 931823, dated 2 November 1932, transferred to Volume 5823 Folio 1164426. Tenants in Common meant that each person had a right to sell or transfer their own portion, as compared to Joint Proprietors which meant that if one partner died the survivor(s) became the owner of the deceased's share.

509 *Australasian,* 30 October 1909, p12; *Herald,* 20 March 1929, p5; *Alexandra and Yea Standard, Gobur, Thornton and Acheron Express,* 24 October 1902, p2.

510 *Herald,* 20 March 1929, p5.

511 Certificate of Title, Volume 5823 Folio 1164426 dated 2 November 1932 and 5 November 1937; PROV, VPRS 28/ P3, Unit 3953, Item 352/929; VPRS 7591/ P2, Unit 1240, Item 352/929 probate and will of Philip L Aitken; *Argus,* 18 April 1944, p2; Age, 22 July 1954, p9.

512 'Dunvegan' Isle of Skye.com. https://www.isleofskye.com/dunvegan, 1999-2021 (accessed 2 July 2021).

513 *Australasian,* 24 March 1928, p44; *Argus, 29 August 1928, p18; Numurkah Leader,* 1 June 1937, p3.

514 *Australasian,* 24 March 1928, p44.

515 *ibid.*

516 *ibid.*

517 *Leader,* 8 January 1887, p11; *Leader,* 26 November 1887, p11.

518 'Australian Oats: Breeding, Farming, Extension' in http://www.australianoats.com.au/oats/p-09.htm, no date; *Daily Examiner,* 10 March 1916, p2; *Murrumbidgee Irrigator,* 28 April 1916, p12: 12; *National Advocate,* 19 July 1916, p1; *Stock and Land,* 3 December 1918, p3.

519 *Leader,* 26 November 1887, p11.

520 *Age,* 9 November 1872, p5; *Australasian,* 1 February 1879, p25.

521 *Leader,* 18 June 1898, p12; *Leader,* 23 January 1904, p6.

522 *Australasian,* 24 March 1928, p44.

523 *Argus,* 29 August 1928, p18; *Australasian,* 1 June 1929, p54; *Age,* 5 November 1931, p5.

524 *Australasian,* 24 March 1928, p44.

525 H. J. Sims, "Pye, Hugh (1860–1942)", *Australian Dictionary of Biography,* National Centre of Biography, Australian National University, https://adb.anu.edu.au/biography/pye-hugh-8138/text14219, published first in hardcopy 1988.

526 *Argus,* 5 May 1928, p20.

527 *Argus,* 5 May 1928, p20; *Cairns Post,* 18 March 1929, p12.

528 *Cairns Post,* 18 March 1929, p12.

529 *Argus,* 5 May 1928, p20; National Archives of Australia (NAA), Series A627, Item 11223/1928, Application for Letters Patent for an invention by Edward Fancourt Mitchell, titled—An improved method of and means for packing livestock for conveyance in transport vehicles (cognate with 8930/1927).

530 *Argus,* 5 March 1936, P9; *Argus,* 11 December 1936, p9; *Age,* 19 May 1937, p21; *Numurkah*

Leader, 1 June 1937, p3.

531 Certificate of Title, Volume 5823 Folio 1164426.

532 *Argus,* 27 June 1938, p18.

533 *Age,* 23 September 1939, p3.

534 *Argus,* 7 October 1939, p6.

535 Certificate of Title, Volume 5823 Folio 1164426.

536 Nelson, P., and Alves, L., *op.cit., p301.*

537 *ibid.*

538 PROV, VPRS 5714/P0, Unit 776, Item 356/12.

539 *ibid.*

540 PROV, VPRS 5714/P0, Unit 776, Item 356/12, letter dated 17 May 1919.

541 PROV, VPRS 5714/P0, Unit 776, Item 356/12, dated 23 May 1919.

542 *ibid.,* assessment dated 18 December 1919.

543 PROV, VPRS 5714/PO, Unit 776, Item 356/12, items dated 29 January and 18 February 1020.

544 *ibid.,* item dated 4 March 1920.

545 PROV, VPRS 5714/P0, Unit 776, Item 356/12, items dated 13 March 1920, 1 April 1920 and 18 April 1920.

546 *ibid.,* items dated 19 April 1920 and 25 May 1920.

547 *ibid.,* items dated 25 May 1920 and 2 June 1920, 18 June 1920 and 27 September 1920.

548 *ibid.,* items dated 30 September 1920 and 14 December 1920

549 *ibid.,* item dated 1 April 1921

550 *Australasian,* 5 March 1921, p42; PROV, VPRS 5714/P0, Unit 776, Item 356/12, items dated 9 May 1921 and 14 May 1921.

551 PROV, VPRS 5714/P0, Unit 776, Item 356/12, item dated 7 October 1922.

552 *ibid.,* item dated 20 January 1923.

553 *ibid.,* item dated 28 January 1923.

554 *ibid.,* item dated 17 January 1923; *Victoria Government Gazette,* 21 February 1923, p652.

555 PROV, VPRS 5714/P0/Unit 776, item dated 27 February 1923.

556 *ibid.,* item dated 4 August 1925.

557 *ibid.,* item dated 17 August 1925 and 19 August 1925.

558 *ibid.,* item dated 17 August 1925.

559 *ibid.,* item dated 17 August 1925.

560 *ibid.,* item dated 19 August 1925.

561 *Victoria Government Gazette, 7* March 1923, p790.

562 *Victoria Government Gazette,* items dated 9 March 1923 and 10 April 1923 and 7 March 1923, p790.

563 *ibid.,* item dated 16 April 1923.

564 *ibid.,* item dated 16 April 1923.

565 *ibid.,* item dated 16 April 1932.

566 *ibid.,* items dated 15 May 1923 and 31 March 1925; *Victoria Government Gazette,* 8 April 1925 p1144.

567 PROV, VPRS 5714/P0, Unit 776, Item 356/12, item dated 29 July 1927.

568 *ibid.,* items dated 29 July 1927 and 11 August 1927.

569 *ibid.,* item dated 11 August 1927.

570 *ibid.,* item dated 13 August 1927.

571 *ibid.,* items dated 11 August 1927 and 13 August 1927.

572 *Victoria Government Gazette,* 24 August 1927, p2594; *Victoria Government Gazette,* 31 August 1927, p2653.

573 PROV, VPRS 5714/P0, Unit 776, Item 356/12, item dated 5 September 1927.

574 'Name Index' Birth, Arthur Kirke Dyson Holland, record RGD33-1-77p243; Victorian Marriage Index, registration number 2160 of 1890, Libraries Tasmania.

575 *Weekly Times,* 18 April 1914, p26; B2455, Dyson-Holland Arthur Kirke, National Archives Australia.

576 *Australasian,* 30 October 1909, p12; *Herald,* 20 March 1929, p5; *Alexandra and Yea Standard, Gobur, Thornton and Acheron Express,* 24 October 190, p2.

577 PROV, VPRS 5714/P0, Unit 776, Item 356/12, item dated 13 October 1927.

578 PROV, VPRS 5714/P0, Unit 776, Item 356/12, item dated 21 October 1927.

579 *Victoria Government Gazette,* 2 November 1927, p3386; PROV, VPRS 5714/P0, Unit 776, Item 356/12, item dated 3 November 1927.

580 *ibid.,* item dated 3 November 1927.

581 *ibid.,* items dated 3 November 1927 and PROV, VPRS 10381/P0, Unit 342, Item 3499, items dated 7 November 1927 and 27 May 1928.

582 NSW Marriage Index, Registration number 9688 of 1928.

583 PROV VPRS 10318/P0, Unit 342, Item 3499, item dated 13 May 1930.

584 PROV, VPRS 10318/P0, Unit 342, Item 3499, item dated 14 March 1931.

585 A6770, Item Dyson-Holland Kirke, NAA. He died in Darwin in 1954 as a result of a bite from an octopus, see *Courier-Mail, 20 September 1954, p1.*

586 PROV, VPRS 10318/P0, Unit 342, Item 3499,

item dated 30 June 1933.

587 *ibid.*, item dated 30 June 1933. A 'shandy' crop is a mixed crop, as in oats and wheat sown together. See image caption, *Age,* 20 November 1941, p4.

588 PROV, VPRS 10318/P0, Unit 342, Item 3499, item dated 24 November 1933.

589 *ibid.,* Item 3499, item dated 4 April 1934.

590 *ibid.,* Item 3499.

591 *ibid.*, item dated 29 January 1934.

592 *ibid.*, item dated 13 January 1936.

593 PROV, VPRS 10318/P0, Unit 342, Item 3499, item dated 30 March 1936.

594 *ibid.,* items dated 1 April 1936 and 25 March 1936.

595 *ibid.,* Item 3499, item dated 1 April 1936.

596 *ibid.,* item dated 20 April 1936.

597 *ibid.,* items dated 20 October 1936 and 16 December 1936.

598 PROV, VPRS 5714/P0, Unit 776, Item 356/12, item dated 4 May 1937.

599 PROV, VPRS 10318/P0, Unit 342, Item 3499, item dated 11 January 1937, 18 February 1937, and 21 March 1927.

600 PROV, VPRS 10318/P0, Unit 342, Item 3499, item dated 18 May 1937.

601 *ibid.,* item dated 25 June 1937

602 *Herald,* 10 March 1937, p3; Victorian Marriage Index, registration number 2841 of 1895; Victorian Death Index, registration number 1207 of 1952; *Age,* 25 May 1925, p1.

603 PROV, VPRS 10318/P0, Unit 342, Item 3499, item dated 25 June 1937.

604 PROV, VPRS 10318/P0, Unit 342, item dated 25 June 1937.

605 *ibid.,* item dated 5 August 1937.

606 PROV, VPRS 5714/P0, Unit 776, Item 356/12, item dated 20 October 1937.

607 *ibid.,* item dated 20 October 1937.

608 *ibid.,* item dated 19 February 1939.

609 PROV, VPRS 5714/P0, Unit 776, Item 356/12, item dated 12 April 1939.

610 *ibid.,* item dated 12 April 1939.

611 *ibid.,* item dated 3 October 1939.

612 *ibid., i*tems dated 9 April 1940, 19 June 1940, 27 June 1940 and 3 July 1940.

613 *ibid., i*tems dated 29 January 1941 and 24 May 1941.

614 PROV, VPRS5714/P0, Unit 776, item dated 31 October 1941.

615 *ibid.,* leases Volume 1106 Folio 221068 and Volume 1160 Folio 231940.

616 *ibid.,* item dated 3 October 1941.

617 *ibid.,* item dated 31 October 1941.

618 *ibid.,* item dated 2 February 1942.

619 *ibid.,* item dated 17 July 1942.

620 *ibid.,* item dated 24 September 1946.

621 *ibid.,* item dated 5 August 1947, 12 October 1949, 7 September 1950, 23 January 1952, 9 September 1952, and 19 November 1952.

622 *ibid.,* item dated 5 August 1947.

623 *ibid.,* item dated 30 March 1955.

624 PROV, VPRS 5714/P0, Unit 776, Item 356/12, items dated 15 April 1955, 9 May 1955, 16 May 1955, 28 May 1955, 10 June 1966, 18 June 1955.

625 Victorian Certificate of Title, Volume 8085 Folio 444.

Select Bibliography

Government and Archives

ACT Heritage Library

Australian War Memorial

National Archives of Australia

National Library of Australia

Public Records Office, Victoria

State Library of Victoria

New South Wales Government Gazette

Victorian Government Gazette

Anglican Diocese of Melbourne Archives

Our Lady Church Sunshine History Group Archives

The R J Simmie Collection

The R J Collection contains extensive business records, images, family records, certain ephemera, memorabilia, heirlooms and farm machinery.

Books, Articles and Reports

Barrow, G., *Canberra's Embassies,* ANU Press, 1978

Billis, R V and A. S. Kenyon, A S., *Pastoral Pioneers of Port Phillip,* Macmillan & Co., Melbourne, 1932

Booker, C., 'Brutalist Footscray 'bunker' built by mysterious architect wins heritage protection', *Age*, 23 May 2020 in https://www.theage.com.au/national/victoria/html.

British Sheep Breeds: Their Wool and its Uses, British Wool Marketing Board, Yorkshire, 1984.

Bull, M., 'Soils of Melbourne' in *Flora of Melbourne* (4th ed.), Hyland House, Victoria, 2014.

Clark, I D., *Place Names and Land Tenure—Windows into Aboriginal Landscapes: Essays in Victorian Aboriginal History*. Ballarat, Heritage Matters, 1998.

Collins, John T., *Yuroke*, State Library of Victoria, 1976.

Coulson, H., *Echuca-Moama Murray River Neighbours*, McCabe Prints: Wangaratta, 2009.

Fitzgerald, A., *Canberra in two centuries: a pictorial history*, Clareville Press, c1987.

Foley, J., Pyke, 'Sir Louis Frederick (1907-1988)' in *Australian Dictionary of Biography*, 2012.

Ford, O., *Harvester Town: The making of Sunshine 1890-1925*, S&DHS, 2001.

Forge, W., *Koch, John Augustus Bernard 1845-1928*, MUP 1983.

Foskett, A., Johnstone, P. & Andrew, D., *On Solid Foundations*, Canberra Tradesmen's Union Club, Canberra, 2001.

Francis, C., 'Winneke, Henry Christian (1874–1943)', in *Australian Dictionary of Biography*, 1990.

Freeman, P., *Thoroughly Modern: The Life and Times of Moir + Sutherland Architects*, Uro Publications 2021.

Garden, D., *Victoria A History, Melbourne:* Nelson, 1984.

Gibney. H J., *Canberra 1913-1953*, AGPS, 1988.

Hamblin, M., *A Family History of Cornelia Creek Run & the Simmies*, South Melbourne, 2020.

Horner, D., *The Gunners: a history of Australian Artillery*, Allen & Underwood, 1995.

Keast, W R H., *A History of the Master Builders Association of Victoria*, MBAV, 1994.

McKernan, M., *Here is Their Spirit—A History of the Australian War Memorial 1917-1990*, UQP, 1991.

'Moonee Valley Thematic Environmental History', for the City of Moonee Valley, Living Histories 2012.

Moloney, D & Johnson, V., *City of Hume: Heritage Study of the former Shire of Bulla District*, 1998.

National Farmers' Federation Australian Agricultural Year Book 1986, Melbourne, Publishing and Marketing Australia, 1985.

Neil, J., *Canberra: dream to reality*, Mullaya, 1975.

Nelson, P., and Alves, L., *Lands Guide: A Guide to finding records of Crown land.* Melbourne: Public Record Office Victoria, 2009.

On Solid Foundations—the building and construction of the nation's capital 1920 to 1950, Canberra Tradesmen's Union Club, August 2001.

Overall, J, *Canberra: yesterday, today & tomorrow: a personal memoir,* FCPA, 1995.

Preistley, S., *Echuca: A History*, ASP, c2009.

Raworth, B., *Analysis on the building stock on the land known as 169 Noone Street, Clifton Hill etc., Report on the Melbourne study area,* Land Conservation Council, Victoria & The Council, Melbourne, 1973.

Report to the City of Yarra, September 2005.

Sims, H J., 'Pye, Hugh (1860–1942)', *Australian Dictionary of Biography,* 1988.

'Spotswood & South Kingsville Profile', Hobsons Bay City Council, 2011.

Steele, D., 'A Prominent Australian Builder & His Contribution to the Neighbourhood Character of 519 Mount Alexander Road', Moonee Ponds, 20 July 2012.

Survey of Post-War Built Heritage in Victoria: Stage One Volume 1: Contextual Overview, Methodology, Lists & Appendices, prepared for Heritage Victoria, October 2008.

Templeton, J., 'Jones, Harold Edward (1878-1965)', *Australian Dictionary of Biography,* 1983.

The Master Builders that built Canberra: 100 years of building in the nation's capital, Canberra MBA ACT, 2013.

'USA Chancery, Residence and Precinct', R068, RSTCA-ACT, 1984.

Vincent, K., *On the Fall of the Hammer: A personal history of Newmarket saleyards,* SLV 1992.

Watson, F., *A brief history of Canberra, the capital city of Australia,* FCPA, 1927.

Wigmore, L., *The Long View: a history of Canberra, Australia's National Capital,* FW Cheshire, 1963.

Willis, J, 'Health and Children' in Lewi, H & Goad, P., *Australia Modern,* Thames & Hudson, 2019.

Zachariah, R., *The Vanished Land,* South Australia: Wakefield Press, 2017.

20th Century Buildings Register, RAIA Vic.

'519 Mount Alexander Road, Moonee Ponds Statement of Significance', Moonee Valley Planning Scheme, MVCC May 2019.

Newspapers & Magazines

Advocate

Age

Alexandra and Yea Standard, Gobur, Thornton and Acheron Express

Argus

Australian Builder

Australasian

Bacchus Marsh Express
Bell's Life in Victoria and Sporting Chronicle
Bendigo Advertiser
Building
Building & Construction
Bulletin
Cairns Post
Canberra Times
Construction
Courier-Mail
Daily Examiner
Decoration & Glass
Elmore Standard
Expanding Horizons
Farmers' Advocate
Film Weekly
Flemington Spectator
Herald
Horsham Times
Leader
Melton Express
Messenger
Murrumbidgee Irrigator National Advocate
Numurkah Leader
Port Phillip Patriot and Melbourne Advertiser
Port Phillip Gazette and Settler's Journal
Record
Riverine Herald
Stock and Land
Sunbury News
Sunshine Advocate
Sydney Mail & New South Wales Advertiser
Wodonga & Towong Sentinel
Weekly Times

Internet

'Dictionary of Unsung Architects' in http://www.builtheritage.com.au/dictionary.html

https://au.usembassy.gov/embassy-consulates/canberra/ambassadors-residence/

https://en.wikipedia.org/wiki/Mark_Oliphant

http://www.builtheritage.com.au/dua_milston.html

https://www.lodgebros.com.au/project/melbourne-shrine/

https://archives.unimelb.edu.au/explore/exhibitions/past-events/melbourne-architecture/music-bowl

https://forgottenaustralianactresses.com/category/cowper-murphy-appleford/

https://www.parliament.vic.gov.au/component/fabrik/details/24/842.

http://roosen.com.au/Background/Free_Christian_Church.html

https://en.wikipedia.org/wiki/Sunshine,_Victoria and

https://en.wikipedia.org/wiki/Hugh_Victor_McKay

https://www.ayton.id.au/gary/History/H_Aust_Vic_Sunshine.htm

https://collections.museumsvictoria.com.au/articles/12510

https://military.wikia.org/wiki/HMT_Southland

https://en.wikipedia.org/wiki/Harold_Edward_Elliott

https://en.wikipedia.org/wiki/Hotel_Canberra

https://www.architecture.com.au/wp-content/uploads/r015_albert_hall_rstca.pdf

https://www.architecture.com.au/wp-content/uploads/r022_screensound_australia_rstca.pdf

https://en.wikipedia.org/wiki/John_Wren

https://www.stmonicasparish.com.au/history-of-st-monicas.html

https://www.architecture.com.au/wp-content/uploads/r055g_parade_ground_and_associated_buildings_group.pdf

https://www.architecture.com.au/wp-content/uploads/r102_house_at_3_wilmot_crescent_forrest_rstca.pdf

https://adb.anu.edu.au/biography/small-sir-andrew-bruce-11714.

https://www.dfat.gov.au/publications/countries-economies-and-regions/60th-anniversary-australia-malaysia/60-years-australia-in-malaysia/introduction.html

https://adb.anu.edu.au/biography/shakespeare-thomas-mitchell-8393

https://www.scotch.vic.edu.au/greatscot/2005maygs/46obit.html

https://heretoday.blog/tag/wystan-widdows/

https://en.wikipedia.org/wiki/Norm_Gallagher.

https://collections.museumsvictoria.com.au/articles/4573

https://en.wikipedia.org/wiki/Comeback_sheep

https://collections.museumsvictoria.com.au/articles/4573.

https://www.architecture.com.au/wp-content/uploads/r056_rg_menzies_building_rstca.pdf.

https://www.ozatwar.com/locations/albertparkbarracks.htm

https://bih.federation.edu.au/index.php/Trewhella_Foundry, 15 November 2016

http://www.australianoats.com.au/oats/p-09.htm

Index

A

A J Galvin Pty Ltd 108
Abbey, Robyn Jean – see Simmie, Robyn 140, 145
Aberline
   – Ron 75
   – Janet – see Montgomery, Janet 3, 18
ACME 128
ACOA Building, ACT 100
Acton, ACT 30, 87
Ada Mary A'Beckett Free Kindergarten 67
Ainslie Public School, ACT 44
Aitken, Walker & Strachan 195
Albany Court 55, 57-58
Albert Hall, ACT 26-28, 30, 173
Alexander Smith Building 21-22
Alfred Lawrence & Co 64
Alleyne, Isabella Forbes – see Simmie, Isabella

American Legation – see US Embassy
Andronas, Arthur 163
Anglican National Memorial Library, ACT 91-92
Apple and Pear Board, ACT 86
Ashburton 75
Association of Cost Accountants of Australia 44
Athlea, see Properties
Aubrey, James David 26
Auditor-General 16
Australian Glass Manufacturers 74
Australian Imperial Force
   – 4th Field Artillery Battery 12
   – 21st Infantry Battalion 13-15
   – 24th Infantry Battalion 15
   – HMT *Southland* 13
Australian
   – Ballet 27

– Institute of Secretaries 16, 74
– Mutual Provident Society 5
– National University/ANU 87, 94, 98, 100-101
  ~ R G Menzies Library 94, 98-99
  ~ Ursula College 100
– Plaster Industries Pty Ltd 82
– War Memorial/AWM, ACT 38, 41, 45-48, 76

B

Ball, Keith 110-111
Ball, Susan – see Simmie, Susan
Bank of Australasia 30
Barlow, Marcus 55
Bega Cooperative Society Ltd, ACT 94
Belconnen, ACT 87
Belmont, see Properties
Bethesda Hospital 55
Bhutan Cypress 163
Black Jack – see Simmie, John Ernest (1923-1994)
Black Mountain Reservoir, ACT 38, 40
Blandfordia, ACT 49, 51
Borrowman, Thomas (Tom) 40
Boucher, George 75
Braddon, ACT 29, 87, 98
Bradshaw, David 143
Braybrook 79
– Hotel 77
Brighter Homes 151
Brighton 24, 74
– Yacht Club 138
Brisbane Building, ACT 90
British Australian Lead Manufacturers 79
British Automatic Telephones 82-83
British Xylonite 67
Brock
– Alexander 132
– Elizabeth (Bessie) 132-133
– Granny – see Elizabeth (Bessie)
– May Isobel – see Gamble, May Isobel
– William Joseph Clarke 132-133
Brocklands – see Properties
Brodie
– coat-of-arms 188
– David 183-187, 190
– George 179, 182-185
– James Sinclair 182
– Richard 179, 182-183, 186
Brooklyn 79, 108
– Quarries 82
Bruce Small Pty Ltd 75
Bruce, Prime Minister Stanley 27

Brunswick 55, 69, 77, 187
- Hospital 167

Budd, Frank Alan 74

Bulla Bulla 119, 179-182, 184, 188, 192-193, 201, 203, 206
- Cemetery 168

Bundoora 84, 132

Builders Labourers Federation 91, 93, 98, 111

Builders Workers Industrial Union 91, 93, 96, 98

Bureau of Mineral Resources, ACT 101

Burwood 67, 69, 206

C

Cahill, Dr Arthur James 29

Caldwell, David L 105

Camberwell 64

Campbell, ACT 96

Canberra, ACT 24-51, 84-101, 173-176
- Aerodrome 49-50
- Advisory Council 34
- Club 90
- Community Hospital 86
- Golf Club 29, 138
- Grammar School 98, 100
- Chapel of Christ the King 98
- Horticultural Society 42
- Hotel 26, 96
- Master Builders 34
- Men's Hockey Association 34
- Relief Society 27
- Repertory Society 27
- Shops Ltd 30
- Society for Arts and Literature 27
- Telephone Exchange 86
- Theatre Centre 27
- University of Canberra 30

Canberra Times 25, 30, 38, 86, 96, 98

Capital Motors Ltd, ACT 44, 86

Capitol Theatre, ACT 42

Carlin, Jack 75

Casey, Sir Richard G 93

Cemetery Works and Grassmere Investments 101

Centennial Hotel, Kensington 78

Chandler, Charles and Elizabeth 49

Chartered Institute of Secretaries 16, 74

Chevrolet 94, 135

Chic Salons Pty Ltd, ACT 90

Chiller, John Thomas 204-205

Christian Brothers Juniorate 82, 84

City Abattoirs 77

Civic Centre, ACT 25-26, 49, 90, 173

Civic Theatre, ACT 35, 40, 42-43

Clancy, Pat 91

Clarke
  - Sir William of Rupertswood 132
  - Elizabeth – see Hurst, Elizabeth
Clarkefield 126
Clarks Shoes 107
Clements, Bishop Kenneth John 100
Cliff, Herbert 121
Cliveden House – see Residential
Closer Settlement Act 179, 193
Closer Settlement Board 193-194, 199
Collard, Clark & Jackson 98
Collegiate Church of St Mark's, ACT 91
Colonial Spark Plug Company 24-25, 45, 69
Colvan Products 102
Commercial Bank of Australia 30
Commercial Banking Co. of Sydney 25, 30
Commonwealth
  - Administration Offices, ACT 28
  - Aircraft Factory 107
  - Bank 25-26, 30, 67, 80
    ~ Blackburn 82
  - Club, ACT 138
  - Cordial Co Ltd, ACT 87
  - Institute of Accountants 16, 49, 74
  - Institute of Auditors
  - Motors, ACT 94, 96
  - Offices, ACT 87
Conciliation & Arbitration Commission, ACT 89, 98
Conway Frank 75
Cooinda – see Properties
Coopers & Lybrand 111
Cornelia Creek Run 3
Council for Scientific and Industrial Research, ACT 29, 32, 40
  - Botanical Laboratories 34
  - Entomology Laboratories 29
Cowper, Murphy & Associates 80
Crabtree & Sons 106
Crabtree Vickers 108
Craigieburn 117, 124, 128, 141, 148, 174, 179
Craig's Buildings 67,
Crestknit 102
Croydon 54, 55,
Crust, John 45, 47-48

D

Darley Camp 65
Dawkins, William J 119
Deaf and Dumb Institute 67
Deep Creek 126, 179-182, 185
Deepdene 69, 77

Delacombe
- Lady Eleanor 106
- Governor Sir Rohan 106

Dempsey, Michael 171

Deniliquin 2-3

Deniliquin and Moama Railway Company 3

Department of the Interior 86

Department of Works and Housing 86, 91

Dickies Ltd 106

Dickson, William Hay Baker 42, 44

Dodge 140

Donald Cameron Home for Elderly Women 84

Dorset Horn Stud – see Harpsdale

Dutch Embassy – see Netherlands

Dyson-Holland
- Arthur Kirke 117-119, 121-125, 129-132, 141, 147, 150, 154, 174, 205-206, 208-212
- George Harold Wollaston 205
- Leila 118-119, 206
- Lillias Frances 205

Duke and Duchess of York 24

Duke of Edinburgh 98

Dunhelen, see Properties

Dunvegan Pastoral Company 195-196, 206, 209

E

Earp, George H 119

Eastlake Tennis Club, ACT 29

East Thornbury 69

Echuca 1-4, 7-8, 136, 141, 144, 192
- State Primary School 7

Edgell, Lillian – see Montgomery, Lillian

Elderly Citizens' Club 108

Elders Clip of the Sale 158

Electricity Meter Manufacturing Company 67

Elmore 2, 3, 5, 7-8, 18, 140

Elliott, Senator Harold Edward 26

Emerald Country Club 37, 117, 138

English, Raymond Walter 150

Entomology Laboratories 29

Erskine House 37

Esmond's Garages Ltd 32, 42

Esmond Motors 42, 44, 94-96, 135

Esmond, John 32

Essendon 53-54, 69, 130, 210
- Airport 143
- Anglican Grammar School 84, 108, 142, 150
- Technical School 108

Evans, Gwilym Thomas 44, 49

Eyelets 60, 63

Exhibition Building
- Palais Royal 74

F

F T Jeffrey Pty Ltd 108, 110
Fairfield 75
Family Trees
- John Ernest (Jock) 145
- John Ernest (Red Jack) 177
- Simmie Family 18-19
- William, John, George 20

FCT Investments Ltd, ACT 44
Federal
- Capital Commission 28, 30, 32, 34
- Capital Territory 44
- Republic of Germany Embassy 93
- Capital Hockey Association 34

Federated Master Builders Assn. of Australia 22
Federated Pharmaceutical Service Guild 77
Federation of Malaya 93
Festival Hall – see West Melbourne Stadium
Finance & Guarantee Co Ltd 98
Fisherman's Bend 67, 82
Fitzroy 102, 108, 183
Flemington 68, 84, 152, 185
Flinders Council 108
- Shire Office and Civic Centre 108

Foale, Kath – see Souter, Kath
Folko Kooper Tasmania 169
Fordson 123
Footscray 67, 75
Football Ground 107
- Psychiatric Hospital/Centre 108-109
- Swimming Pool 108
- West Footscray Hospital 108

Forrest, ACT 29, 34-35, 41, 44, 49, 51, 87
France 13-16, 29, 144
Fraser, Prime Minister Malcolm 100
Free Christian Church 7
Freemasons 4-5
- Australian Chapter 87
- Broadmeadows Lodge 89
- Millewa Lodge 47
- Naval and Military Lodge 49
- Peace and Commemoration Lodge 76, 89
- Remembrance Mark Lodge 43-44
- Royal Arch 34
- Uniting Grand Lodge of NSW 32
- Capital Lodge 612

Fyshwick, ACT 94, 101

G

G A Carter & Son 135
Gallagher, Norm 111

Gallipoli 12-13, 15-16, 26, 54, 137
Gamble
   – Bill 129
   – Desmond 130, 132, 138
   – Edward Alexander Clarke (Ted) 20, 126, 138, 139, 145, 154-155
   – Helen – see Souter, Helen
   – Jean Elizabeth – see Simmie, Jean
   – Joyce Shirley – see Simmie, Joyce
   – Kathryn Anne (Kate) 78, 145, 155, 168
   – May Isobel 132
Garema Place, ACT 96-98
Geere, Arthur Edward 24
Gerd and Renate Block 93
German Embassy – see Federal Republic of Germany
Glenroy 80, 102
Gordon Institute 67
Goornong 3
Government Printing Office, ACT 38
Grandview Hotel, West Brunswick 79
Granny Brock - see Brock, Bessie
Greenvale 128, 132, 169
   – Sanitorium 124
   – state school 130
   – Tennis Club 128, 130
Green Room Club 102-103
Griffith, ACT 41, 86, 91
   – Infant School 89
   – Primary School 89

H

H B Dickie Ltd 106, 108
H Rowe & Co 80
H V MacKay Massey Harris 123
Haileybury College 141-142
Harper, Jamesina Alice – see Simmie, Jamesina
Harpsdale
   – Land to 1906 179-188
   – Land to 1940 189-197
   – To 1968 117-145
   – Dorset Horn Stud 117, 119, 124, 157
   – To 2000 146-164
   – To 2022 165-176
Harrison, Sir John 28
Hawkesbury Sandstone Company, NSW 46, 48
Hawkins, Stanley Theo 125
Hedderwick, David Balderinnie 21
Hedderwick, Fookes & Alston 21
Henry Bucks 135
Hibernia 2
Holland, George 100
Holt, James and Annie 7

Holt's Matrimonial Agency 7
Holy Spirit Church, East Thornbury 69
Hopetoun Kindergarten and Nursery 67-68
Hotel Kingston 49
Hotham Gardens 82
Housing Commission 77, 79, 82
Howard, Philip (Phil) 148
Howe
   – Keith 63, 101, 137
   – Dorrie 135, 137, 155
Humber Snipe 123, 135
Huntly Shire Council 3-4
Hurley, Bert 75
Hurst
   – Elizabeth 132
   – Granny – see Elizabeth

I

Illustre 94
Institute of Anatomy, ACT 29-31, 42
Irons
   – Arthur John 18
   – Mary – see Simmie, Mary

J

Jack Burt & Co 124
Jacka, Albert VC 54
Johnston Fred 75
Jones, Lieutenant-Colonel Harold Edward 42, 87
Joyce
   – Emily 35
   – Ivy Eliza Ann – see Simmie, Ivy
   – John James (Jack) 35, 80, 102
   – Joyce & Howe Shoes 101-102, 137

K

Keilambete 3
Keilor 84, 194, 203
Keith Parlon 135
Kensington 10, 17, 23, 64, 75, 78, 111-114
Kent, Oliver 171
Kew 21, 67, 69, 84, 108
Kildonan Children's Home 69
Kiloran, see Residential
Kindergarten Teachers Training College 67, 108
Kingston Heath Golf Club, ACT 63, 138
Koch, John Augustus Bernard 174, 184-185

L

Lancedene - see Properties
Lariston Building, ACT 30
Lariston Investment Company 26
Law-Smith, Sir Robert 157
Leighton Contractors 101
Lewis, Professor Brian Bannatyne 87
Liberal Party Headquarters, ACT 100

Liberty Theatre 74, 80
Lillingston, Constance – see Simmie, Constance
Ling/Lang, Henry H 16
Lister, T. 40
Lloyd
– Alfred (Alf) 65, 101, 107, 110
– Edward 107
Lording, Stanley Gordon 193-194, 199-204
Lorne 37
Lowther Hall 108
Lyneham Motors, ACT 94

M

Macarthur
– Archibald Norman 194-195
– Lillias - see Dyson-Holland, Lillias
Macarthur and Macleod 194-195, 205, 209-211
Mackenzie, Professor Colin 30
Macleod
– Christina Elizabeth – see Turner, Christina
– William Edward Brock 194-195, 205
Maize Products Pty Ltd 67
Malaysian High Commission, ACT 93
Malvern 74, 77, 152
– Library 107
Malvern Star 75
Malley's 106

Mann, Eileen – see Simmie, Eileen
Mannix, Archbishop Daniel 54, 65
Manuka, ACT 34, 42, 44, 86
Marco Polo 1
Maribyrnong 138, 180
– Explosive Factory 66
– Ordnance 66
– River 180-181
Marshall Shoes 101
Mason, Ailsa Lynette Noel – see Simmie, Ailsa
Master Builders'
– Association of the ACT 89
– Association of the Federal Capital Territory 28
– Association Victoria 63, 78, 82, 138
– Federation of Australia 89
McAliece, Andrew 145, 166, 168-169, 177
McAuliffe, William (Willie) 121, 136
McCaughey Court - see University of Melbourne
McClusky, Rowan 124, 143
McDonald, J. 40
McKay, Hugh Victor 8
McKay's Harvester Works 8-10
McKenzie & Holland 82
McNamara, Jack 84

Melbourne
- City Council 21, 74, 102
- College of Textiles 152
- Distillery 74
- Glass Manufacturers 74
- Metropolitan Tramways Board 77

Menzies, Prime Minister, Sir Robert 48
Messines, Belgium 15
Methodist School Hall, ACT 32, 34
Metropolitan Meat Market 130
Mickleham 120-121, 179-181, 184-185, 188, 200
- state school 141

Millar
- Joan 128, 139, 169
- Mavis 128, 137, 139

Milston, Ernest Edward 75
MLC Building, ACT 94-95, 97
Moama
- Municipal Council 3-4

Moir
- Malcolm Johnstone 26, 31, 34, 42, 44, 91
- Heather 49
- and Sutherland 84, 87, 94
- Ward + Slater 94
- and Slater 96, 98

Monash University
- Farrer Hall 102, 104
- Engineering building No 6 108

Mont Royal – see Royal Park
Montbrehain, France 15
Montgomery
- Albert Reid (Bert) 8-10, 12
- Eric Ford Aberline 18
- Janet 7-8, 17, 35, 117, 129, 136
- John Ford 7-11, 17-18, 35, 117, 136
- Lillian 136
- Violet Christina 10

Moonee Ponds 102, 110, 128, 205
Moorabbin 67
Moore, William Watson & Sons 8
Mount Royal Hospital 102
Muir, Lill 143
Mühlstein, Ernst Israel – see Milston, Ernest
Mutual Life and Citizens Assurance Co Ltd 94
Mt Martha 139-140

N

Narrabundah, ACT 86, 89
National
- Bank 105
- Library, ACT 39-40
- Museum of Zoology 29
- Sheep Dog Trials 125

– Trust 171
Nelson-Slee, Leila - see Dyson-Holland, Leila
Neon Electric 79
Netherlands Embassy, ACT 40, 90
Newmarket 119-122, 124-125, 197
Nichol, John 158
North Melbourne 75, 79, 82, 84, 108, 130, 135
North Suburban Club 102
Northcote 77
   – Plaza Theatre 55-56
Notting Hill 80
Nutter, Daniel and Edith 96

O

Oak Hill – see Residential
Oaklands 181
   – Hounds 186-187, 189-190, 197
   – Hunt Club 138
Oakleigh 21
O'Brien, Bernie 158
O'Connor, ACT 87
   – Patrick Joseph 64-65
   – Youth Hostel 100, 144
Odeon Theatre 73-74, 80
Oldsmobile 129, 135, 141
Oliphant
   – Professor Marcus and Rosa 87, 100

– Kenneth Henry Bell 26, 29, 90
Ormond College, see University of Melbourne
Our Lady of Good Counsel Church 69, 71-72
Our Lady of Immaculate Conception Church 64-65
Oxford University Press 83-84

P

Palais Royale – see Exhibition Building
Parkville 102, 108
Parliament House, ACT 24, 26, 29, 86, 91
Penleigh Girl's School 130, 150
Penny, Flora – see Simmie, Flora
Pharmacy College 108
Philip Fire Station, ACT 100
Philippines Embassy, ACT 94
Plane, Robert (Bob) 158
Plaza Theatre – see Northcote
Plottel, Joseph 64
Poole
   – Reg. Hartley 121
   – William Henry 124, 125, 187-189
Port Melbourne 74, 79
Pozières, France 14-15
Preece, 'Nugget' 40
Preston 75, 132
Properties

- Athlea 119
- Belmont 124-125, 129, 131-132, 138-139, 141, 148, 150, 151, 153-154, 159, 161-162, 166
- Brocklands 130, 132
- Cooinda 126, 137, 154, 157
- Dunhelen 128, 182,
- Harpsdale, see Harpsdale
- Kalkallo 124
- Lancedene 125
- Ruthven 2-3, 5
- Springfield 125
- Weetangera 87

Prospecting Board, NSW 38
Pyke, Sir Louis Frederick 23-24, 45, 69
Pyke-Simmie Pty Ltd 69, 101

Q

Qualeta House 61-63
Queanbeyan 32, 38, 42
- Rifle Club 40
- Football Club 41

Queen Elizabeth II 74, 98

R

R & W H Symington 55, 59
Raggatt, Harold and Edith 49
Rahman, Prime Minister Tunku Abdul 93
Red Hill, ACT 29,

Red Hill Outlook 100
Red Jack – see Simmie, John Ernest (1925-2012)
Redd, Marge 142
Reid, ACT 29
Reinforced Concrete and Monier Pipe Construction Ltd 64
Repatriation Department 16
- Industrial Scheme 17

Reserve Bank 108
Reservoir East 77, 79
Residential
- Cliveden House 132
- Kiloran, Mt Martha 139
- Oak Hill, Preston 132
- 1 Kororoit Street, Sunshine 10, 136
- 3 Wilmott Avenue, Forrest 44
- 4 Normanby Crescent, Deakin 49
- 5 Baudin Street, Forrest 35, 50
- 16 Roberts Street, Essendon 130
- 38 Holmes Crescent, Campbell 96
- 42 Halifax Road, Brighton 35, 36, 117
- 43 and 45 Melbourne Avenue, Forrest 87
- 58 and 60 Arthur Circle, Forrest 49-51
- 199 Dryandra Street, O'Connor 87-88, 100
- 519 Mount Alexander Road, Moonee Ponds 110

Returned Soldiers' Club 49
Returned Soldiers & Sailors Imperial League of Australia
   – Canberra 28-29
   – Sunshine 16
Returned Services League/RSL
   – Caulfield 144
   – Flemington-Kensington 106
R G Menzies Library – see Australian National University, ACT
Richards, Maurice (Maurie) 40
Robert Hutchinson & Co 102
Romsey 132, 180, 182
   – Shire 126, 148, 151
Rosebud 108
Romberg and Boyd 107
Romney Cross 120
Rowntree 77
Royal
   – Agricultural Show Society 63-64
   – Australian Air Force
      ~ Canberra 49
      ~ No 1 Store Tottenham 108
   – Ballet 27
   – Canberra Golf Club, ACT
   – Insurance 150
   – Melbourne Hospital 157, 159
   – Military College Duntroon, ACT 43
   – Park 64
   – Victorian Eye and Ear Hospital 159
Rugby Union Club, ACT 94, 98
Ruthven - see Properties
Rydge, Norman Bede 74

S

Scarborough, John Francis Deighton 98
Scotch College 119, 127-128, 142
Shakespeare
   – Annie 34
   – Arthur 34
   – Thomas Mitchell 34, 98
Shrine of Remembrance
   – 1939-1945 Forecourt 75-77
Sides, R. 40
Simmie & Co
   – Establishment 21-24
   – Canberra 1926-1941 24-51
   – Canberra 1942-1969, 84-101
   – Melbourne 1924-1941 51-66
   – Melbourne 1942-1978 67-84
   – Closure Canberra 100-101
   – Simmie Nominees Pty Ltd 111
   – Liquidation Melbourne 112

Simmie
- Ailsa Lynette Noel 145, 152, 177
- Annie 18, 102
- Constance (Connie) 17, 110, 129
- Eileen 17, 20
- Flora 1, 18, 102
- George (1828-1906) 2-4, 6-7
- George (1862-1937) 102
- George Herbert (1895-1944) 2-4, 6-8, 10
  ~ War Service 12-13, 16-21
  ~ Family Tree 20
  ~ Business 23-24, 45
- Ivy Eliza Ann (1894-1952) 20, 145
- Isabella Forbes 19
- James (1865-1897) 2
- James (1979-) 150, 155
- Jamesina Alice 2, 18
- Janet – see Montgomery, Janet
- Jarrod 150, 153, 155, 157
  ~ Jean Elizabeth 20, 128, 130, 145, 177
  ~ John (1823-1867) 1
  ~ John (1857-1915) 2
  ~ John (1860-1950) 8, 102
  ~ John Ernest (Jock) (1892-1968)
    > Early Life 2-4, 6-11
    > War Service 14-16
    > Simmie & Co 24-51, 84-101
    > Family Trees 20, 145
    > Farming 117-144
    > Who's Who entry 144
  ~ John Ernest 'Red Jack' (1925-2012) 16, 36
    > Family Tree 177
    > Farming 121, 147-162, 167
  ~ John Ernest 'Black Jack' (1923-1994) 17, 36, 107, 111, 128-129, 142
  ~ Joyce Shirley 36, 126, 137, 139, 151, 154
  ~ Lisa 150, 153, 155, 177
  ~ Mary Ann (1864-1959) 18, 141
  ~ Peter John (1950-) 133-134, 137, 139-142, 145, 150, 152-155, 159-160, 162, 166
  ~ Philip Edward (1952-) 133, 137, 139-142, 145, 150, 152, 155, 157-158, 160, 162, 170, 177
  ~ Richard James (1954-) 133, 137, 139, 142-143, 154, 155, 157, 159-160, 162-172, 177
  ~ Robyn Jean 150, 152-153, 155, 159, 177
  ~ Roy William (1920-2004) 17, 20, 74-75, 101, 107, 110-112, 128-129, 142
  ~ Sarah 150, 155
  ~ Shirley 17, 20, 129
  ~ Susan 110
  ~ William (1825-1901) 1-3, 5

~ William James (Bill) (1890-1986)
  ~ Family tree 20
  ~ Early Life 2-4, 7-8, 11
  ~ War Service 12-17
  ~ Simmie & Co 21-24, 51-84, 101-112, 102
Slim, Governor General Sir William 90
Smith, Ernest (Ern) 40
Smyth, Anna 167, 169-170
Snow's Corner 30
Society of Missionaries of the Sacred Heart Monastery 54-55
Sodersteen, Emil 45, 47
Soldiers Land Repatriation Committee 199-200
Soldier Settlement 117, 179, 203-204
  – Board 118
Souter
  – Helen 131-132
  – Kath 133
South Australian Dorset Fair 149
Southampton General Hospital, UK 159
South Melbourne 24, 55, 75, 79, 84, 102-103, 106, 108
South Yarra 75, 77
Spotswood 74, 82,
Stadiums Pty Ltd 80
State Electricity Commission 82
Stevenson, Noelle June 137-138, 148
St Andrew's Presbyterian Church, ACT 32-34, 41
St Andrew's Presbyterian Hospital 64-66
St Alban's Anglican Church 102, 105-106
St Anthony's Convent 84
St Claire's Catholic School 84
St Francis' Church 69
St Joseph's Convent 69
St Joseph's Parish Church 69-70, 84
St Kilda 54, 74, 84, 107
  – Sea Baths 52
St Michael's Church 108
St Michael's School 107
St Monica's Church 53-54
St Quentin, France 15
St Theresa's Church 69
St Vincent De Paul School 69
Stubington, Edward George 94-96
Sunbury High School 108
Sunshine 8, 10, 12-17, 35, 64, 66, 117, 136
  – Sunshine-Braybrook Football Club 9-10
  – District Cricket Club 11
  – Technical School 67, 102
  – Harvester 123
  – Harvester Works 8-9, 11
Sunshine Advocate 136

Sutherland, Heather – see Moir, Heather
Swanston Used Cars 64

T

T R & L Cockram 65
Telopea Park School, ACT 87, 89
Tempel Beth Israel 84
Thompson, Lou 65
Thompson, W 40
Thompson & Chalmers 65
Tobler, Conrad 84
Tomlins-Simmie Flour Pty Ltd 101-102, 144
Toyota Corolla 140
Toorak 74
Troodos 117-109, 118-119, 125, 148-150, 174, 193-194, 197, 206, 212
Troutbeck, Hutton 121
Turner
 – Christina Elizabeth 210
 – Primary School, ACT 91

U

University of Melbourne
 – McCaughey Court 107
 – Ormond College 107
Ursula College – see Australian National University
US Embassy, ACT 84-86

V

Vauxhall 135, 147
Veale, Raymond 75
Victoria
 – Barracks 16
 – Hotel 82
 – Markets 21
 – Racing Club 138
Victorian Benevolent Home and Hospital for the Aged and Infirm 63-64
Victorian Butter Factories Cooperative 63

W

Wake's Mail Order Co 64
Walker, Clarence Albert 101, 105, 110
Warner, Elizabeth – see Brock, Elizabeth (Bessie)
Webster
 – James Anthony 194-195
 – Senator James 128-129
West Brunswick 55, 70, 79, 84, 150
West Footscray 75, 108
West Melbourne Stadium 80-82
Weston Creek Primary School, ACT 101
Westridge, ACT 49
Widdows, Wystan 105-106
Wilson
 – Arthur Chesney 192-194, 199-201

– Isabella Forbes – see Simmie, Isabella Forbes
– Keith 150
Winneke, Chief Justice Sir Henry 119
Wolfdene 171
Woods, Archbishop Frank 106
Woollybutt Pty Ltd 165
Works and Railways Department 21
Wren, John 54, 80
Wright Brothers London Ltd 94

Y

Yarralumla 86, 93
Yates, Ron 75
Yellow Cabs of Australia 21
Ypres, Belgium 13
Yuncken & Freeman 100
Yuroke 158, 179-180, 182

www.ingramcontent.com/pod-product-compliance
Lightning Source LLC
Chambersburg PA
CBHW061127010526
44116CB00023B/2995